THE ROOTS OF RITUAL

THE ROOTS OF RITUAL

edited by

James D. Shaughnessy

WILLIAM B. EERDMANS PUBLISHING COMPANY
Grand Rapids, Michigan

Library of Congress Cataloging in Publication Data

Main entry under title:

The Roots of Ritual.

Most of the contributions were first presented at a
Conference at the University of Notre Dame.
Bibliography: p.
1. Ritual. I. Shaughnessy, James D., ed.
BL600.R64   264   72-96405
ISBN 0-8028-1509-X

To
Mr. and Mrs. George Murphy

Introduction

This collection of essays is designed to illustrate how persons working in a variety of disciplines view ritual. Despite differences in approach and concern, the authors' corporate opinion is that ritual, so far from being a matter of mere ecclesiastical ceremonial, is a basic human language rooted in man's social nature and pervading his social environment.

Until recently this matter has been the almost exclusive concern of historians of religion and certain kinds of anthropologists. In religious circles, where one would have expected to find particular concern with the demands and possibilities of ritual as a genre of behavior and communication, little formal attention has been given the matter. This is astonishing, considering the extensive work Christian churches have done during the last decade in reforming and redeveloping their worship traditions. Such reforms have been instituted for the most part on the basis of theological and historical methods — methods that were primarily those of liturgical and pastoral studies in the past. The result has been generally good reform, but it may be argued that adaptation and development of Christian worship traditions of the past into new cultural dimensions cannot be well served by theological and historical methods alone.

This is so because liturgical worship is ritual by nature,

and ritual behavior has its own grammar and syntax. If these go unlearned, the liturgical act itself not only suffers but those who engage in it may well find themselves split rather than united by it. If these go unlearned, the power of ritual for evil as well as for good goes unfactored, and those who engage in it may find themselves unknowingly gripped by the viciousness they would not rather than the good they would.

Not only is ritual habit forming, it is power laden. We are also immersed in it — to such an extent, indeed, that it takes an extraordinary degree of perception even to note its presence, much less to analyze its influences on us. This presence and its effects are nonetheless real, and they are not confined to stadiums on Saturday afternoons, to military parades, to inaugurations, or to Sunday services in church. Even less is ritual an arcane phenomenon that survives only in societies we call "primitive."

Architecture, for example, is both a response to the ritual patterns by which people live together and a cause that effects such patterns, for better or worse. On both counts, architecture is ultimately embedded in the ritual patterns through which people socialize. It rises out of those patterns as a practical art by which space is defined by, for, and among those who enact the patterns over and over again. The same might be said of other social institutions — such as the theater, schools, systems of jurisprudence and politics, and religion — except that these processes (none of them are merely "things") deal with other significant aspects of socio-cultural definition that affect us all.

What these other significant aspects are is the scope of the chapters that follow. None of the chapters pretend to be exhaustive, nor does the collection itself pretend to be definitive. Perhaps the only point on which the several authors agree totally is that ritual is not a need of man that may or may not be retained but an inevitability coextensive with man's social nature. On this basis the authors tackle the grammar of ritual behavior from various points of view and attempt to suggest something of ritual's scope and effects in the ways we live.

As the one who originally organized the conference at the University of Notre Dame, at which most of the contributions to this volume were first presented, I am obliged to acknowledge the debt I owe to the work of Professor Erik Erikson of Harvard for the concept of the conference. Thanks are also due to Mrs. Ann Lauer and Mr. Richard Humbrecht, both of the Murphy Center for Liturgical Research at Notre Dame, and to the Center's director, the Reverend James Shaughnessy, for their generous and untiring work in seeing the volume into print.

Aidan Kavanagh, O.S.B.
Notre Dame, 1973

Contents

1

Ritual and Culture:
Some Dimensions of the Problem Today

by

BRIAN WICKER

ONE OF THE MOST IMPORTANT FACTS ABOUT LIFE TODAY IS
that there is no longer any major society being made up
by immigration. By this I do not mean that there are not
population shifts. I mean that there is no society being
continually made and remade by the need to absorb new,
well-defined cultural minorities who see themselves as
coming to some kind of promised land, some unformed
space which it is theirs to create and sanctify with their
own labor and their own life. Even the recent immigration of West Indians and Asians into Britain and that of

Brian Wicker is Senior Lecturer in English and Resident Tutor for
Birmingham, Department of Extramural Studies, University of Bir-
mingham, England. His books include *Culture and Liturgy; Culture and
Theology* (American edition, *Toward a Contemporary Christianity*); and
First the Political Kingdom.

Jews to Israel is not really a journey to the unknown, but rather a return home or a request for an established right of entry to be acknowledged. Certainly America does not have to face, in (quite) the old sense, the problem of immigrant minorities trying to achieve a sense of identity within the host community. The problem it does have to face is that of an already established minority that feels excluded, but not of any substantial, united minority that wishes to enter *from outside*.

At some point for every immigrant community there comes a crisis of identity. It comes at the point when its wish to be accepted as part of the host society (and thus to soften some or all of its own cultural peculiarities) becomes as powerful as the desire to retain a sense of cultural unity precisely by insisting on those peculiarities as marks of special concern. The whole process of Americanization has consisted in the facing and solving of this crisis by each successive wave of immigrants.[1] But in a secular society like America, which has no official and universally acknowledged religious rituals for establishing personal or group identity, there is really very little room for maneuver on the part of any incoming group that is trying to find a footing. Eventually, and paradoxically, in order to survive, the group must relinquish its cultural *differentia*, its *raison d'être*. This means that, in the end, it has to disappear as a cultural entity, maintaining only the trappings of its old distinctive forms. Yet a society that is created by immigration has one resource that helps to soften this blow for each successive incursion — namely, the arrival of the next group of immigrants. As long as there is some other group that is newer, and even less sure of itself, than the one that is undergoing its crisis of identity *now*, there is at least somebody against whom one can identify negatively. "At least we are more American than they are," each

1 Philip Gleason, "The Crisis of Americanization," in *Contemporary Catholicism in the United States*, ed. by Philip Gleason (Notre Dame: Univ. of Notre Dame Press, 1969), pp. 3-32.

group can say to itself and to the host society; by so doing it can ease the burden of losing its old personality and taking on a new one. The special, critical problem today, however, is that there are no more new waves of immigrants against which it is possible to identify. Hence, the national crisis of identity that is affecting America now is due, at least in part, to the knowledge that according to official ideology and plain fact the people against whom one finds it necessary to identify are fully as American as oneself. This is why the problem of finding an identity, which faces the black American or the young American everywhere, is also, and to exactly the same extent, a problem for the white American and the middle-aged American. What began as a crisis for each group in turn has become a crisis for the whole society.

I have referred to the problem as special to a secular society. What I mean by this is that a religious society has certain rituals of initiation by which it can cope with the identity crises of its new members (whether they are immigrants or merely the young). These rituals are of fundamental importance in preserving the stability of the society (which of course is not always a good thing). But what matters is that they do so by transforming the whole problem of personal identity. To put it very simply: religious initiation is a means by which the social and psychological crisis is turned to positive, creative use. The essence of this process is that the individual or group is led to believe that relinquishing all that it holds dear, and taking on some other set of values that makes a new world of experience accessible, is a positive ethical duty, requiring a profound personal rebirth. By translating the identity crisis into terms of death and rebirth, and by making the enduring of this agony the basis of the whole social and moral structure of society, the sense of loss and bewilderment that is bound up with the crisis is turned into a sense of joy — the joy that lies on the other side of despair. Where some kind of baptism becomes the foundation of a society's morals and politics, the personal identity crisis ceases to be a problem and becomes an opportunity.

This is why a society that fails to sustain a psychologically valid religious initiation process, or ceases to believe with any conviction in the old-established rituals that used to give effect to it, must inevitably be faced with a crisis on a global scale. The coming of such a crisis in most Western societies today seems to me quite obvious and easily predictable. In fact it has been so obvious for so long that many attempts have been made to deal with it, or at least to show how to deal with it. Roughly speaking, two kinds of solution have been offered: those which amount to the invention of new rituals or the resuscitation of old ones, and those which amount to saying that man is now mature enough to put away such childish things and cope with his own problems simply by making use of his own secular knowledge of himself.[2]

One of the most interesting and at times catastrophic features of the twentieth century has been its preoccupation with the revival of dead or moribund rituals, and the creation of new ones, as means of filling the vacuum left by secularization. One might mention several different, but sometimes overlapping, examples.

The first was, of course, *fascism*. Fascism could be called an atavistic substitute for Christianity. The rituals of fascism, extending from relatively harmless children's games to the most unspeakable crimes, succeeded in appealing to large sections of a secularized and industrialized society, giving them a sense of identity and providing people with methods for coping with personal crises — utilizing, of course, as an auxiliary, the technique already mentioned of identifying negatively by rejecting certain groups as beyond the boundaries of legitimate society, e.g., the Jews.

---

[2] Perhaps I should say here that Christians are deeply divided between two opposing camps, and there is certainly no one "Christian" attitude to the problem.

Secondly, one might mention the so-called liturgical revival among organized Christians. This revival had a good side — in that it stimulated mature and scholarly thought about the fundamentals of Christianity and an understanding of the depths to which secularization had gone. But it had a bad side too — the side that made it possible in some places for the Christian liturgy inside the church and the fascist liturgy outside it to coexist, or even at times to cooperate with each other. The liturgical revival was, in its origins, a conservative or even reactionary movement, liable at times to delusions of grandeur. This gave it a certain sympathy for the trappings of fascism and made the essential atheism of the latter harder to nail down. It is perhaps not surprising that those Christians most opposed to Hitler were often those least touched by the new liturgical ideas — either intellectual protestants like Dietrich Bonhoeffer, or simple tridentine-formed peasant-Catholics like Franz Jägerstätter.[3] Neither is it surprising that many post-fascist secular theologies of Europe and America (including those developed under Catholic auspices) have today turned away from liturgy as a source of inspiration or hope, or have even given it up as a bad job altogether.

Thirdly, one must mention the various attempts by individuals or groups (usually intellectuals) to imagine or even practice some wholly new kind of ritual life, not based on concepts drawn from Christianity in any form. Perhaps the most spectacular and instructive of these was the great attempt by D. H. Lawrence, in his Mexican phase, to encompass in thought and word a civilization based on the recovery of pre-Christian Mexican religion. It is a mistake to think of *The Plumed Serpent* — the novel in which Lawrence outlines his ideas most fully — as an overt return to barbarism. It is an attempt to imagine a *new civilization* with a religion that is no longer

[3] Gordon Zahn, *In Solitary Witness: The Life and Death of Franz Jaegerstaetter* (New York: Holt, Rinehart and Winston, 1964), passim.

based on what Lawrence felt to be the enervating and self-destructive principle of universal, indiscriminate Christian "love." But what is most important about Lawrence's vision is that he finds it absolutely necessary to invent a ritual in which to embody his new, or renewed, religious principle and that, in doing so, he simply produces a Cecil B. de Mille scenario made up of an incoherent riot of words and a banal sub-Hollywood action. Lawrence's grandiose attempt, and his failure (which is more than just a failure of art), should help to show us that there is something fundamentally wrong with the whole notion of a more or less artificial invention of a religious ritual to fit the supposed needs of a society that has lost its old one.

These examples, however, belong to the recent past. What of the strictly contemporary world? Are we presented today with anything equivalent to these earlier attempts at reestablishing rituals? I think we are. As one example I might mention the avant-garde theater. "Off-off-Broadway" productions like *Dionysus 69* and *Paradise Now* seem to be characteristic, and typically reactionary, examples of the general trend. They represent a return to the obscure origins of drama in the murky past of mystery religion and ritual enactment. Their object is not to "imitate" but to transform mankind. They are liturgies rather than plays, and their ambience is that of the sanctuary or the shrine rather than that of the theater or the auditorium. The disused garage off-off-Broadway in which Dionysus was being redeified in 1969 was turned into a temple rather than a playhouse. It is true, of course, that the dramatic theories of an earlier generation — the theories of Brecht and *Waiting For Lefty*, not to mention pantomime and music hall — demanded at times active participation by the audience. For the most part, however, participation did not spill over into conversion. Dramatic catharsis did not entail a religious *metanoia*. Drama, it might be said, began when *seeing* was freed from the shackles of *believing:* when understanding became possible without an immediate interior change of heart. Today the theater seems to be returning to the bondage of its religious roots. In understandable reaction to the post-enlightenment amputation of drama from religion and politics, the theater seems now to be engaged in an attempt to reestablish some kind of primordial, unified vision that would get beneath or behind both drama and politics. But in trying to do this, the theater is perhaps failing to recognize that the detachment of drama from ritual, of "seeing" from "believing," was a tremendous liberation as well as a dangerous dissociation. To be able to pity, sympathize, and understand without being forced into direct action made possible that enlargement of experience without which civilization, with its demands for mutual acceptance and political maturity, could hardly begin. In this sense it is possible to see the current mood in the theater of the avant-garde, like current moods in other compartments of life, as profoundly reactionary and potentially fascist. It is a glance over the shoulder towards a primitive terror rather than a movement of rational hope or promise for a different kind of future.

The most pervasively familiar of all contemporary ritualizations, however, is undoubtedly to be found in the products of the advertising industry. The paradox of modern advertising is that although what it proclaims is always the latest, the most up-to-date, the most fashionable, its manner and ambience is that of the routine incantation, the never changing utterance of the same familiar spell. When the proclamation of the arrival of the newest-of-the-new becomes a predictable routine that continues day after day, and the demand for ever more exciting, unfamiliar, and exotic methods of presentation becomes ever more pressing, the final product turns out to be the purest of all conservatisms: an eternal round of ecstasies and orgies and priestly incantations designed simply to bolster up a tired society. Advertising today is a strictly "religious" activity, and the advertising agents

are the high priests of the modern mysteries. Their work
has the essential character of *priestcraft,* in the pejorative
sense of that term. They are a cultivated, sought-after
elite caste within commercialized society. Their spells
enable us to enter into magical dreamworlds of exotic
experience, to banquet with the gods, so to speak, but
thereby they only help society as a whole to remain
exactly where it always was. Their claim to have access
to secret knowledge is characteristic of all priesthoods;
their research files on the opinions and attitudes of the
public — which are plausibly said to contain far more
useful information about society than all the words of
disinterested social investigators put together — confirm
the claim.

Advertising, then, is the supreme instance of modern
society's thirst for ritual. We are so drenched by its magic
that we can hardly imagine a truly religionless, ritual-
free secular world at all. Of course, disinterested, concrete, factual publicity is always potentially revolutionary
in its power to disillusion and expose; modern advertising is, in every way, designed to bind us ever more
tightly to our traditions, our illusions, our false hopes.
Its very proclamation of secularity and freedom is the
utterance of a priesthood ruthlessly dedicated to its own
continued power over us. Insofar as our society is now
definable as the society of advertising, it has become
priest-ridden. We cannot imagine how we could possibly
do without advertising's routine offerings. Its orgiastic,
magical drug is truly the opium of the people.

If the attempts to invent new religious rituals of initiation have obviously failed, deliberate attempts to do
without them altogether by inventing secular theologies
have met with no greater success. This is because there
is something essentially esoteric about a secular theology.
The very phrase "secular theology" (and its various
equivalents) expresses a paradox which it takes an intellectual to swallow. At any rate, the man in the street
remains stolidly unimpressed. Wherever he does take

any notice of modern theology in its secular guises he usually dismisses it as just another piece of mental trickery by which unbelievers manage to hang on to lucrative or respectable jobs in the religious establishment without paying the price of real belief. No doubt the man in the street is unfair. But the point is that there *is* something wrong with a purely esoteric or elite religion.

As far as its embodiment in ritual is concerned, religion is of its very nature a popular, as well as a conservative, affair. The liturgy, in Christian terms, was ideally the thing that levelled everybody. The Christian altar was the one table where the lord and his servant, the capitalist and his wage-slave, sat down together. If they didn't, people knew that there was something wrong. Peasants and theologians might be leagues apart in their spirituality or their politics or their productive labor,[4] but in the presence of the sacramental food equality before God actually meant something. In fact, public ritual, of its very nature, is popular. Either it is rooted in a common culture or it is nothing. When it ceases to be popular, it ceases to be authentic.[5]

The fact that the twentieth century has witnessed in fascism an almost unprecedented outburst of pseudo-religious ritualism at the very heart of its own secularity suggests that the notion of religion without ritual is a contradiction in terms. This is not to say that there is no such thing as "religionless Christianity." That phrase has its own importance, in emphasizing that Christianity is not a religion in the same sense that ancient Mexican civilization was a "religion." There is a certain secularity about the Christian gospel that does make it a fitting

---

[4] On Christianity as an egalitarian community in "consumption" only, see Adrian Cunningham in *Catholics and the Left* (Springfield: Templegate, 1968).

[5] I do not mean that it has to be a majority activity — there are minority rituals of protest, just as there are rituals of the "establishment." But genuine religious ritual does have to be accessible to the unsophisticated and the naive.

outlook for a secular age. All the same, the question
arises whether a Christianity that is without ritual embodiment is really Christianity at all, and whether it can
survive as a popular cult. The history of secular theologies in recent decades is not encouraging in this respect.
Like other revolutionary movements, each has tended
to outbid the last in radicalism of thought without managing to interest that "contemporary secular man" whom
secular theology is supposed to serve. Insofar as secular
theologians have tried to make Christianity intelligible
and significant to "modern man," I think that they have
failed.

The reason seems fairly clear if one accepts the broad
outline of the argument pursued thus far. There is no
such entity as the secularized modern man beloved of
the secular theologians. He only exists in the minds of
theologians themselves, because he is a picture of themselves: a person without beliefs or convictions about God
(or about himself) but deeply interested and worried
about this absence of belief. George Orwell once said
that "it is not easy for most modern writers to imagine
the mental processes of anyone who is not a writer."[6]
Neither do theologians find it easy to imagine the mental
processes of anyone who is not a theologian. Not only is
the modern man the theologians conjure up not really
there, but also the totally secularized landscape in which
he is supposed to exist is not to be found either. By this
I do not mean to suggest that we are all really still
basically Christian. Perhaps we never were, and certainly
that kind of apologetic is still as suspect as it always
was. What I mean is that it is a mistake to invent an
all-embracing mental landscape as the background for a
good idea, and then expect to find its embodiment in
the real world exactly in that form. Certainly we live in
a secularized society, but this secularity is a far more

---

6 In a review of Graham Greene's *The Heart of the Matter.* Cf. George
Orwell's *Collected Essays, Journalism and Letters,* ed. by Sonia Orwell
and I. Angus (London: Secker and Warburg, 1968), IV, 443.

varied, complex, and subtle thing than any single mind can begin to comprehend. All one can do is to understand that part of it which is reasonably accessible to oneself, and begin from there without too large a pretension to universality.

This is why I want to consider just one area of the modern secularized world and what it suggests to us about the meaning of ritual today. The area I have chosen, that of higher education, is the one I know best, and it happens to be crucial in a number of ways. Not only is higher education a matter for constant comment and public debate; I suggest that it is also the locale of some of the most potent and interesting rituals of initiation in the whole of human history. I think I need no excuse for discussing it as one of the areas where we find the ritualization of life still going strong, despite the secular context which the modern university claims and to which it aspires.

In speaking of rituals of initiation, I am talking as an amateur anthropologist, as one who has only the barest and vaguest knowledge of the subject. But it seems to me that we can distinguish three elements that have traditionally been associated with the religious and social process of acceptance into adult society.[7] These are, first, a period of what may be called enforced *retreat* from society; second, a personal, interior *revolution* — the recognition by the initiate of something in himself that has to be purged away; and third, a public rite or *ordeal* to symbolize society's acceptance of the new, purified individual. These three elements go naturally together. The young initiate is first of all taken out of the society in which he has hitherto been brought up, and is sent away into a spiritual, or even a real, wilderness. In this period of retreat he is instructed in the demands the adult society will make upon him, and is helped to rec-

---

[7] On these, cf. Mircea Eliade, *The Sacred and the Profane* (New York: Harper and Row, 1961), pp. 184-201.

ognize its laws and customs. He has also to interiorize them so that, instead of merely taking them for granted in an external, unthinking way, he is now ready to adhere to them consciously and conscientiously. This sense of personal, interior adult responsibility does not come simply from a smooth development and growth. To achieve it requires a certain interior and personal crisis. (With women, the onset of menstruation makes the crisis point obvious; with boys it has, perhaps, to be artificially induced.) In any case, initiation is a catastrophic affair: the crossing of a boundary between two worlds, childhood and adulthood. Accumulated defilements and guilts inevitably go with the explosion of adult potentialities upon the child — particularly, of course, of sexual potentialities. Initiation is the resolution, after a period of crisis, of the conflicts associated with this passage from one world to another.

These conflicts are moral, physical, and psychological, and their resolution is possible only by a kind of self-purification that is both interior — the personal recognition, admission, and transformation of past "sins" — and exterior — a public purification that is the essential prelude to public acceptance. This, it seems to me, is the fundamental logic of the process of religious initiation. The Christian sacrament of initiation (the catechumenate and baptism-confirmation) is no exception. Its original form, still just visible under the accumulated debris of ecclesiastical tradition, reveals all these elements quite clearly. The catechumenate was, essentially, the period of retreat into "the wilderness" for instruction and for the making of that interior, personal revolution which was necessary for the real elimination of "original sin." This retreat culminated in the public profession of faith and the public rite of washing and purification: a symbolic death to the old sinful existence, and resurrection to a new form of life — life now lived fully within the mature society of "the saints."

One reason why baptism-confirmation has lost most

of its religious significance and has come to seem an
artificial and alien curiosity is, of course, that initiation
into adulthood has for a long time been telescoped with
initiation into life itself. The habit of infant baptism
has long robbed the rite of its aspect of personal, interior
revolution. That necessary revolution was then indefinitely postponed; when it did occur, as often as not it
took the form of a revulsion against the whole Christian
"thing" rather than a turning against the self and the
accumulated conflicts and "sins" of childhood and im-
maturity. Today only those fortunate enough to have
escaped being made Christians until after attaining a
certain personal grasp of themselves as adults can understand fully what baptism as a personal revolution in the
interior life really means. Recognizing this, twentieth-
century liturgical reformers have sometimes struggled to
re-create that sense of a personal crisis more or less artificially. Either they have rejected the whole concept of
infant baptism and returned to the practice of baptism
at the moment of personal maturity, or they have attempted to create some analogous rite — a separate "confirmation" procedure perhaps, or even a kind of secular
equivalent — that they hope will mean something to the
adolescent on the verge of maturity. But everyone, I
think, realizes that this is only tinkering about on the
fringe of the problem. For the fact is that one cannot
artificially create a rite of initiation that will mean as
much as the rite that is already there in the secular
world. And the major form of that rite, in an advanced
society, is the process of higher education.

Education provides, first of all, that temporary retreat from full commitment to society at the time of
emerging maturity which, I have suggested, is one characteristic of the typical initiatory procedure. This re-
treat-period is devoted, theoretically at least, to the in-
doctrination of the initiate into the ways and possibilities of adult society — a socializing of the former child
for his new role. It also attempts, at any rate used to at-

tempt, to transmit the central values, traditions, myths, and sagas of society to its students in order to give them a basis for grasping the problems of the present and the future. In this respect, then, the university, at any rate in theory and even to a certain extent in practice, provides the first and basic element in the true process of initiation.

The modern university, however, is disastrously split today in its actual initiatory functions. The public rituals of acceptance into the adult world that it offers have been cut adrift from the process of bringing to a head the personal, interior crisis that is a necessary preamble to the effective celebration of such rituals.[8] The university offers many rituals of acceptance, of which the whole apparatus of degree-giving, with its attendant rites of grading, testing, job placement, and status validation, are only the culminating moments. Equally significant, if less openly acknowledged, are the multifarious rites of a traditional kind associated with college life: the ritual activities of societies and clubs; the myriad sporting activities, which act as means for institutionalizing and containing violence and aggression; traditional and ritualistic modes for tolerating deviance within a strictly ordered system, ranging from the semi-official recognition of ways of getting into Oxford colleges at night when the doors have been locked, to the old-fashioned panty-raid; and of course the teaching situation itself and its attendant myths and customs. But for many students these rituals no longer focus or symbolize that interior spiritual revolution which is the basic and overriding purpose of the retreat from society that precedes public initiation. On the contrary, these rites are all now fully incorporated into the way of life of the wider society and its system. So far from being celebrated in secret, away from the glare and publicity of the wider

---

8 This splitting apart of the routine, public ritual and the interior, personal revolution is, of course, a characteristic feature of a religion that has degenerated into mere ceremonialism.

world, and fully intelligible only to those directly involved, they have become an important part of that world, indeed a center of interest within it. Essentially worldly concerns — symbolized above all by the incorporation into the university itself of the most worldly of the world's preoccupations, the promotion of *business* — have contaminated these traditional and sacred rites, taming and distorting them. So far from constituting a visible, sacramental embodiment of its role as a retreat-house for secret instruction, and as a scenario for coping with the personal crises of emerging adulthood, the university's official ritual has become the property of the outside world, and has taken on the values of that world.[9]

It is true that the university has *unofficially* retained a hold upon its traditional role, but only by a partial rebellion against this worldly appropriation of its being. The contemporary rituals of student protest and demonstration; the intensive but unofficial discussion, *outside* the strictly academic situation, of all the crucial personal concerns of those awaiting initiation; quasi-religious devotion by "dissenters" to various cultic, ascetic, or ceremonial practices as ways of expressing the interior revolution which they feel the need to undergo and by which they can be purified from the sins of having been brought up as children of "the system" — all of these represent legitimate and proper concerns of an initiatory process in the traditional sense. These unofficial rites cannot, however, be fully accommodated *within* "the system." Hence in the modern university the two essential and complementary processes of personal interiorization and official ritual have been split apart from each other. The official rituals tend to become meaningless and mindless ceremonies, captured for all intents and purposes by

---

9 Of course, this "secrecy" which is properly associated with university teaching has nothing to do with restricting the publication of results. It rests on the fact that the academic community is concerned with the preservation of values — scholarly integrity, disinterested research — that belong to it in a special and even exclusive way.

"the system"; while the interior and personal revolution
has lost its *social* significance as an essential preamble
to adult life, and is in danger of being regarded, both by
its devotees and its opponents, as a mere eccentricity to
be tolerated by an officially liberal society as long as it
causes no significant social disturbance. Should it do so,
it is to be put down with vigor.

Meanwhile, what is left out of all this turmoil is precisely the scholarly and academic role of the university
itself. Or rather this role too has been divided, and thus
ruled, by forces outside itself. One part of the academic
system, it has been discovered, can without fuss be fully
and effectively incorporated into "the system" of society
as a whole. For instance, the study of economics, of the
sciences, of sociology, and even of philosophy and lan-
guages *can* be brought under that system's control by
being interpreted merely as the essential *tool* of society's
most important concern — namely, business. Academic
study can thus be lured away from the straight and narrow path of scholarly detachment and academic rigor,
and brought into collaboration with "the system." So
the university becomes an organ of commerce or government, or a training ground for those destined to manage
"the system" in the future. The other side of the academic life can then be left to stew in its own juice. That
is to say, disinterested study of the humane disciplines
can now be left alone, so long as this does not become
too expensive. It can even be seen to be useful as a safety
valve, drawing off energies that would otherwise be used
to make a radical, disinterested, and thorough critique
of "the system" as a whole.

*   *   *

I have spoken of the new rituals of dissent as legitimate expressions of that need for a spiritual revolution
which the individual must undergo as part of any genuine initiation into adult life. There are, however, many

serious obstacles to the maintenance of these rituals as valid expressions of such personal upheavals. In the first place, in the modern mass-communications world, any ritual, however genuine its conception, can easily be cheapened before it has had time to focus its meaning properly. Rituals become dead before they have done their job. This danger is especially threatening in a closely knit community such as a university, or among groups of like-minded people such as students. What begins as a genuine symbol of revolt becomes a mere label for membership in a herd. The beards and the beads, the sit-in and the demonstration, the cultivated scruffiness and the ritual indulgences in drugs or sex, the automatic flexing of muscles at police or disciplinarians soon become worn-out symbols for a merely ersatz revolution. Like all other rituals, those of the modern student movement, necessary and legitimate though they may be as the expression of the university's role as provoker of an initiatory personal crisis, are always suspect. Indeed, they have already, in many cases, been captured by "the system" itself. The student demonstration has become a public spectacle and a predictable bore; threat of it becomes an occasion for the media-bought agents of "the system" as they are to represent it as a tolerated (or intolerable) exercise in youthful arrogance and irrationality, and this very fact becomes itself an inextricable part of the whole calculation, a fact that cannot be ignored. There is a constant temptation for the revolution within the revolution to become merely a competition in yet more extravagant rituals and symbols, each group or individual trying to get further to the political, social, or psychological left than the group or individual next door. The student revolution becomes almost a tourist attraction, on a level with those exhibitions of peasants in native costume doing obsolete dances that some countries put on for the benefit of tourists.

The second obstacle to a genuine personal revolution comes from the nature of the new ritualism itself, and more particularly from its connection with what may be called the ethic of immediate personal gratification, and from the profoundly puritanical overtones of that ethic. The starting point for the new ritualism is, of course, a sense of having been defiled by contact with, or even by being born into, the prevailing "system." This defilement is, of course, recognized as inevitable, but it is also rejected as evil. What we have here is, in fact, something like an admission of the guilt of original sin, put into modern language. But, of course, to be of any permanent value, the recognition of a universal, inescapable, and guilt-laden defilement by contact with "the system" must first be applied to oneself. Only by facing this defilement in oneself and by coming to terms with it can the individual find either the charismatic authority or the sense of long-term commitment that is needed successfully to transmit this sense of sin to others. It is at this point that contemporary student dissent tends to break down, because of an internal contradiction that needs to be exposed. Traditionally, the sense of original defilement and guilt has been particularly associated with illicit personal pleasures in general, and with sexual behavior in particular. Now I am fully aware of the excessive emphasis on these aspects of "sin" in the Christian tradition in the past, and of the enormous psychological damage that a distorted emphasis upon them has done to the collective psyche of modern man. It is wholly understandable that, associated with the sense of sin already discussed (that is, the sense of having been guiltily defiled by participation in "the system" understood in its social, political, and economic terms), there should be a revolt against what is taken to be the accompanying notion of "bourgeois morality." In the current post-Ibsenesque mood of disillusionment, it is wholly understandable that, for instance, people should take for granted that one part of a liberation from "the system" will be a liberation from the restraints of traditional sexual ethics, even to the point of asserting the freedom to copulate, where, when, and with whom one pleases, simply for the sake of immediate pleasure. This part of the contemporary revolt seems to be all of a piece with the rest of it. As Orwell saw, in some extreme circumstances even sex undertaken purely for instant, animal gratification can become a potent political weapon, an act of symbolic defiance.[10]

Yet it remains true that this aspect of the contemporary ritual of revolt, the pursuit of pleasure and of exotic experience for their own sakes, is in fact an unconscious collaboration with, not a rejection of, "the system." For the immediate gratification of such pleasures is one of the fundamental values that sustain the magic dream-world of pop and advertising, and hence of "the system." The new hedonism offers one of the most convenient means for siphoning off energies that would otherwise become dangerously subversive to "the system." In proclaiming a total liberation from traditional personal morality, the extreme left wing of the youthful revolt has in fact sold out to, or been sold down the river by, the advertising agents. In so doing it has attacked one of the few relics of the older generation's life-style that is *not yet* fully incorporated into "the system," and it has thereby compromised its claim to be a prophetic minority dedicated to a higher and more humane morality than that of "the system" itself. It is at this point that the Christian concept of sex — based upon a lifelong, unconditional, and willingly undergone self-exposure by one person to the dense and intricate reality of another — needs to be recognized as a genuinely revolutionary model of social relationships. The true Christian insight into sex is that there can be no genuine sexual encounter without a profound revolution on the part of both partners. To be united in this sense is to be faced with just that kind of identity crisis which the process of initiation itself demands. Indeed, the two are part of the

---

10 Cf. George Orwell, *Nineteen Eighty-Four* (New York: Harcourt, Brace, 1949), p. 128.

same thing. Marriage, like birth and adolescence, is a new world entered only through a kind of personal death and resurrection.

But it must also be insisted that the cult of immediate gratification, which is shared by Yippie and huckster alike, and which both proclaim to be a rebellion against puritanism, is itself a return to puritanism — to the puritanism of the wholly pure. Both proclaim, simultaneously, liberation from reason and from sin. This is perhaps obvious in the case of the huckster. His outlook is simply that pleasure is happiness, and that happiness is the ultimate end of life. "To a smoker, happiness is the taste of Kent." In saying this the advertiser is being both sophisticated and naive: sophisticated in appealing to our wish to be free from guilt, and telling us that in effect sin can be washed away, along with the dirt on our clothes, by the incantation of some magic detergent formula; naive because the whole appeal is rooted in a childish, but potent and appealing, belief in the possibility of a total human innocence. The same is, perhaps, less obvious in the case of the Yippie. The link is to be found in the essentially religious basis of the new dissent. Perhaps this suggestion needs some explaining.

There is a paradox in the idea of religious initiation. On the one hand it is a process for acknowledging maturity, but on the other it is a return to the womb, to original innocence; it is in the conflict between these two that much of our trouble lies. Maturity connotes, among other things, a recognition of the complexity of life. It refuses to oversimplify the moral dilemmas that face us and tries to find tolerable ways of accommodating the irreducible differences between men. Maturity is a "liberal" thing — it asks us to connect the prose and the passion. But it is also a "catholic" thing, using that term not in its denominational sense but as signifying a certain universality of outlook within which all kinds of divergent views can be reconciled, or at least put up with, and which has within itself the means for coming to terms with conflict in such a way as to prevent total disruption. In placing tolerance at its center, the ideal of maturity is placid rather than revolutionary. It involves a generosity of mind, a refusal of immediate judgment, that comes from seeing beyond the limits of one's own background or viewpoint. It rests, perhaps, on that liberation of "seeing" from "believing" to which I have already referred. It proclaims the sovereignty of reason, especially in dealing with moral problems. For example, the medieval casuistic tradition of moral rationality based on "natural law" was "mature" as well as "catholic" in the sense that, by drawing what it took to be necessary rational distinctions, it helped to make sense of the conflicts among men without falling into sheer moral laissez-faire. The just war tradition, for instance, was designed to reconcile the facts of human violence and political ambition with other opposite facts —namely, the brutality and futility of war.[11]

Religious initiation, it must be stressed, also works in the opposite direction. In seeking original innocence, it is not aiming at maturity or catholicity, but at purity and simplicity. In his retreat from the world, the initiate goes back to the womb to be reborn. Initiation is a return to childhood, and the wisdom it seeks is not that of the mature man of the world, but that of the newborn innocent whose intuitive understanding confounds, by its sheer simplicity and directness, the wisdom of the old. In his new-found purity, the man reborn cuts through all the complexities rational discourse has tried laboriously to unravel: he solves all his problems by the simple invocation of some instant prophetic power. Only those who have become again as little children can enter the kingdom of heaven. The mature, with their tedious preoccupation with realism, and politics, and the peaceful resolution of conflict, are from this point of view

---

[11] I should insist here that in saying this I am not giving an outline of the actual history of traditional casuistry but suggesting what in ideal circumstances would have been its natural tendency.

simply loaded with sin and guilt. They are the tired businessmen who cannot recognize what Chesterton called "The Ethics of Elfland."[12] Their very tolerance is a crime against the truth, and their reluctance to destroy established institutions is not genuine veneration of the sacred but a blind rejection of the clear call of God.

If, then, there is a profound ambivalence about the whole concept of religious initiation, it is not confined explicitly to religious forms. The secular equivalents in our own day show exactly the same ambiguity. Perhaps this is because it is not the religious aspect of initiation that brings the tension to a head, but simply the logic of inexorably conflicting claims. Old and young, the established and the as-yet-unestablished, faculty and students, are inevitably opposed to each other: precisely because one of the poles of the paradox is the spirit of tolerance and reconciliation itself, there can be no third term, no higher order of things that can embrace both kinds of wisdom and reconcile them in a kiss of peace. The spirit of reconciliation, it seems, has already been captured by one side. Because there can be no final superior wisdom to act as referee in the struggle, the paradox modulates into a dilemma.

*   *   *

I hope that this analysis helps to show why it is correct to regard the extreme libertarianism of the dissenting left in higher education today as a kind of militant puritanism: not the dreary grey puritanism of the nineteenth-century bourgeoisie, but the fanatical and enthusiastic puritanism of the seventeenth-century sects, driven by a genuine, naive belief in the purity of their own cause and the purity of their members. It is this spirit of militant puritanism which calls for the elimination of all competition in education, for the abolition of all rules and regulations in college dormitories, for the annihila-

---

12 Cf. G. K. Chesterton, *Orthodoxy* (London: Lane, 1908), ch. 4 passim.

tion of the difference of status between teacher and student, for the elimination of all external restraints in public expression and in the performing arts, and for the destruction of everything associated with the word "administration." These are puritanical demands because they come from people who think that man is capable of living without rules in sheer, pristine innocence, face to face with himself. The rituals of dissent are embodiments of this idea, and the uncut beards and the cultivated nudity are symbols of the shameless naiveté of prelapsarian man.

It is only against this background of tensions between catholic and puritanical tendencies in the new ritualism that we can properly evaluate the insistence on the essentially sinful nature of "the system" that lies at the root of much of the current unrest. To put it in a nutshell, what the dissenters choose to call "the system" is more or less what St. John consistently referred to as "the world" — a connected order of things that is systematically given over to itself, to the seeking of its own ends apart from God. I think "the world" in St. John's sense of the term has to be understood today as that whole tendency of any complex society to dissociate its various activities, to keep them from understanding each other, to disconnect the prose from the passion just where the divine and human imperative insists they must be connected. Western society today seems to want to refuse that creative connection, preferring to drug itself with pseudo-religion and with idle but commercially profitable dreams — most obviously the public fantasies of the advertising industry. We have been manifestly failing collectively to accept the links between private affluence and public squalor, between white privilege and black subjection, between metropolitan prosperity and colonial deprivation, between the trivialization of public debate and the commercialization of public language, in short between morality and politics. It is just this connection that the doctrine of original sin is designed to bring out into the open. The crucial thing about original sin is that it asserts that there is a sense in which the world is a connected order opposed to God, turned in upon itself — not just incidentally or in certain minor respects but systematically. There is a sense in which each individual, whether he recognizes it or not, is responsible to God for this state of affairs and is in need of that internal revolution of spirit which alone can release him from the ensuing guilt of complicity.

Understood in this way, many of the arguments of the "dissenters" about "the system" begin to appear as simple restatements of a familiar Gospel theme. When the postliberal student rebel insists that, however well-meaning his professor may be (and however good his voting record), he is still part of a system that needs to be opposed and overthrown, he is merely rewording, although in a highly uncomfortable way, an essential piece of Christian wisdom. But it is a wisdom that is not of "this world." And of course it is a wisdom that cannot be turned to genuinely creative account as long as it is founded upon that puritanical spirit which refuses to see that it applies first of all to oneself.

If the revolutionary wisdom that is Christianity has nothing in common with a fanatical and arrogant puritanism, neither does it seem to have much in common with what we may call rational morality. It is here that I think we have to see the positive role that may be played by the reversion to ritual behavior exemplified by certain dissenting groups in our society. Perhaps there is after all an eschatological meaning to this trend that runs counter to, and perhaps even cancels out, the reactionary possibilities of the new ritualism. If those who espouse the new rituals of revolt seem on the face of it simply to be retreating into the comfortable womb of unthinking "commitment" and animal instinct, it may yet be that this is only the agony that must precede a rebirth into a new kind of morality.

This suggestion is, of course, purely speculative, but

there are some elements in the contemporary situation that, perhaps, require us to interpret it in these large terms. There seem to be two connected features of life in the advanced countries of the West, especially in the United States, that lie beneath the particular battles over racism or Vietnam or whatever, and upon which contemporary dissent is rightly and properly focused. The first is an overwhelming sense of personal impotence in the face of the all-powerful and self-perpetuating forces of technological progress. The second is the radical divorce of modern politics from rational morality. Against these immense obstacles to a decent human life the old concepts and institutions seem powerless. Neither the church nor the elected political assemblies seem able to make themselves felt as representatives of humanity over against the huge impersonality of technology and the momentum of world conflict. At the most elementary level, the breakdown of a humane existence is epitomized by the manifest incapacity of the servicing and repairing industries to cope with modern gadgets. It is far easier to make a reliable repair in a ten-million-dollar airliner or an orbiting space station than it is to get a broken part replaced in a gas stove or to feel confident about the diagnosis of a faulty transmission. The ordinary person today is more and more at the mercy of the expert, while the expert is becoming less and less able to serve him.

This is, perhaps, a rather trivial example. It may be only a matter of time before things catch up with themselves, but I think not. For what I have alluded to is only one aspect of a far larger fact — namely, the rise of the megalopolis or super-city, and the kind of life this development implies. The city, of course, is the epitome of "civilization." In certain strains of Christian tradition it was the very model of heaven itself. The city of God was the only stronghold capable of withstanding the onslaught of the world: the celestial city was the ultimate object of man's quest. Yet it is also clear that in the same traditions the city was a diabolical invention. The city of Babylon was the name for chaos and disorder. For St. Augustine the city of God was at war with the city of Satan, and Bunyan's pilgrim could attain the celestial city only by fleeing from the city of destruction. The city, as such, was then an ambivalent institution. It nourished *civilization* but was at the same time profane and self-destructive. The modern super-city embodies this contradiction to an extreme degree. Here we have a *totally* transformed world, in which the surface of the earth, the depths beneath, and even the sky above are made over into human creations. Nature is everywhere transfigured, indeed polluted and uprooted, in order to be given up to human life. At the same time, however, it is only in the city that one can assemble all the resources of human invention. Modern life is there, in the city: its richness as well as its chaos and profanity. The city is where creative and destructive conflict exist simultaneously.

This is hardly a new discovery. H. G. Wells, as long ago as 1908, could describe London as a place whose growth was that of a cancer (not a healthy development) and could ask himself: "Will those masses ever become structural, will they shape indeed into anything new whatever, or is that cancerous image the true and ultimate diagnosis?"[13] Today this question is even more pressing. Beyond all the efforts of urban renewal, is there really anything ultimately worth having about the modern super-city, strangling itself with its own size and complexity? The traffic jam is a kind of cancer, the rush hour a malignant growth that stems directly from the fact of the city itself. It is somehow beyond human control. Planners, architects, social and civil engineers, and politicians alike are helpless in the face of it. Every plan that is adopted is out of date before it is even begun. Only by the imposition of an iron dictatorship that can

---

13 Cf. H. G. Wells, *Tono-Bungay*, Book 2 (Boston: Houghton-Mifflin, 1966), p. 84.

cut through the multitude of private interests and personal considerations by ruthless fiat is it, perhaps, possible to envisage a city that could regain human control
of it own life. But to go that way would simply be to
destroy the city itself as a *polis* — a civilized community
dedicated to humane ends. Here, it seems, we come up
against a barrier of an apparently new kind: a barrier to
human control that emerges just at the moment of maxi-
mum technical mastery of the environment.

I wish to suggest that here we are bumping up against
what I can only call the sense of the "sacred" in a new
form. And it is for this reason that, paradoxically, the
new ritualism seems capable of positive, creative action
within the contemporary milieu. This needs a more detailed explanation.

The sacred has always been associated, I suppose, with
the recognition of taboos — that is, with absolute limits
that must be observed if life is to be maintained. In the
past, these limits were necessary for the demarcation of
the sacred from the profane world,[14] and for the establishment of a kind of security through access to the
divine. In a diluted sense, the moral rules elaborated in
the Western tradition of rational morality can be seen
as secular versions of the same thing. But the important
difference is that primitive taboo was not a utilitarian
or metaphysical inference. It was a simple intuition or
sense of danger. "If you put your hand in the fire you
will get burnt." "If you eat of the forbidden tree you
will die." Taboo, in its essence, was based on as automatic a chain of cause and effect as that. And this was
because it was concerned largely with reconciling man
to the simple, ineluctable facts of life. At a later stage,
perhaps, morality had to become more rational in response to man's ability to control his environment. Because the outer world presented fewer terrors, the focus
of the sacred became the human individual himself. His

---

14 Cf. Mircea Eliade, *Sacred and Profane,* passim.

own person and life, or even the quality of that life, was
the thing that had to be protected and held sacred. So
it was the sanctity of persons rather than gods or natural
objects that mattered. Could not, then, the free individual, unlike a natural object, voluntarily forfeit his
right to this sanctity by his own act? Could he not put
himself beyond the pale?

Looked at in this oversimplified way, I think the
whole apparatus of moral theology in the Christian tradition might be described as concerned with working
out some accommodation between a purely *religious*
sense of the human person as simply and unconditionally
"sacred," and therefore immune from violation, and the
rational recognition of the free human being as able,
deliberately, so to violate the rights of others as to lose
his own right of immunity in return. Thus, as man develops, religious taboo gives way to moral law, and then
as morality itself becomes touched by Cartesian dualities,
objective behavior gives way to subjective intentions and
signs as the main topic of moral argument. For example,
in the post-Cartesian world "innocence" ceases to mean
"not doing any physical harm" and becomes rather "having no malicious thoughts, feelings, or intentions." The
absolute physical immunity of the "innocent" human
person — for instance, his immunity from attack in war-
time, as in the just war tradition — is replaced by "innocent" intentions on the part of the attacker, as the criterion for discrimination.

The results of this gradual erosion of religion by
rational morality have been paradoxical. Within the
older religious scheme of things, some persons were simply and unconditionally immune — namely, sacred persons such as kings or priests. There was here a limit to
violence that was as irrational as it was absolute. Calcu-
lations about means and ends were simply irrelevant in
that case: what mattered was simply that a taboo was
broken and had to be atoned for. But once this sense of
taboo was lost, rules had to be devised for distinguishing

those whose personal record or subjective condition of mind still qualified them for immunity. The whole apparatus of the modern just war ethic as a rational moral system was thus one inevitable product of the erosion: while its purpose was to limit and humanize war, its actual effect was to make war more terrible. War became, in certain cases, morally legitimate, and "progress" was thereafter only a matter of widening the limits, in response to political demands and technical inventions, in order that ever more brutal wars could be brought under the umbrella of "justice."

With the coming of the just war theory, war then ceased to be a religious ritual or religious duty and became simply a secular means to a secular end — the continuation of politics by other means. In short, the limits that were set to human violence were now reduced to that feeble and ineffectual kind which we now call, without much qualification, "moral." Thus, with the erosion of clear and undeniable taboos and their replacement by merely moral rules, the hope of ever recovering that demarcation of boundaries, which is the essence of the sacred, seems to have disappeared.

The recent history of Western ethics, then, might be summed up as the steady erosion of any limits to what man may do without fatal hurt to himself. But what this really means is that, when pushed to the limits, rational morality has become irrational morality; the harm that is brought to the individual by the breach of a moral rule becomes invisible, not only to himself, but also to the public at large. A merely rational morality is for this very reason unable to hold back the tide of autonomous economic and technological development. It is not surprising, therefore, that today an ethic of self-fulfillment through the absence of any "moral" restraints would seem best to express man's unbounded confidence in his own technical powers. For what we appear to have almost within our grasp is a world in which we can do what we like without having to fear any uncontrollable consequences for ourselves. We can take care of all our follies through birth control, abortion, drugs, psychotherapy, group dynamics, sensitivity training, fertilizers, tax allowances, hidden subsidies, antipollution agents, brainwashing, advertising, nuclear terror, and, if necessary, genocide. All of these have become simply techniques, morally neutral and equally legitimate.

But at the very moment when we glimpse this apparently limitless future, the political facts rise up against us in all their incomparable intractability. If we have moved out of the age of *moral* limitations, we have moved into a world where a sense of *political* limits is taking its place. We have, for practical purposes, removed all "moral" limits upon violence to the human person only to find that this violence is rebounding upon us as the due expression of the facts of this postmoral era. The violence of the modern world is an apt symbol and revelation of its inner reality. Violence in the city, for example, reveals nakedly the problems that traditional techniques apparently cannot solve. Violent crime and violent anticrime on the streets are the natural ritual activities of the super-city, creating in reality what they signify as symbols. They are the sacramental actions, complete with attendant mythologies, hierarchies, and ascetical disciplines, of the contemporary urban community. Similarly, at the international level, the diplomatic and ideological statements — Vietnam, the Middle East, Czechoslovakia, Latin America, all locked together at their apex by the massive overarching and perilous balance of nuclear terror — are equally fitting symbols, ever liable to become destructive facts, of the same political frustration. What we must now recognize is that this sense of frustration is not merely a "hang-up" to be dissolved away by some new breakthrough in technique. It is a kind of political *taboo*. The huge menacing cloud of violence and threat that hangs over us all is the veil of a numinous, appallingly fearsome, and hideously real presence in the political area. This new cloud, like the cloud of old that hung over Mount Sinai, is both a shield and a revelation of the terrible power cloaked within it. Its white-hot radiance of nuclear threat and brutal menace is a warning against man's attempt to go beyond what is politically possible. The H-bomb, one might say, needs to be seen not as a useful weapon or a bargaining counter for political transactions, to be handled with care, but as a tabooed object that it is quite simply too hot and dangerous for anybody to touch at all, something which it is forbidden to him to have any truck with.

It is here that the ritualism of the new dissenters can be positively beneficial. Against a threat and a power that holds the very future of mankind itself in the balance, the weak and disorganized verbal sallies of a rational morality and political reality never come within shouting distance of each other. As far as is discernible to the world at large, for example, none of the moral prohibitions that have been enunciated in the last few years by bishops, popes, or councils concerning war have had any effect whatever on the conduct of wars in that period, though they may have had a marginal effect on the kind of propaganda put out by warring sides to impress the world generally. It is not that in these cases the politicians and strategists have come up with arguments to prove the invalidity of the old just war prohibitions. The impression is, rather, that morality and war simply inhabit two quite different realms. The one is the realm of practical reality, the other of academic theory. The two, it seems, can never meet.

If political reality and moral theory never meet in international conflicts, neither do they have much more intercourse with each other in the field of domestic economics. For example, it seems clear enough that the whole economy of a country like the United States or Britain depends upon the advertising industry. In other words, the very life of a modern, commercialized society depends upon accepting the proposition, to quote Orwell's words, that "the public are swine"; and as a corollary, that "advertising is the rattling of a stick inside a swill bucket."[15] Without this rattling of the stick, we are told, the economy would perish. Yet to go on with it involves us in reducing people to the level of pigs. In order to survive we have to allow all the work of parents and teachers, in trying to instill such virtues as frankness, sincerity, intelligent discrimination, and respect for the natural grain of the language, to be systematically undermined. Of course, advertising does not corrupt us by meeting our professed ideals head-on in a frank confrontation of opposing principles: it works sideways, by a process of subtle distortion and gradual corrosion. It deliberately sets out to numb us at the point when alertness is most needed for decent human values to survive — especially for the survival of literature and art. The essence of advertising is not lying, but the mass-organization of insincerity. Sherwood Anderson, one of the few writers of any note who actually worked for a long period as an advertising agent's copywriter, knew this well enough. "When I am being corrupt," he said, "perverting the speech of men, let me remain aware of what I am doing . . . hypocrisy in this matter, this believing your own bunk, is the real sin against the Holy Ghost."[16]

The paradox of the situation here sketched is evident. To invoke the categories of rational morality is to commit social, economic, and political suicide. Yet the situation is itself suicidal. What kind of protest can be mounted against such a paradox if not an equally paradoxical form of direct action? If what is needed is an awareness of an absolute taboo, the observance of which is a *sine qua non* of survival, perhaps only the breach of

---

[15] Cf. George Orwell, *Keep the Aspidistra Flying* (London: Secker and Warburg, 1954), p. 66.

[16] Quoted in Irving Howe, *Sherwood Anderson* (New York: Sloane, 1951), p. 52.

some less absolute rule will be sufficient to bring the society to its senses.

This, I take it, is the argument for the new ritualism, the new religion of symbolic action. It is not my task here either to defend or to attack it. That it has its own immense dangers is perfectly obvious. There is only a hair's breadth of difference between creative and symbolic rule-breaking and destructive and real society-breaking, but it is also the difference between legitimate revolution and collective suicide.

What is clear, however, is that the university is bound, of its very nature, to find itself at the center of the storm. For the twin pillars of the university's structure are, or should be, the primacy of reason and the exploration of reality. When reason and reality seem to have fallen apart where does the university stand? If it gives up either, it merely ensures its own collapse. To avoid making any kind of choice is to be condemned to irrelevance. The paradox of the university is the paradox of the contemporary situation itself. How the universities manage to cope with this paradox will be a sign of how society as a whole will cope with it. What is certain is that, whichever way history goes, the new ritualism will have had a great deal to do with the outcome.

2

Ritual and the Development of Social Structure: Liminality and Inversion

by

CHRISTOPHER CROCKER

RITUAL IS A STATEMENT IN METAPHORIC TERMS ABOUT
the paradoxes of human existence. In this paper I wish
to consider the theoretical background and the two prevailing schools of anthropological interpretation of this
definition: the view that regards ritual as a type of political action, and that which sees it as an expression of
belief.[1] In both cases the particular content of action and

1 I wish to thank Professors T. O. Beidelman, W. La Barre, D.
Maybury-Lewis, T. Turner, J. Peacock, and J. Fox for helping me
develop the ideas reflected in this paper.

Jon Christopher Crocker teaches Sociology and Anthropology at Duke
University. His publications include *Social Organization of the Eastern
Bororo;* "The Southern Way of Death," in *The Not So Solid South:
Anthropological Studies in a Regional Subculture,* ed. J. Kenneth Mor-
land; and "Men's House Associates among the Eastern Bororo," in the
Southwestern Journal of Anthropology.

belief is interpreted as a related characteristic of a given social structure, but the nature of this relationship is precisely the disputed element. The ritual-as-action theorists assert that certain culturally stereotyped behaviors, despite their ostensible reference to various cosmological esoterica, are but statements about the statuses of persons relative to one another. Thus, the required (in some increasingly limited segments of our society) doffing of masculine headgear to a lady implies a certain quality of deference in male-female relationships that a native informant might characterize as respect. In the opinion of the action-oriented anthropologists, however, such an "actor interpretation" is totally irrelevant as an explanation of the custom; the beliefs held by participants in it are seen as epiphenomena or, in Durkheim's phrase, symbolic representations of social reality. The ritual-as-belief theorists maintain that understanding of a given rite must derive from knowledge of the entire conceptual system of the society; ceremonies must be analyzed in terms of the categories by which the society attempts to order the inchoate world of experience, or action. This approach emphasizes the partial independence of belief from social structure, the lack of causal relationship between the two, while the action school seeks to demonstrate the structural content of ceremonial events.

To continue with the preceding example, the former would examine the symbolic significance of hats, the uncovered male head, the bow and curtsey, while the latter discuss male-female relations in general, or statuses in which sex has no relevance in determining whether or not the hat should be raised — royalty and children respectively. My tactic in this paper shall be that traditional scholastic device, a combination of the two interpretations that attempts to show them as mutually complementary rather than antithetically opposed. The possible virtues of the synthesis will be illustrated by reference to various ceremonies of the Bororo, a Brazilian tribe that I have studied. In this society a man becomes through ritual something that is totally the opposite of his usual social identity and in the process establishes the principles that found group and personal identity. As I said, ritual involves paradox.

I must emphasize that the implicit unity of opinion expressed by the reference to "schools" scarcely exists. There are as many definitions of ritual as there are anthropologists; we seem to have replaced those notorious angels by totems. There is as little substantive consensus on what we mean by social structure as on the attributes of ritual. Many anthropologists, however, appear to agree on certain basic characteristics of each, and my interpretation of these shall be utilized here as a basis of departure. For most of my colleagues, ritual expresses those fundamental categories by which men attempt to apprehend and to control their social existence — categories that refer both to social positions and to mystical entities. We assume that man is a rule-making and order-seeking creature to whom transition and change represent a challenge, if not actual threat. The cataclysms that menace the fabric of social coherence range from epidemics and assassinations to the transition from youth to manhood, birth to death, and spring into winter. Societies tend to meet these situations of crisis with ritual, which presents the enduring validity of certain principles of order. Symbolic action affirms something: it makes a statement about the conditions of existence in terms of the relations of persons and groups. Ritual, then, is essentially communication, a language in which societies discuss a variety of matters. It deals with the relationships a man has to other men, to institutions, spirits, and nature, and with all the various permutations of which these themes are capable. Our immediate problem thus becomes, exactly what is ritual communicating? How do we discover what a savage is saying, to himself and his fellows, when he parades about in feathers and paint, or what we mean when we use a fork to eat certain vegetables but our fingers to deal with corn-on-the-cob?[2] Moreover, ritual not only says something; it also does things: it changes one season into another, makes boys become men, transforms ill persons into healthy ones, and the ghosts of the dead into the souls of the ancestors. Anthropologists agree that these functions of ritual are merely various perspectives of a nondifferentiated, dynamic whole, but differ as to how communication relates to transformation and the mechanisms involved for both.

*   *   *

Early attempts to establish the significance of ritual focused on context. Perhaps the best known example of this was Durkheim's assertion that social action could be distinguished in terms of those behaviors directed to the sacred and those oriented to the profane. Such a contrast derived, however, from the assumptions of the late nineteenth-century positivists, and these in turn were conditioned by the particular climate of opinion and the society in which they wrote. These men — I have in mind Frazer, Tylor, Fustel de Coulanges, Spencer, W. Robertson-Smith, and their intellectual precursors — were confronted in their documents with the uncomfortable problem that while primitive man clearly expressed an awareness of deity in ways that were not incompatible with nineteenth-century Christianity, this expression was bound up with such barbarisms as tree worship, human sacrifice, fetishism, and a great deal of feathers and paint.[3] How could a man chant gibberish over a rock one moment and the next establish through sacrifice a blood covenant with a spirit that stressed

---

2 This example is not as farcical as it may seem. Lévi-Strauss has recently (*L'Origine des Manières de Table;* Paris: Plon, 1968) shown the relevance of the codes through which nature is incorporated into society, such as "table manners," to the understanding of cultural systems.

3 The following discussion owes much to Steiner (*Taboo;* London: Cohen and West, 1956, pp. 50-115), Douglas (*Purity and Danger;* New York-London: Praeger, pp. 7-28), and Beidelman (private communication).

self-abnegation and the public weal? A variety of attempts were made to solve this dilemma. Robertson-Smith, a theologian and minister in the Free Church of Scotland, began by first sharply distinguishing beliefs (dogma or mythology) and practices (ritual); since the former are explanations of the latter, any analysis must begin with the practices, the actual ceremonial behaviors. He thus implicitly attacked those scholars, such as Tylor, who held that religion was the outgrowth of speculative thought that attempted to explain such phenomena as dreams, birth, and the passage of the seasons. Smith also emphasized the close relation between religious acts and the moral values of primitive communal life. In doing so he confronted the problem mentioned above, the apparent mixture of paganistic magical practices addressed to myriads of demons with such manifestations of faith as sacrifice to a clan or tribal god who embodied the highest social good. His solution was to contrast "magic" to "religion."[4] This emphatic distinction between magic and religion was taken over by Durkheim and incorporated into the sacred-profane dichotomy. Thus he defined religion as "a unified system of beliefs and practices (rites) relative to sacred things, that is to say, things set apart and forbidden — beliefs and practices which unite into a single moral community called a Church, all those who adhere to them."[5] Those actions and concepts which

---

[4] W. Robertson-Smith, *The Religion of the Semites* (London: Black, 1889), p. 55. "From the earliest times religion, as distinct from magic and sorcery, addressed itself to kindred and friends who may indeed be angry with their people for a time, but are always placable except to the enemies of their people or to renegade members of the community.... It is only in times of social dissolution ... that magical superstition based on mere terror or rites designed to placate alien gods invade the sphere of tribal or national religion. In better times the religion of the tribe or state has nothing in common with the private and foreign superstitions or magical rites that savage terror may dictate to the individual. Religion is not an arbitrary relation of the individual man to a supernatural power; it is a relation of all the members of a community to the power that has the good of the community at heart."

[5] Emile Durkheim, *The Elementary Forms of the Religious Life* (Glencoe: Free Press, 1953 [1912]), p. 47.

do not have reference to this moral community and which are oriented to the individual rather than to the society are clearly magic and belong to the realm of the profane. Magic is characterized by the lack of a church, the absence of a common union of all believers, antagonism to the sacred, and frequently has to do with the problem of pollution, of separating (or combining in alchemic ways) those substances which are somehow antithetical to one another.[6] Later thinkers, following Frazer's scheme, added that magic was also profane in being a sort of misplaced, fallacious science. Since primitive man was technologically unsophisticated, he attempted to do through spells and potions what he could not accomplish by utilitarian means. Thus there was magic for curing disease, or enticing game to the hunter, or insuring the fertility of crops. These techniques were quite distinct from religious acts, which established the dependence of individuals and groups on the moral order of society through rituals expressing their relationship with the gods that embodied such order. All of this fit rather neatly into the evolutionary dogma of the time, for it followed that as man progressed, science would slowly edge out magic until religion was purified of its nonmoral, utilitarian, and paganistic elements.[7]

The heritage, then, of these early thinkers was an association of the irrational, mystical expression of transcendental social values with the sacred, and the identification of secular, utilitarian, experimental efforts to coerce reality with the profane. However, as anthropologists began working in the field with actual primitive

---

[6] *Ibid.*, p. 338. "The things which the magician recommends to be kept separate are those which, by reason of their characteristic properties, cannot be brought together and confused without danger."

[7] Again, Douglas and Steiner must be credited with developing this insight. On the general problem of the epistemological assumptions of the early anthropologists, see Edmund Leach, "The Epistemological Background to Malinowski's Empiricism," in *Man and Culture*, ed. by R. Firth (London: Routledge and Kegan Paul, 1957), pp. 119-137; "Golden Bough or Gilded Twig?", in *Daedalus* (Spring, 1961), pp. 371-387; "On the 'Founding Fathers,'" *Encounter*, XXV, 5 (1965), 24-36.

peoples, rather than deriving their theories from travel-ogues and garbled accounts of "savage practices," they immediately observed that such distinctions simply did not accord with the observable facts. Members of those exotic societies did not have separate terms for "magic" and "religion," no more than for "sacred" and "pro-fane"; nor did their actions indicate any rigid demarca-tion of the two spheres. Objects treated as highly potent and with mystical forces on certain occasions were at other times handled casually and even cavalierly. As Evans-Pritchard points out: "The Zande cult of ancestors is centered around shrines erected in the middle of their courtyards, and offerings are placed in these shrines on ceremonial, and sometimes other occasions; but when not in ritual use, so to speak, Azande use them as convenient props to rest their spears against, or pay no attention to them whatsoever."[8]

This does not deny that men categorically distinguish between the "dangerous" or "mystically potent" and the "secular" or "normal," but rather that they are contextu-ally flexible about such contrasts. The social definition of a particular situation establishes which of its elements are fused with power and which are not, but any given element is unlikely to retain its "sacredness" in all situa-tions. For such complex matters the magic-religion con-trast is simply not very helpful. For example, the sup-posed "magical" treatment of illness might involve the ingestion of various "medicinal" substances, the expia-tion through sacrifice of a prior state of sin or pollution, the visitation of a spirit through the agency of a shaman or other ritual intermediary, formal communal gestures of sympathy and good-will toward the afflicted person, and so forth. That the holy and sacred is an integral part of the most ordinary, mundane activities is a common-place from pulpits of all persuasions.

By obliterating the sacred-profane distinction and re-

---

8 E. E. Evans-Pritchard, *Theories of Primitive Religion* (Oxford: Clarendon Press, 1965), p. 65.

placing it by a situationally specific orientation, we may have operationalized our approach to the subtleties of contextual categories, but we are no further toward the problem of understanding the meaning of any particular ritual action. Nearly all anthropologists, I find, continue to assume Durkheim's and Robertson-Smith's emphasis on the strict relationship between the sacred and the social. We may not accept the original argument that divinities are created in the image of societies, that cosmological categories are the product of social classifications,[9] but it is in the interpretation of those symbolic representations presented in ritual that the action and the belief schools diverge. The latter feels that meaning must be derived from the interpretation of the believing actors. The action group points out that the same ritual may be interpreted in contrasting and even opposing terms by various participants: a young man's explanation of a fertility dance is likely to be quite different from an old matron's. One eminent member of this group, Edmund Leach, even states, "With minor variations the ritual of the Christian Mass is the same throughout Christendom, but each individual Christian will explain the performance by reference to his own sectarian doctrine."[10] Even though I would take issue with this, the comparative problem Leach is implicitly raising is a very serious one. Precisely the same rites may be found in cultures which give them very different interpretations but which do not resemble each other in organization or ecology.[11] The lack of correlation between belief,

9 Emile Durkheim and Marcel Mauss take this argument in *Primitive Classification*, trans. and introd. by Rodney Needham (Chicago: Univ. of Chicago Press, 1963 [1903]). Cf. also Introduction, pp. vii-xlvii, for one modern response.

10 Edmund Leach, "Ritual," in *International Encyclopedia of the Social Sciences*, ed. by D. Sills (New York: Macmillan-Free Press, 1968), pp. 520-526.

11 Arnold van Gennep pointed out many years ago that rites of passage seemed to have the same structure and even some of the same symbolism (such as death and rebirth) in nearly all societies; see *The Rites of Passage* (Chicago: Univ. of Chicago Press, 1960 [1909]).

act, and structure is analogous to the absence of a causal relationship between language and society. We may learn to speak and understand Bonga-Bonga without ever sharing Bongese beliefs or participating in their institutions.[12] But even if the ritual-as-language view is accepted, how can this language be deciphered?

First, it might be noted that a focus on ritual as the communicative aspect of behavior completely obviates the sacred-profane dichotomy, for the emphasis is on what is being said about relations and social structures in all contexts. It is this characteristic which underlies one widely used technique for establishing the vocabulary of ritual language, first developed by Radcliffe-Brown. He demonstrated that the meaning of a given symbol could be derived only by comparing all instances of its formal, obligatory usage.[13] By noting the interpretations of a symbolic act and comparing all the contexts in which it appears, we may come to comprehend not only its significance but also that of a particular ritual, which combines a series of such acts to produce a subtle, multi-layered whole.

Such an approach presumes some amount of consistency and an awareness of contradiction on the part of the society's members. Apparent exceptions to this may constitute one of the most important characteristics of ritual — the ambiguity of its symbols. We would normally associate the color white with occasions of joy: a bride's

---

12 The problem of "translation," making the rules and meanings employed in one society intelligible to members of another culture, is sometimes regarded as the central problem of anthropology. The moot point is the degree to which one may understand the Bongese through their language alone, *without* direct participation in their institutions.

13 "That is, weeping and crying may be intuitively held to express sorrow, but among the Andamanese persons are required to weep upon such diverse occasions as marriages, homecomings, births, feasts, funerals and so forth —as, indeed, Americans are." A. R. Radcliffe-Brown, *The Andaman Islanders* (Glencoe: Free Press, 1964 [1922]), pp. 239-241. He concluded that ceremonial weeping affirms and establishes a social bond between two or more persons, and creates the solidarity that must prevail in social relationships.

dress, a birthday cake, springtime. On the other hand, we clothe the dead in white shrouds, portray ghosts as arrayed in white sheets, and say someone is "pale with fear" or "white with anger." The anthropologist would say that while the various connotative meanings given the color are distinct, they all derive from a common underlying denotation; equally, the contexts in which white is used, no matter how apparently different, all have something in common. Consequently, each meaning affects the others, and a shadowy network of associations is established during each encounter of ritual whiteness. This gives great psychic and cognitive force to the experience, as any reader of Joyce knows. I shall return to this theme of ambiguity later; at the moment, we should note that the comparative techniques of discovering ritual meaning are very much like those used by linguists in deciphering both the semantic content of speech events and the rules of syntax that determine the particular forms taken by them.

For the ritual-as-action group, the symbolic acts that compose the vocabulary of ritual are interpreted as statements about the right, ethical relationships between individuals and groups, and about the moral principles of social organization. Social life depends upon such definitions of who I am, what I expect of you, what you may expect of me, and how our recent behavior toward one another has affected these expectations. It is crucial that such messages be understood, that they compose part of a formalized system or code, for when the ritual code of expectations is no longer able to communicate, the pathological state of disorganization known as *anomie* occurs.[14] As Leach says, "Our day-to-day relationships depend upon a mutual knowledge and mutual acceptance of the fact that at any particular time any two individuals occupy different positions in a highly complex network of status

---

[14] Strictly speaking, *anomie* results from contradictions in the normative system such that goals and the institutional means to obtain them are in conflict.

relations; ritual serves to affirm what these status differences are."[13] Thus the more status relevant to the occasion, the more stereotyped clothing and bearing, from morning coats at weddings to cap and gown at commencement. In many primitive societies ceremony can be seen as an assertion of authority that embodies the continuing, most widely held values of the community. The well-known complexities of Hindu ritual pollution, in which various social positions are pure or defiled in relation to those roles and natural entities above or below them in the caste hierarchy, provide an exceedingly elaborate language for the discussion of relative status and of the preeminent ethical principles that control the relations of groups.[16]

The English social anthropologist Max Gluckman has emphasized the crucial importance of ritual in resolving the conflicts generated by the very nature of primitive social life. In his view, such life is characterized by a juxtapostion and overlapping of functionally distinct roles. In the confined world of the village the same man may be required to act simultaneously as a father, a brother, a husband, a priest, and a farmer. The expectations involved for each of these roles conflict to some degree with one another. Thus, at times a woman must choose between the demands of her lineage brothers and the needs of her own children. Since two persons may be related in a variety of ways, irresolvable problems seem

---

15 Edmund Leach, "Ritual," p. 524.

16 Concluding a general discussion of African social organization, E. E. Evans-Pritchard and Myer Fortes in *African Political Systems* (Oxford: Clarendon, 1940), p. 21, say: "[Africans] think and feel about it [their social system] in terms of values which reflect, in doctrine and symbol, but do not explain, the forces that really control their social behavior. Outstanding among these values are the mystical values dramatized in the great public ceremonies and bound up with their key political institutions. These, we believe, stand for the greatest common interest of the widest political community to which a member of a particular African society belongs — that is, for the whole body of interconnected rights, duties, and sentiments; for that is what makes the society a single political community."

built into the social organization; what must a man who is responsible for his lineage before the ancestors do when his own son defies his authority? Since all of these relations are articulated in a coherent system, necessary to one another and in close daily contact, failure or conflict in any given role threatens the entire social fabric. Because the natural order is closely identified with the social one, such disruptions are reflected in droughts, epidemics, floods, eclipses, and so forth. Conversely, these events are often thought to derive from, or be caused by, improper social relations, from confusions in the multiplex, confounded roles.

Gluckman does not make the mistake of many social scientists in claiming that mystical punishments are a sort of substitute for legal sanctions against those who defy communal laws. For him, man is a moral creature who values the coherency and stability of his cultural mode of being. Incest, even with a very distant member of one's own clan, represents a basic confusion of the categories that regulate the interaction of social groups who marry one another. The incestuous pair may sicken and die, but their actions may also bring about disaster for every member of society. Consequently, Gluckman argues, ritual and a variety of formalized behaviors (which he breaks down into various types of ceremony and etiquette) serve to differentiate roles which might otherwise become confused and liable to conflict.[17] In contrast, modern society clearly segregates roles from one another. A man's performance in the office is irrelevant to his capacities as a husband or as a bowler; even though events in any of these may ultimately come to affect one another, they do so only through the individual himself. Some vestiges of

---

[17] Max Gluckman, "Les Rites de Passage," in *Essays on the Ritual of Social Relations,* ed. by M. Gluckman (Manchester: Manchester Univ. Press, 1962), pp. 1-52, states: "When a Tsonga man, who is normally a cultivator, goes hunting or fishing, he changes his role and affects his whole social milieu; his new role is segregated, by passage rites and by taboos to be observed by his family and himself, from the intrusion of his other roles" (p. 29).

ceremony remain, as in the distinctions of clothing apparent in a hospital staff and in the seating arrangements in a company cafeteria. But these "do not pass into that mystical association by which tribal peoples often believe that breach, default and misdemeanor, and even vicious feeling, will bring misfortune to one's fellows, so that ritual dealing with mystical forces and beings is necessary to redress the equilibrium at any alteration of social dispositions."[18]

In accounting for the ways in which ritual prevents and reconciles role conflict, Gluckman has emphasized the importance of rituals of rebellion. In these, persons are able to act out roles normally denied them, and thus such ceremonies are one example of the ritual inversion that I shall discuss later. In certain African kingdoms, during the passage from one season and mode of social arrangement to the next, the normally revered figure of the king may be mocked, taunted, and scolded, becoming the figure of obscene jests and humiliating acts.[19] On the village level, rituals of rebellion may be found in those rites in which women act the parts of men, herding cattle and behaving obscenely and/or aggressively, while men perform tasks normally allocated to women. In Gluckman's approach, then, ritual may accomplish its integration of society either by stressing which particular role out of many possible ones an individual is performing at that moment, or by some form of psychological catharsis the precise mechanisms of which remain obscure. Not only for Gluckman, but for all of the ritual-as-action theorists, ritual is assumed to both communicate and achieve. It accomplishes some transformation in the secular world of roles and statutes, whether this be to resolve conflicts between sociological positions or to transform their character, as in initiation.

There is considerable divergence among this set of

---

18 *Ibid.*, p. 38.

19 Thomas O. Beidelman, "Swazi Royal Ritual," *Africa,* XXXVI (1966), 373-405, gives a brilliant interpretation of such kingly rituals.

anthropologists in terms of assumptions they make regarding the motives, processes, and consequences on the part of the actors in these ceremonial dramas. Some, like Gluckman, follow Durkheim in asserting the preeminence of commitment to realization of those moral principles which regulate social organization. Others, of whom Leach is a particularly adroit spokesman,[20] hold that ritual is just a complex metaphor through which persons attempt to gain political power.[21] The Tiv concept of *tsav,* which combines political and mystical power in a single ambiguous whole, substantiates such an identification,[22] and the Parsonian theory of consensual power represents, in my opinion, the most sophisticated way of reconciling such insights with the views to be described later.[23]

*   *   *

Both this and other formulations of those who emphasize the connection between rites and status encounter two crucial problems. First, ritual is addressed to forces or entities that might be characterized as mystical or supernatural. Their conceptual attributes and the entire cosmologies in which they figure simply do not relate that closely to social institutions. Writers such as Gluckman and Leach tend to ignore this intellectual content of

[20] Perhaps the most complete expositions of Leach's general approach can be found in *Pul Eliya* (Cambridge: Cambridge Univ. Press, 1961) and *Political Systems of Highland Burma* (Boston: Beacon Press, 1965 [1954]).

[21] Leach himself would identify such power with that addressed in ceremonies. "Every action by which one individual asserts his authority to curb and alter the behavior of another individual is an invocation of metaphysical force. The submissive response is an ideological reaction, and it is no more surprising that individuals should be influenced by magical performance or religious imprecations than that they should be influenced by the commands of authority. The power of ritual is just as actual as the power of command." "Ritual," p. 525.

[22] Paul Bohannan, "Extra-Processual Events in Tiv Political Institutions," *American Anthropologist,* LX (1958), 1-12.

[23] Cf. Marc Swartz, Victor Turner, and Arthur Tuden, "Introduction," in *Political Anthropology,* ed. by Swartz, Turner, and Tuden (Chicago: Aldine, 1966), pp. 1-41.

rituals, treating the symbolic, cognitive elements in them as nothing more than epiphenomenal metaphors for "real things" such as economic or political transactions. This is an exceedingly arbitrary limitation to analysis. If nothing more, Lévi-Strauss has demonstrated that the structures of mythical thought and conceptual order have a very emphatic reality that transcends institutional expressions while correlating with them. Such intellectual antitheses as those between nature and culture, raw and cooked, heaven and earth, are structural polarities that may be expressed in different images by various societies while retaining a pan-cultural coherence. We have agreed that ritual defines social order by delineating the categories by which experience is organized. An examination of the content of the categories seems essential to a comprehension of the principles of that organization. As Van Gennep, Mauss, Tylor, and other early anthropologists demonstrated, the ideas about spirit, creation, mystical transformations, and so forth pose fascinating problems in their own right.

The second objection derives from the posited function of ritual to "do something." This "doing" cannot be explained in terms of communication about status and duties. Why do so many societies, confronted with the problem of passing a nonsexual boy into the status of a sexual man, insist on going through all the rigamarole of initiation? Why can they not merely announce the change and mark it with legal sanctions? Why cannot a community of believers just discuss their ideas, instead of gathering to perform all sorts of peculiar actions? I suggest, following the ritual-as-belief group, that these two aspects of ritual, the symbolic and the transformational, must be explained in terms of each other.

A culture's methods of treating affliction and calamity provide one case for demonstrating that the significance of ritual cannot be limited to communication about status and relationship. For example, when a man becomes sick, his whole social *persona* is reflected in the ceremonies that transpire. Various relatives are obligated to perform certain ritual acts, and the curing rites may vary according to the social position, sex, age, and so forth of the patient. In many societies, the illness may be ascribed to a breakdown in proper social relationships. Its treatment then consists of remedying these institutional conflicts and reestablishing a right relation between men and the mystical forces identified with social integration. Recent studies of witchcraft[24] emphasize that, in case after case, the person accused of being the witch and the patient stand in the same relationship to one another. This consistency is assumed to derive from structural tension in these roles that is not alleviated by other mechanisms; the curing rites then emphasize "clearing the air" and creating the proper normative relationship. Since the conflict, however, is built into the very institutional arrangements, it is only a matter of time before a new illness crops up and the rituals of solidarity must be repeated.

Very often the roles most suspect of exerting malign influence on persons and groups are those of individuals who are in some sense structurally ambiguous, who mediate between two groups and whose loyalties are divided.[25] Thus a wife may be an unwitting agent of contagion and malign influence in her husband's group. She is necessary to its continuity, but she never becomes entirely a part of it. One never knows whether her ties with her own kin may not outweigh her allegiance to her husband and children. The social disruption known in our society as "going home to mother" may be expressed in another culture as fears of the "witch mother." The important point is that the curing rituals focus pre-

---

24 John Middleton and E. H. Winter, eds., *Witchcraft and Sorcery in East Africa* (London: Routledge and Kegan Paul, 1963).

25 Mary Douglas, *Purity and Danger,* states: "Witchcraft ... is found in the non-structure. Witches are social equivalents of beetles and spiders who live in the cracks of the walls and wainscoting ... the kind of powers attributed to them symbolize their ambiguous, inarticulate status" (p. 102).

cisely on the sociological positions of the actors, utilizing various symbolic devices to represent the integration of maternal with paternal principles by propitiating through sacrifice both matrilineal and patrilineal ancestors.

But these ancestors have their own characteristics, which in some ways transcend their sociological relevance. The mystical powers that are set loose in witchcraft must be handled on their own terms, independent of social implications. Furthermore, the ancestors and the powers are represented by symbols that stress not so much the unique character of specific roles or one group, but rather general moral principles: the dependency of man on the total community of ancestors, the cleansing benefits of sacrifice, the dangers of sexuality. I must emphasize too that while these ideational aspects may involve the non-utilitarian mystical world where the ritual operations are out of sensory control,[26] this does not mean they are irrational. Since Levy-Bruhl, many anthropologists have emphasized that the belief systems of primitive societies are eminently logical and coherent, although the terms and operation of their logic is very different from our own.[27]

A belief in witchcraft does not imply any abandonment of the rational processes of thought. A person may be accidentally killed by a jaguar; he may succumb to a heart attack or tuberculosis. In a society in which witches are deemed to be the causal agents of misfortune and death, people will acknowledge that the actual, efficient cause of death was the wounds dealt by the beast, or the

---

26 E. E. Evans-Pritchard, *Witchcraft, Oracles and Magic among the Azande* (Oxford: Clarendon Press, 1937), p. 12.

27 I follow Evans-Pritchard in maintaining that Levy-Bruhl has been often misunderstood on this point: his "pre-logical thought" is only "prior" to the particular scientific logic of the Western world. Primitive mentality, he showed, is eminently rational but proceeds in a style very different from our own standards of proof, deduction, and meaning. If a man asserts that a parrot is his brother, he may be saying that the soul of a deceased sibling is incarnate in the parrot, or that the relation between him and the parrot, a totem of his clan, is comparable to that between brothers, or any variety of perfectly coherent assertions.

stopping of a heart, or the various organic traumas conditioned by the disease. But why, they ask, did this particular man happen to encounter such a jaguar at that moment in time and space? Why did his heart stop now, rather than two years ago or ten seasons to come? The sufficient cause of death must be witchcraft. Our concept of "accident," "luck," or "fate" is as irrational, in one sense, as a belief in witches; all such concepts explain the unforeseen, the random, or unpatterned by relating such incidents to a prior set of beliefs.[28]

In many ways the American devotion to psychological, even Freudian, explanations and to derived treatment procedures closely resembles in logical structure witchcraft beliefs and curing techniques. A psychoanalyst says that a certain ego is "ill" because his relationships with certain crucial "alters," such as parents, was or is now disturbed, abnormal, wrong. Treatment requires the abreaction, through the therapeutic process of identification, of the feelings that give rise to the behavioral abnormalities that are termed "sick." In family therapy an attempt is made to change directly the interaction patterns that are disturbed or "neurotic" through participation in a highly formalized situation in which all behaviors are invested with a symbolic meaning. Such techniques are nearly identical with those used in curing rituals for persons afflicted by witchcraft or other forms of magic. Furthermore, are such concepts as ego, id, identification, projection, abreaction, repression, and the like any more based on "scientific" procedures and induction than the ideas of witch, fetish, taboo, and curse? I think not. To belabor the point a minute longer, at least one psychoanalytic school identifies the wife-mother as the crucial figure in the genesis of schizophrenia,[29] and, as I noted

---

[28] See Robin Horton, "Ritual Man in Africa," *Africa*, XXXIV (1964), 85-104.

[29] Gregory Bateson et al., "Toward a Theory of Schizophrenia," *Behavioral Science*, I (1956), 251-264.

above, the mother is often a liminal and suspect category in the rituals of affliction following witchcraft.[30]

If the rituals of psychological treatment cannot be understood without reference to the complex body of psychoanalytic theory that lies behind them, so too, *mutatis mutandi*, the rituals of primitive curing cannot be approached without an appreciation of the cosmologies they reflect. This is not to say that we must accept the view that belief is logically prior to action. It seems, rather, that any rigid dichotomy between thought and deed ultimately confronts the insoluble mind-body problem and should be avoided. Accepting, then, the insoluble mixture of these two elements, what results can be obtained by focusing on the totality of primitive ritual? That is, what results occur supposing that belief and action be taken as two levels or aspects of a series of ceremonial behaviors?

One of the most suggestive attempts to achieve this synthesis is that represented by the work of Victor Turner, who has based his interpretations on the analysis of one society, the Ndembu of northwestern Zambia (formerly Northern Rhodesia).[31] He has emphasized that the structure of ritual symbolism has three characteristics wherever it occurs. First, each culture has a limited number of basic, elementary symbols. These occur over and over again in rites directed to very different social ends and involving a vast range of spirits. Such symbols tend to be organized through various sets of combinations in which each takes on subtle implications due to its juxtaposition with the rest. Second, each symbol has a wide spectrum of referents (or denotata), which are in them-

---

30 I do not mean to imply that "mothers" or "wives" are *per se* categories that are universally ambiguous and suspect, but that these roles seem particularly difficult to reconcile with the exigencies of many social structures.

31 See particularly Victor Turner, *Schism and Continuity in an African Society* (Manchester: Manchester Univ. Press, 1957); *The Forest of Symbols* (Ithaca: Cornell Univ. Press, 1967); *The Drums of Affliction* (Oxford: Clarendon Press, 1968).

selves diverse and ambiguous. (The color white, to pursue the earlier example, is so commonly used in ritual because it is defined as the lack of color, the absence of all sensuous reference, and hence can stand for all matter of things.) There is a vast power attached to that which is neither "fish, fowl, or good red herring," which is at once man and animal, spirit and flesh,[32] and which can thus mediate between contrasting entities. Third, the particular meaning of a symbol in a rite depends on which of its many referents are mobilized. This in turn reflects the social context in which it is utilized, the effect of other symbols in the immediate ceremonial environment, and the sweeping penumbra of shadowy associations that result from its other referents and the situations in which it appears. While much of the explicit content of Ndembu ritual is bound up with the structure of that society, Turner concludes that very much more must be understood on another level, in terms of cognitive and affectual processes.

Thus, much Ndembu religious practice centers around "cults of affliction." These are concerned with various illnesses and misfortunes inflicted on people and their matrilineal clans by the souls of their matrilineal ancestors. These spirits are concerned that the unity of the lineage be maintained, and they punish those who imperil it through quarrels with lineage mates or through endangering the stability of its relations with other groups. Each kind of illness has its own special ritual, a separate cult, and its rites are directed to the particular ancestor who, usually in alliance with one or another variety of male nature spirit, is responsible for the disease. For example, when someone has the illness known as Chihamba, this is interpreted to mean that a female ancestress, together with the male spirit Kavula, is the source of infliction. The rites of the Chihamba cult are supposed to institute a new, beneficent relationship between the

---

[32] This theme is discussed at length in later sections.

patient, the social groups with which he is involved, and these spirits.

Kavula is certainly associated with many basic aspects of Ndembu social structure. He is said to be the "grandfather" of cult members, and thus stands for the authority of the elders. He controls the fertility of women and the growth of the crops on which the continuity of the lineage is dependent, and therefore is represented in lightning, rainfall, and success in hunting.[33]

At one point in the Chihamba ceremony, the candidates who are entering the cult are told to reverence a shrine that is claimed to hold the actual spirit of Kavula. They are then instructed to strike it and to kill the spirit, and his blood is shown them as proof that they have, indeed, destroyed the beneficent force. But on the next day it is revealed to the candidates that Kavula is not dead, that he was transformed and is present in many different persons and objects. No longer the unitary personality he was before the death, he may be comprehended in many new ways. "It is clear that his death is no more than a metaphor for radical change in his mode of manifestation ... For Ndembu, physical death does not mean extinction: it means the passage from a visible to an invisible mode of existence ... Both life and death depend upon and are permeated by the ineradicable act of being."[34] This paradox is accompanied by other contradictions and ambiguities. Before the killing the candidates are called guilty; they are treated in humiliating

---

[33] Yet, according to Turner, Kavula is a great deal more than the sum of these sociologically derived attributes. "The ethical and spiritual values he represents and sanctions are no mere product of the social process. Indeed, Ndembu religion has its own set of ends, which clearly transcend the social category" (*Chihamba: The White Spirit*, Rhodes-Livingston Institute Papers, No. 33 [Manchester: Manchester Univ. Press, 1962], p. 83). Turner interprets these ends in terms of a Thomistic distinction between act-of-being and concept-of-being, between *esse* and *id quod est*. He sees ritual as seeking to establish man's awareness of this contrast, and of the dimensions of spirit as act-of-being, through paradox and metaphor. This thesis is documented through an analysis of native symbolic exegesis and of the ritual sequence.

[34] *Ibid.*, p. 85.

ways and said to be "shamed." But after they have killed
the god they are innocent and are acquitted of all shame.
Everyone rejoices in his new state and seems to take
quiet satisfaction in the successful outcome of a dangerous proceeding.

I cannot do justice here to the conceptual richness of
the data Turner brings forth to show how the symbols
used in the rite interact with one another on many levels
to create one poetic metaphor after another. His analysis
relies very heavily on the exegetical explanations of the
Ndembu themselves, and his interpretations are not
immune from criticism.[35] Such objections, in my opinion,
do not touch the usefulness of his main theme: "that we
have in Chihamba, the local expression of a universal-
human problem, that of expressing what cannot be
thought of, in view of thought's subjugation to essences."[36]
Kavula represents a pure act of being rather than an
object or an essence, and as such he can only be grasped
in terms of acts. Therefore the symbolic personalities of
spirits like Kavula, or mystical forces generally, are symbolic dynamos, generating countless particular symbolic
representations that can never be exhausted "precisely
because such a symbol is an attempt to give visible form
to the invisible act-of being."[37]

*   *   *

Such a theme is by no means unique to Turner. Ten
years before his appearance, Evans-Pritchard's descriptions of Nuer religion emphasized the dichotomy between
the Nuer categories "spirit" and "creation" in ways that
identified them as act-of-being and essence.[38] The difficulty with such approaches, however, is that they very often

35 Horton, "Ritual Man in Africa."

36 Turner, *Chihamba: The White Spirit,* p. 87.

37 *Ibid.,* p. 82.

38 E. E. Evans-Pritchard, "The Nuer Concept of Spirit in Its Relation
to the Social Order," *American Anthropologist,* LV (1953), 201-214; "A
Problem of Nuer Religious Thought," *Sociologus,* IV (1954), 23-41.

develop into an exposition of cosmological subtleties alone. The structure of the beliefs may be thoroughly and laboriously documented without any reference to social structure. As most who have attempted to analyze myths know, it is nearly impossible to decipher them without some ethnographic knowledge of the society that produced them. Or the account may deal with the theology of one or two highly gifted informants. The criticism of the ritual-as-action school mentioned earlier is relevant here: how can we account for rites willingly performed by many highly diverse people in terms of one individual's idiosyncratic views? The categories of spirits, the natures of the various mystical processes, the concepts of the afterlife and so forth are much more than abstract intellectual games. They figure in the daily lives of people and constitute the very definitions of social action. The "reification error" is often extremely difficult to avoid, for it may be very hard to show the social relevance of such esoterica as throwing a few drops of one's own blood to stop a rainstorm[39] or telling how the leopard got his spots. Recently a number of anthropologists, including Turner, have dealt with this problem by developing the implications of liminality, or structural ambiguity. This depends on the following considerations.

Societies attempt to achieve an orderly, coherent universe through the maintenance of a system of categories that organize perceptual data in terms of various classifications. (This is, of course, very similar to Gluckman's emphasis.) We would not even be able to think, let alone interact, if we could not identify the messages of our senses as establishing what something was like, what it was unlike, and how these things were related logically. Every set of categories operates by abstracting certain attributes of the objects or experiences as relevant to the classification, and discarding many other possible ones. In constructing zoological taxonomies biologists regard

---

[39] Rodney Needham, "Blood, Thunder and the Mockery of Animals," *Sociologus,* XIV (1964), 136-149.

only morphology as relevant, ignoring such things as length and color of hair, relative weight, diet, and so forth. Some entities and processes, however, have the attributes of two discrete categories and cannot be firmly assigned to one or the other. They do not fit into the classifications; they are betwixt and between, in Turner's phrase. Such anomalous things seem to have great cognitive and psychic power. We have already encountered two examples: the "witch" whose social roles overlapped, and the spirit of Kavula with its range of paradoxical associations. As these two cases imply, the power of liminality is neither good nor evil, but amoral — a dangerous force that may confer social benefits but also threatens coherency. Since ambiguous entities have the characteristics of mutually opposed categories, they are able to mediate between them. To bridge the gap between man and spirit, something must have the characteristics of both while being neither.

The curious element here is that liminal entities appear to shift and blend into one another, as one might expect of something that cannot be clearly defined. In many societies a saint and a madman or witch have many of the same attributes, for all these figures are between human society and the mystical world.[40] It is also common that liminal social roles are associated with liminal symbols; a prophet or boys in initiation are expected to be dirty, with long, filthy hair, and a diet of roots and insects, wandering out in the desert or jungle far from social constraints. It has been argued that our own notions of "dirt" are really statements that things are out of place, disorganized — they are no longer ordered through the proper categories.[41] Pollution results when such anomalous "dirt" is spread about, which is why so much primi-

---

40 Joan of Arc was identified by the French as divine but proclaimed by the English to be a mad heretic; each classification used precisely the same characteristics from slightly different perspectives. I am indebted to T. O. Beidelman for suggesting this illustration.

41 Douglas, *Purity and Danger*, passim but especially chs. 1, 2, and 3.

tive ritual seems designed to restore things to their proper, categorical place. The products of the human body — hair, fingernails, saliva, blood, excrement, and so forth — are in this view very much liminal products. They are products of the body but not part of it; they express its boundaries and may threaten its integrity. But why then should so much of ritual (and included here is magic) be involved with the deliberate utilization of these substances and other anomalous entities? Why should the initiates be required to be filthy and engage in markedly asocial acts? Precisely because the achievements of ritual derive from generating and utilizing the tremendous power of liminality. Suppose a boy must be passed into the status of a man, a transformation between two opposed categories. All former elements of the old role are obliterated by making the boy as nonsocial as possible, through associating him with dirt, blood, and disorder. Only then may he be incorporated into his new position. Very clearly this process operates on psychological as well as cognitive levels in ways that anthropologists are just now beginning to explore.[42]

*   *   *

I have attempted to show how the action and belief approaches may be combined through focusing on the common quality that the mystically potent, whether this be a conceptual category, a substance, or a role, all share. To demonstrate that this sharing is also an association, it is necessary to utilize a recent article that shows the intimate connection between the conceptual entities of religious creed and the particular forces in social life. Beidelman notes that the Nuer, a people who normally go about quite without clothes, rigidly prohibit nudity

---

[42] See Victor Turner, "Colour Classification in Ndembu Religion," *Anthropological Approaches to the Study of Religion,* ed. by M. Banton, ASA Monographs, No. 3 (London: Tavistock), pp. 47-84; Thomas O. Beidelman, "Some Nuer Notions of Nakedness, Nudity and Sexuality," *Africa,* XXXVIII (1968), 113-132.

in the presence of certain categories of relatives. He relates this to the general characteristics of Nuer religion noted by Evans-Pritchard: its concern to avoid any possible confusion between the opposed but complementary spheres of spirit and creation and its attempts to deal with entities that do so confuse. Such things as twins, lightning, and birds partake of both realms and are at once sacred and dangerous. The Nuer say that their behavior toward such liminal items must express "respect," or *thek*. In precisely the same way, a Nuer male or female is said to show *thek* toward his relatives by marriage, or affines, by covering the genitals and by not eating in their presence.

In Beidelman's analysis, the Nuer are seen as equating the ingestion of substance and the social ingestion of human fertility through marriage, which incorporates persons (wives or husbands) into groups to which their own stand opposed. Both of these processes tend to blur or break down the crucial boundaries that distinguish the clans upon whose differentiation Nuer social order is based. The basic contrasts between kin and nonkin, "our clan" and "not-our-clan," just as those between spirit and creation, involve "sets of categories which are linked through medial objects, which by their mediality draw attention to, and yet jeopardize, these distinctions. Thus the genitals (sexuality) of spouses relate to the uniting and yet divisive aspects of Nuer marriage and domestic groups."[43] He goes on to show, through a marvellous bit of analysis, that the male genitals must be covered by the skin of a civet cat. Now, such creatures are among those which express a confusion of spirit and creation and which Nuer must *"thek"* in their own right. Further examples of the insights generated by the liminal synthesis of diverse approaches to ritual could be added on top of one another.

---

43 Beidelman, "Some Nuer Notions of Nakedness, Nudity and Sexuality," p. 126.

Appendix

I wish to devote the rest of this paper to an examination of the relationship between the kinds of social inversions Gluckman described and liminal processes in the society I know best: the Eastern Bororo of north-central Matto Grosso, Brazil.

Bororo society may be apprehended as a structure of positions and a system of statuses. The positions are defined by the unique complex of relationships that is established for each individual by the social facts of descent, marriage, birth, abilities, ritual events, and the like. The statuses are related to the institutional structure of Bororo society, to the corporate groups that compose it, and to their organized, normative relations with one another and with the world about them. The positions, consequently, refer primarily to sets of individual, unique persons, while the statuses derive from group membership and affiliation. Bororo ceremony and cosmology is interpreted here as a means of integrating these two levels of analysis.[44] To show this requires an exposition of Bororo ethnography. Every Bororo village should be composed of eight clans, arranged in a circle around a central plaza and a men's house. Each clan has a specified position in the village circle — its unique spatial identity — for the circle is bisected by an east-west axis that divides the village into two halves. Each half, or moiety, includes four clans and is characterized by a name (Tugarege and Exerae) and certain social and symbolic attributes. The clans in one moiety must marry members of clans in the other moiety, and such exchanges of spouses are only one part of a highly diverse series of economic, political, and ritual transactions between the moieties. Each clan is divided into three subclans and each of these into three

---

[44] This is by no means the only possible method of representing Bororo social structure. It could also be seen as sets of transactions between corporate groups, or in terms of cosmological assumptions implemented in various fashions, or as a series of adaptations to a particular natural and social environment.

to six named lineages. Membership in these social units is gained by possession of a personal name taken from a stock of such names associated with one's mother's lineage and clan. Thus the Bororo are matrilineal: a male ego's father, wife, and children are all members of the opposite moiety while his sister's children are members of his own clan and are his legal heirs. Social existence for the Bororo is impossible without the collaboration of the other moiety: from it come one's own life (through the father), one's spouse, and, for men, one's children. Not only do the moieties provide each other with food, gifts, and such services as the burial of the dead, but it is only through the other moiety that a man is enabled to participate in the ritual life of his community.

The clans are differentiated from each other by a complex system of property rights. Each clan has the right to utilize specified types of ritual paraphernalia, songs, and dances, and each is associated with a limited number of totems including animal, fish, plant, and bird species as well as meteorological phenomena and a particular category of spirits. From these totems are derived the clan's name, the titles of the lineages, and the stock of personal names mentioned earlier. For example, an individual of the Armadillo clan (Bokodori Exerae) and the Red Armadillo subclan might be called "Red Spotted Running Armadillo."[45] The names are, therefore, the foundation of an individual's total social personality. They refer both to his general membership in the clan and lineage, which themselves determine many of his relationships, and also to his unique identity within these units. These names also reflect the rights possessed by the clan, which are the ritual means by which persons and groups communicate their relationships to each other. This is so be-

---

[45] Lévi-Strauss has pointed out that such parallels between the hierarchies of zoological taxonomies and social classifications appear to be a fundamental element in totemic thought (*Savage Thought* [London: Weidenfeld and Nicholson, 1966], pp. 166-177). Similar nomination systems are found in numerous Brazilian tribes, including some quite close to the Bororo.

cause the rituals associated with each clan are those which represent its various totems through costume, dance, mimicry, and song. Thus the Armadillo clan has ceremonies that personify armadillos and other creatures.

Curiously, however, the members of the clan never represent their own totems, but instead invite persons from other clans in the opposite moiety to do so. The clan that owns the ritual paints and decorates the other group so that they become, symbolically, armadillos, jaguars, monkeys, or spirits. To be thus allowed to represent another group's totems — the very foundation of its social character — is a very great honor, perhaps the most valuable gift that one group can bestow upon another. Due to such transactions, the Bororo say, the clan that owns the ritual may marry women in the performers' clan "without shame." In other words, the gift of the ritual establishes certain rights and obligations between the groups involved, fixing their status relative to one another. Of course, the performers have their own totemic representations with which they honor clans in the other moiety, and thus gain the right to wives. The great bulk of Bororo ceremonial life consists of these ritual transactions, which, as I mentioned earlier, have the result that any Bororo can participate in the religious life only through the office of the other moiety. Moreover, since members of this division are the only persons who can embody the clan's social identity, it is only through the other moiety that one can express the basic definition of self.

All these transactions operate within a cosmology that parallels, but does not derive from, the social order. Again, this realm is ordered by two opposed and mutually complementary categories, this time of spirit rather than of society: the *bope* and the *aroe*. The first category, the *bope,* include several dozen varieties of nature spirit or natural force, such as the rain spirits *(Butao-doge)*, the *Maereboe* (which often transform themselves into vultures and snakes) , and the *Tupa-doge,* who are less hos-

tile to man than the other types of *bope*. Some types of
bope live on this earth, abiding in rocks or trees, or
merely wandering about; others reside in one or another
of the three levels of heaven. In the top-most heaven
(*baru kaworureu*, blue-green sky) dwells the "Father of
the *Bope*," *Maereboe-Doge Etu-o*, who is responsible for
the creation of the world and all things in it. One of
his manifestations or attributes is *Meri*, the sun, while
his younger brother reveals one aspect of his multiplex
character in the moon *(Ari)*. Both of these images of
spirit, like the category of *bope* in general, closely resemble the attributes of spirit Turner describes for the
Ndembu: they are modes-of-being that transcend any
concrete representation. While they express many basic
principles of Bororo society, they cannot be reduced to
mere reflections of that society, as I shall show later.

The *bope*, as a generic concept, are credited with controlling all fertility — they cause humans and creatures alike
to reproduce,[46] institute rain, drought, earthquakes, solar
and lunar eclipses, extremes of heat and cold, vegetable
germination, and all processes of creation and growth.
But they are also responsible for decay, destruction, and
death because for the Bororo, as for the Ndembu, death
and life are indissoluble aspects of a unitary force. Every
case of sickness, accident, and death among the Bororo
is ultimately attributed to the *bope*. These spirits are
thought to control or oversee all aspects of Bororo trans-
action with the natural world, from hunting and fishing
to the dietary rules that apply during such "natural"
processes as childbirth and menstruation. Men offend the
bope by transgressing the rules that govern the relationships between the natural and cultural worlds, for these
spirits never act capriciously, but always for due cause.

---

[46] The crucial exception here is that the *aroe* are thought to control
all reproductive processes of water creatures, particularly fish. These
spirits are intimately connected with rivers and lakes, and the Bororo
sometimes represent the contrast between them and the *bope* through a
land-sky versus water dichotomy.

The opposed category of spirit is *aroe,* which usually can be translated "soul." Every human has his own particular *aroe* whose permanent departure from the body means death and whose state of health can be affected by various polluting acts — precisely those violations of man-to-man or man-to-nature relations mentioned above.[47] The soul of a deceased Bororo is termed an *aroe,* and the souls of all the ancestors are thought to live together in two villages of the dead from which they periodically depart to visit, invisibly, the village of the living during ritual occasions. Moreover, the totems of each clan are termed its *aroe,* for these categories stand in the same relationship to the perpetual and enduring character of the clan as do the ancestors to the groups of their descendants. In other words, the totems are to the clan as the soul is to the individual: that element which continues through time, expressing the most essential elements of identity and founding the dimensions of relationships. Included among the clan's *aroe,* or totems, are certain types of spirits whose attributes sharply contrast with the characteristics of the *bope.* These include wondrous water creatures living in the rivers and lakes of Bororoland, and other types of spirit that figure very prominently in the society's rituals. Not only are the *aroe* totems represented in ritual form, as described earlier, but certain of these spirits must participate in the great communal rites of name-giving, hunting, initiation, and burial, in order for those events to accomplish their manifest, culturally specified ends.

The *aroe-bope* dichotomy may be interpreted in a number of ways, and the difficulties of these must be clarified before the rituals themselves are explicated. First, the *bope-aroe* opposition cannot be identified with that between the moieties themselves. Every clan in both

---

47 It should be emphasized that generally the *bope* are not credited with punishing man for transgressions against social norms such as thievery, adultery, rape, or even homicide (nor, for that matter, are the *aroe*).

moieties has its distinctive *aroe,* and all men share the same relation to the *bope.* This remains so in spite of the apparent contradiction that a few clans have certain *bope* among their totemic *aroe;* it should be remembered that the two categories are not totally exclusive. The entities that are both *aroe* and *bope* are liminal categories; viewed from one perspective they are form, and from another, process. Again, in certain situations, one moiety might be identified with the *bope* and the other with the *aroe,*[48] but this association changes from one ritual context to another, and expresses the character of the opposition between the halves of society rather than reflecting any of their permanent attributes.

No more is it the case that *bope* and *aroe* may be identified respectively with nature and culture, as an overzealous application of Lévi-Strauss might incline one to do. The *aroe*-totems of the clans include a wide variety of natural species and processes. The totem is the ideal form of the species, the very idea of armadillo or crow. Particular members of these species stand to these totems much as does, in Platonic philosophy, a given chair to the Ideal Chair. Therefore the totem *Bokodori Aroe,* or Spirit Armadillo, can be expressed through a man painted with red and black patterns, by a bow with such markings, by a ceremonial rattle decorated in a similar way, by a neckpiece made from its claws, or by the total ensemble of these as well as by individual armadillos of the species *Prio-dontes giganteus.* But the Spirit Armadillo itself transcends these concrete reflections of its being, which are the only modes whereby man can apprehend its reality. Together, all the Bororo clans figure among their totems nearly all the bird, animal, fish, and plant species found in that part of Brazil, and informants said that everything in the world has an *aroe,* the idea of its

---

48 Most commonly, the *aroe* are associated with the Tugarege and the *bope* with the Exerae, as revealed in the different kinship terms shamans from different moieties use to address the spirits.

essential form, and thus its particular social position.[49] There is one exception to this: the *bope* as a rule have no *aroe* at all, for they are the vital force that transfuses form into life.

The totality of Bororo totems, then, reflects the perpetual universe of conceptual, ordered forms that continually manifest one aspect of themselves in the flawed, partial examples of a bird, a rainfall, or a ceremonial headdress. From this it follows that the *bope* cannot be symbols of natural forces alone. The process of creation and destruction is basic to the continuity of social life, for children must come into this world and be nourished by the slaying of creatures. Growth and aging, with which the *bope* are intimately associated, is seen by the Bororo as a universal process in which a nature-culture is simply not relevant. For these reasons, the most tempting identifications of all, of men with *aroe* and women with *bope*, cannot be consistently maintained. These equations do indeed figure in many Bororo rituals and in some of their cosmology, but again they are specific to the context of opposition and comparison. In situations where men are contrasted to women,[50] the respective characteristics of each category and the physical processes that result from their conjunction are compared to the relationship between the *aroe* and *bope*. At a more general level, however, all human beings are said to be a mixture of *bope* and *aroe* elements. Human beings, in the Bororo concept, have the potentiality both for the destroying power of creation and for establishing the order of system, of form. I believe, then, that the most accurate translation of *bope* and *aroe* is in terms of order and disorder, of form and process. My thesis here is that Bororo "rites of representation" may be understood on

---

49 E. E. Evans-Pritchard, *Nuer Religion* (Oxford: Clarendon Press, 1956), pp. 77-79, has made a similar argument concerning the nature of Nuer totems.

50 These occur in the initiation ceremony and in certain rites connected with the men's house associates.

the ideological level as attempts to control the relationship between the two principles of this dyad through the ritual inversion of social statuses and positions. On the sociological level of action, the rites may be interpreted as expressions of conflict between roles and groups that are resolved through the manipulation of cosmological themes. Only by seeing the two levels as expressions of each other can we understand how the rites achieve liminality and why this should have the effects it does. I shall try to show through a brief account of certain Bororo rituals the utility of this approach.

*   *   *

The *aroe* (meaning the entire pantheon of ancestral souls, totems, and water creatures) have as their chiefs two particular aroe spirits, named *Bakororo* and *Itubore*. They stand in the same relation to the *aroe* as do *Meri* and *Ari* to the *bope,* but, unlike these latter forces, the *aroe* chiefs are expressions of transcendent form and structure. This is manifested in their identification as culture heroes who founded the principal institutions of Bororo society. Before their advent, informants say, people lived without rules, like animals, leaving their dead to rot in the jungle, fighting constantly among themselves, and coupling indiscriminately. In other words, chaos prevailed and social relations were totally confused until the two spirits brought order, regulation, and pattern. They divided men into clans, gave these groups their unique identities through endowing them with ritual possessions, totems, and names, and established the complex scheme of ceremonial, marital, and other transactions that unite the clans. *Bakororo* and *Itubore,* then, stand for those moral principles which insure the continuity of structure and plan: for the temporal permanence of the clan as founded through matrilineal descent, for the ethical rules which generate proper behavior between members of the clans, and which are expressed in marriage and the obligations of kinship. They do this in very specific and concrete ways through the symbols used to represent them. *Bakororo,* for example, is associated with alternate red and black stripes together with such things as the *ika,* a ceremonial trumpet. The red and black colors come from certain plants that are connected with menstrual fluids, female sexuality, and relationships traced through women. To substantiate the mechanisms that achieve the materialization of the abstract would require another paper. At the moment, I must emphasize how such symbolic images as red and black draw on common physical experiences to give great psychic force to the structural ideas represented by *Bakororo* and *Itubore.*[51]

Since without these figures there would be no social form, no structure of positions, it is to be expected that they are invoked on all occasions when the society undergoes some form of transition. As we noted earlier, passage from one position to the next, whether undergone by the society as a whole or by individuals, involves a disordered, threatening period of liminality when the old structure has been left and the new not yet reached. At these times *Bakororo* and *Itubore* appear: during the name-giving for a child (that is, when a new nonsocial thing is incorporated into the social fabric); during funerals, when an individual passes from the living to the dead; during initiations, when boys achieve the status of men. They also appear during the transition from one season to the next, in the corn harvest festival marking the end of the dry season. Their names appear in the songs used to welcome travelers, those who have undergone spatial transition. The participation of *Bakororo* and *Itubore* during these dangerous times of passage in-

---

51 Turner has recently suggested that color symbolism might have certain universal constants due to pan-human experiences with emotionally charged body processes and substances, such as defecation, blood, milk, semen, and so forth ("Colour Classification in Ndembu Religion").

sures the triumph of order; this, at least, seems to be the ideological message.

But what of the mechanism whereby this order is made to prevail? It is here that the principle of inversion combines with the symbolic nexus of psychological and cognitive elements manifest in the ritual figures. The Bororo say that when the "true" spirits of *Bakororo* and *Itubore,* along with the other *aroe,* visit the village during ceremonies (invisible to all save shamans), they often appear upside down, floating on their heads. This vivid metaphor suggests that the very principle of order must be inverted, somersaulted, for liminality to prevail and the structure to be generated anew. I suggest, partly in opposition to other anthropological theories, that the disorganization of the liminal period is not so much a prevalence of chaos but the systematic turning over of principles of organization. The Bororo accomplish this through substituting one social category for its opposite. *Bakororo* and *Itubore,* like all other *aroe,* are associated with specific lineages in certain clans, namely, the *Baitogogo* of the *Arore* and *Borogei* of the *Apiborege.* It is important to be clear here, for much confusion has arisen over the relationships between these and other roles. The original persons known as *Baitogogo* and *Borogei* were the first Bororo chiefs appointed by *Bakororo* and *Itubore*; they were actual, historical beings who were extraordinary men but hardly mystical beings. But the two spirits are not human — they were never born nor can they die. The men who are now ritually associated with them stand to these spirits as expression to principle, rather than as sons or heirs. Members of these clans have the right to utilize names referring to the attributes and powers of *Bakororo* and *Itubore,* and the songs that are the clans' anthems recount their deeds. In sum, they are to the *Arore* and *Apiborege* as all totems are to their associated clans. Where does inversion enter into this complex system?

The spirits of *Bakororo* and *Itubore* are ceremonially impersonated not by members of their associated clans, but by persons in the opposite moiety. Precisely, the *Bakorokudu* lineage of the *Bado Jeba Xebegiwuge* clan must represent *Bakororo* and the *Karia Bokodori* lineage of the *Bado Jeba`Xobugiwuge* clan, *Itubore*. The Bororo express this situation by saying "Bakorokudu is Bakororo but Bakororo is with Baitogogo of the Arore."[52] The common name of the two "performing" clans, *Bado Jeba*, can be translated as "Planners of the Village" and refers to the obligations of their heads to set out the plan and disposition of the huts whenever a new village is built. Since, for the Bororo, this village plan embodies all the moral principles of their organization (the relation of the clans to one another, their spatial and totemic identity, etc.), the title of "village planner" symbolizes the office's formal responsibility for the ceremonial maintenance of social order. The two men who hold the titles of *Bakorokudu* and *Karia Bokodori,* in theory through matrilineal inheritance from an earlier incumbent, are known as "Chiefs of the Village" (*pagimejera*), and it is they who, nominally, impersonate *Bakororo* and *Itubore* during periods of social transition. Although these officers have a limited *de jure* right to these ritual roles, they cannot enact them unless invited to do so by the heads of the clans who have the spirits as totems, the *Arore* and *Apiborege*. Such an invitation must also be confirmed by the entire men's council, composed of the heads of all the clans. Therefore, the chiefs of the village, who embody the most sacred beings of the Bororo cosmology and the principles of village order, do so only at the sufferance of the village as a collectivity, and at the pleasure of those clans who stand in the most intimate connection of identity with these beings, but who can never, in a sense, become themselves. It is only through inversion, of one status being transformed into its complete political antith-

---

[52] Claude Lévi-Strauss, "Do Dual Organizations Exist?", *Structural Anthropology* (New York: Basic Books, 1963 [1956]), pp. 132-163, offers an ingenious elaboration of this point.

esis, that spirit can be made to exist in society. This is true not only for *Bakororo* and *Itubore* but also for every other totemic spirit, as discussed earlier. Among the Bororo, the clans and their associated offices may only be that which others allow them to be, and a man's essence can be personified only through those who stand opposed to him at every level of existence: his fathers, brothers-in-law, and sons.

All of this has, of course, repercussions on the political level that can only be mentioned here. Among the Bororo, legitimate authority is vested in the offices of lineage and clan chief, which are designated by the titles of famous past incumbents, such as *Bakorokudu* or *Borogei* In principle these are transmitted matrilineally, from MB to ZS, but exceptions are more common than the rule. All in the clan must accept the authority of the office-holder, who attempts to secure the allegiance of his kinsmen through a variety of means. This causes sharp competition among close uterine relatives, particularly brothers. However, not even the support of the entire clan confers office on an individual, for in a literal sense it must be extended to him by all other clans in the village. That is, it is only the ritual clan chief who is asked, or permitted, by other clans to represent their most important totemic principles (such as *Bakororo*) . Only through such representations can a man's claim to office be validated, or, as the Bororo put it with their usual wry paradox, "Bakorokudu is only Bakorokudu when he is Bakororo."

Ceremonial inversion, therefore, is basic to the whole political process and the distribution of power. It prevents factions based on clanships or other interest groups from developing[53] and generally checks conflict between groups. Moreover, there is a good deal of change from one ritual occasion to the next, so that all the senior men

---

[53] This is by no means always true, and when the demographic base of the village is highly biased toward two or three clans, such groups do indeed develop.

of a clan might have been "Bakororo for a day" within a few months. Ambitious men are disliked by the Bororo, and it is not uncommon for a relatively obscure person to hold the ritual office of clan chief while his older brother has considerable covert power but no authority. The Bororo political system is characterized by ambiguity, flux, and subtlety, but it usually functions so effectively that political feuds, factional squabbles, and general turmoil are markedly absent. This is due both to the totemic representations, which function on the level of depersonalized status or office to check conflict between groups, and to the ritual inversions derived from funerals that pertain to the individual's unique social position, as distinct from his clan-derived statuses.

Every deceased Bororo is represented during his or her funeral and in subsequent ceremonies by a member of the opposite moiety. This man becomes, literally, an exact substitute for the deceased in terms of his personal relationships (but not of statuses). He is addressed by members of the deceased's clan with the same kinship term formerly used for the dead man — terms meaning "brother, sister, uncle, nephew, mother," and so forth. He is required to act towards them as he does to his own siblings, mother, and other relatives, presenting them with food and other services. His obligations, coinciding with the particularistic set of duties owed by the deceased, extend to persons who are married into or who are otherwise related to his ritual relatives. Thus he must treat the deceased's "father" as exactly that, even though this man might be younger than he and even a member of his own clan, someone whom he has treated up to this moment of ritual inversion as a "brother." Since in Bororo society fathers and sons are strictly enjoined to treat one another with great consideration and fondness, and usually do so, this means the political competition between clan siblings mentioned above is often "defused" by the inversions achieved through funerals. The same also applies to personal conflicts between members of opposite moieties.

Sociologically, then, and contradicting Gluckman's thesis, conflicts are handled not by ritually segregating roles but by confounding them. Cosmologically, this situation reflects the total interdependence of the moieties and suggests that transcendence of self and integration of the community are facets of one another that can only be accomplished by what is, on both formal status and personal levels, the not-self. According to the context, this polarity may be presented through the opposition of women against men, or form against process, or order against disorder, or one moiety against the other. Thus two types of liminality might be distinguished, the one resultng from the transformation of one category into its antithesis, through the *aroe* inversions, and the other deriving from the total absence of category, from the fluid permutations of the *bope*. This situation can be represented diagrammatically by representing the opposition between the moieties by a horizontal line, and the *bope-aroe* dichotomy by a vertical line.

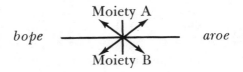

Thus, the totality of Bororo ritual is a transition in each dyad from one term to the other through the intermediary of the second dyad as a totality. It is therefore neither opposition nor synthesis but the transformation through inversion of each term into the other that establishes order and controls the organic process of change.

3

Ritual and Social Crisis

by

MARGARET MEAD

To speak of ritual is to speak of patterns of human behavior. We can also speak of ritual behavior in animals, which provides analogues that are sometimes helpful and sometimes not, but here I intend to discuss primarily human ritual behavior — behavior that is repetitious and different from the ordinary. We do not normally talk about the things that people do every day, although they are both patterned and habitual, as is ritual. Ritual has an extra degree of intensity. Such intensity may be due simply to the fact that the behavior pattern is a contact between the secular and the sacred, or that it has high

Margaret Mead is Curator of Ethnology, American Museum of Natural History, and Adjunct Professor of Anthropology, Columbia University. Among her numerous publications are: *Continuities in Cultural Evolution; Anthropology: A Human Science; Anthropologists and What They Do;* and *Culture and Commitment: A Study of the Generation Gap.*

affective tones, such as death compared with an ordinary parting. Whatever the occasion for the intensity (which differs from society to society), an observer has little difficulty in distinguishing a ritual from a nonritual occasion.

This is true, as far as we know, of all the primitive peoples we have been able to study thus far. Even if a visitor enters a society and culture in which he cannot speak the language and with which he is unfamiliar, he will, nevertheless, be able to sense very quickly whether what he is observing is a ritual action or an ordinary, everyday one. In New Guinea he can usually tell this from the way in which people walk: either they just walk or they walk as if it were a ritual occasion. The anthropologist just looks up and sees people walking in this special way and knows he had better go along because something is going to happen. The people will be dressed in a perfectly familiar style, and they might be carrying a bowl of food, as they do every day. If they are carrying it as a ceremonial gift, however, their gait and posture will be different.

A fair amount of bodily behavior is normally included in a ritual action, although this does not necessarily mean active behavior.

Another thing that is very important about ritual is that it is social behavior. Social behavior, however, does not necessarily require a group of people. The American Indian searching for a vision or the lonely hermit living in a hermitage as a way of serving his God is, nevertheless, behaving socially by the inclusion of the guardian spirit who will come to him or the spirit to whom he prays. On the other hand, an individual who behaves in an intense, habitual, traditional pattern, all by himself, is not necessarily acting ritually. Often this could be merely psychological abnormality, which is a perfectly good description of some ecclesiastical behavior. Such behavior, however, is related to the religious community, and therefore it is accepted as ritual — while the person who performs it all by himself has a compulsion neurosis that needs treatment. One can caricature Durkheim, of course, by saying that religion is everything that people do together, and nonreligion is everything they do alone. I believe that it is much more accurate to say that the presence of another, whether the other is God or a companion of the human sort or many companions, all involved in the same situation, is one of the necessary ingredients of ritual behavior.

I think this would be a useful distinction to keep in mind: ritual is concerned with relationships, either between a single individual and the supernatural, or among a group of individuals who share things together. There is something about the sharing and the expectation that makes it ritual.

Ethologists, those who are concerned with animal behavior, have applied the term ritual to wild animals, using it to denote an adequately determined sequence of behavior in these animals. To apply the term to human behavior meets with disastrous consequences, as in the claims made by Ardrey about man's territorial behavior.[1] Think, for instance, of two bucks locking antlers in the spring confrontation to impress the does. Just at the moment that a deadly conflict seems inevitable, they disentangle their antlers and turn away, pacing along in step. Ethologists speak of this as "ritual." They speak of the courtship ritual among birds, and use the term for such given, instinctive types of behavior that occur in wild animals. Such rituals are always inter-creature, and while this similarity to human ritual is important, we should not carry it too far or we lose sight of the peculiarity of human rituals.

Throughout human history man has employed ritual behavior to deal with critical moments. Which moments are thought of as most critical will vary from society to society, but I know of no people for whom the fact of

---

[1] Robert Ardrey, *African Genesis* (New York: Dell, 1961); *The Territorial Imperative* (New York: Dell, 1966).

death is not critical, and who have no ritual by which to deal with it. I do know of peoples who treat birth very casually; some of them, in fact, attempt to ignore the infant for several months in the hope that the child will be saved from the forces of evil and malice. Some treat marriage as an important event, and others do not. Some treat puberty as deserving of a year-long segregation of the adolescent or for long initiatory procedures, while others treat puberty so casually that no one notices it. Disasters, hurricanes, tornadoes, shipwrecks, volcanic eruptions — all may be handled with a high degree of ritual, or they may be treated rather casually. Although one cannot make any general statements about what constitutes a crisis, it is certain that all peoples have certain moments in their lives that they have dignified with ritual behavior — that is, with a far greater amount of elaboration than is expected on other occasions.

When one talks, then, about social or personal crises, this is culturally relevant. Christianity maintains a certain degree of consistency concerning what events it regards as critical, but even here a certain fluctuation is evident — particularly, for example, in the case of Confirmation and its place in the Christian initiatory procedure. Fluctuation aside, however, consistency of judging what events are critical and of appropriate ritual responses to such events raises the issue of cultural continuity. In anthropological as well as religious language, this issue is one of tradition.

One problem concerns the possibility of creating a new ritual. This is one of the things that is upsetting the world today, because it is of the essence of ritual that those who participate in it have participated before. Not all members of society, of course, participate in it or have participated in it before. Obviously, the baby who is brought to church for the first time and sees the lights on the altar has never seen them before, but the people who bring the child have. The essence of ritual, then, is bringing the same ritual to a particular critical event of previous experience. So, in a ritual treatment of death, for example, each death is related to all the other deaths to which those present have related before. With each death the feeling that they have had at other times resurfaces. The repetition of an act previously experienced will not fall short of the required intensity.

This, of course, is something that everyone who is involved in religious ritual understands. There are moments that should be of high emotional intensity but are not, and the ritual act serves to re-create to some extent the intense emotion experienced in the past. A familiar instance is that of weeping at weddings. People weep at weddings regardless of the particular marriage involved. It may be a perfect marriage or it may be a disastrous marriage, but they weep. Women weep for their own wedding and that may have been a good wedding, too, but all weddings, all brides, all sacrifices of virgins in the past and to come, get mixed up with people's feelings about weddings, so they weep.

Approaching it in a slightly different way, another important aspect about ritual is that its performers have done it before, in some cases to the point of habit. Any change in ritual dislocates the people who have participated in it previously and is, therefore, resisted. Changes inevitably upset one: throw one out of that semi-automatic type of behavior which is only partly conscious and they project the participant into too great a consciousness.

What I am speaking of is *ritual awareness*. An action is not ritual if the participants are not aware that it is ritual. It is this awareness that makes it a ritual occasion when a particular action is performed, however simple, like lifting the bride across the threshold. The action may be very simple, but it is of a different order than just opening a door. For an act to be ritual, in human terms, therefore, one must be conscious that it is ritual, and yet, at the same time, one must not be too conscious, because if the consciousness is too explicit the blend between the past and the present is lost. It is this loss which occurs when changes are made in ritual, which makes it understandable that people fight changes in ritual more fiercely than they fight changes in anything else, except, perhaps, changes in the arts. Antagonism to new visual or audio representations of any kind is extremely fierce, but it is of the same type of behavior as antagonism to changes in ritual. In each case, one is being robbed of the particular state of bliss and security that seemed previously guaranteed. Only if a ritual is conducted in the same way, only if the same words are spoken in the same order and accompanied by the same gestures, will the same feeling of security be present. It is this security which integrates, for all who have previously experienced the ritual, the past with the present, and at the same time exhibits to the novices, who have never before experienced it, what they are to feel.

The first time I experienced the new Low Mass in Australia and the priest turned and said, "And the Lord be with you," and the congregation answered, "And with you," it introduced *a shock.* Such a shock is inconsistent with the guarantee that is associated with ritual. The right things must be done in the right way and as they have always been done. At a formal dinner in England fifty years ago, no one would start smoking before the port, and no one would drink another toast before the King's toast was drunk. Everybody was thus guaranteed a participation in something that would insure a reinstatement of their previous experience of correct ceremonial behavior. Part of this guarantees that when you live in a state of ritual awareness the symbolism will fit.

A religion develops in one climate but moves to another almost inevitably, because the definition of a great religion is that it can cross boundaries — national boundaries, climatic boundaries, racial boundaries. As it moves, however, more and more of the figures of speech become inappropriate. Something of which I am very fond and which I think gives extraordinary insight into the problems of the contemporary generation is a piece from the ceremony surrounding the blessing of the Paschal candle — *The Exultet*:

> This is the night concerning whereof it is written: And the night is as clear as the day; and, Then shall my night be turned to day. The sanctifying power therefore of this night putteth to flight deeds of wickedness, washeth away sins: restoreth innocence to the fallen, and joy to them that mourn: casteth out enmities, prepareth concord, and boweth down principalities. Therefore in this night of grace accept, O Holy Father, the evening sacrifice of this incense: which, by the hands of thy ministers, holy Church doth lay before thee, in the solemn offering of this Candle, made from the work of bees. But we already know the excellency of this pillar, which for the honour of God the sparkling fire doth kindle. Which, though it be divided into parts, suffereth not loss by the borrowing of its light. For it is fed by melting wax, which the bee mother hath wrought into the substance of this precious Candle.[2]

The imagery of the mother bee making the wax for the candle is poetically delightful, but the contemporary generation knows little about candles. The result is that the whole of the symbolism is lost.

Similarly, as a ritual system of any sort crosses national boundaries, or crosses from one hemisphere to another, there occurs an increasing degree of incongruity between the symbols that are used and the feelings they are intended to evoke. I am thinking, for example, of a poem written by Sister Eileen Duggan, entitled *A New Zealand Christmas*.

> What a grace upon it that He chose that country —
> We have kind oxen and our straw is sweet.
> We have shepherds too now and stables and a manger.
> Had we but one imprint of His little feet!
>
> For my heart goes crying through these days of summer,

---

2 *Missale Anglicanum. The English Missal* (4th ed.; London: Knott and Son, 1940).

Through the sleepy summer, slow with streams and bees.
Had my land been old then there He might have lighted,
Here have seen His first moon in the ngaio trees.

And my heart goes crying through these days of waiting
While His lilies open and His tuis sing.
Had my Lord been born here angels might have ringed
    us,
Standing round our islands, wing wide to wing.

Had my Lord been born here in the time of rata
Three dark-eyed chieftains would have knelt to Him
With greenstone and mats and the proud huia feather,
And the eyes of Mary watching would grow dim.

The sky would be a tumble of summer constellations,
Our own, alas, hidden, that cluster of loss,
Exiled from sight by some great thoughtful angel,
Lest He too soon should look upon a cross.

Oh my heart goes crying through these days of waiting,
We too have oxen and our straw is sweet,
We too have shepherds and stables and a manger
Oh for one clear footprint of His little feet![3]

This portrays all the poignancy of the exile of a people
who had left their native lands, a people who went to
New Zealand not because they wanted to leave England,
but because there were too many mouths at the table.
The poetess was trying to express the things that went
wrong and the things that did not fit. She exhibited the
tremendous temptation to project her native landscape
and the stellar constellation seen in the wintry North
into the picture that she had of the birth of Christ. Such
a nostalgic reinterpretation occurs whenever people move,
whenever the liturgy is carried from one place to another,
with the result that the images are no longer expressive
or intelligible to the people among whom they are used.

Another problem is that of continuity. Ritual has no
efficacy without continuity. I am not speaking here of

----

[3] Eileen Duggan, "A New Zealand Christmas," *New Zealand Poems* (New York: Macmillan, 1940).

efficacy in a strictly theological sense, but I mean merely that ritual is not efficacious for the people who participate in it when it is altered and changed.

We tend to underestimate the extent to which ritual, as it becomes increasingly archaic, alienates people from their religion, from their society, and from their family. This is, perhaps, one of the reasons why men have sought for universality, and have relied so heavily on very simple things in ritual: for instance, fire and water, on the one hand, and on the other, the body — the one absolutely reliable cross-cultural reference we can use. There are no people who do not value the hierarchy that comes from an upright position, and who do not build any sort of statement of hierarchical relationships with the body as the reference. There are no cultures in which images built on the body cannot, to some degree, be translated. This may be one factor in the continuation of bodily posture and bodily symbolism in any kind of ritual statement. Mary Catherine Bateson says we are each our own metaphor.[4] It is our understanding of relationships that constitutes relationship; it is our understanding that makes what we would want to say inside and outside identical. Each person as a whole person is a metaphor for the understanding of the universe.

Dependence upon ritual detail has, in the past, been so great that schisms have arisen and empires have virtually fallen apart because of controversies on such small points of ritual as whether the sign of the cross was to be made with two fingers or with three. Ritual offers a way in which people express their tremendous dependence on this continuity for their sense of identity and their ability to draw on their own memories of those around them, and the faith of those around them. It is by drawing on such memories that a sense of identity, security, and continuity is assured.

Today, however, much of this is being lost. We are

---

4 Mary Catherine Bateson, *Our Own Metaphor* (New York: Knopf, 1972).

reaching a very serious state all over the world, but more acutely, I think, in America than anywhere else. Instead of the attrition of beliefs that went on steadily from the time of the Enlightenment — the attrition in the beliefs of people who could no longer find in the conventional religious ritual any meaning for themselves, and who found a complete dichotomy between science and religion — we find something quite different in the experiments of the new generation.

The American attitude toward ritual differs rather sharply from the attitudes toward ritual in the rest of the world (except in some of the nearer English-speaking countries). Over the past century or two, Americans have distinctively and consistently looked down on any kind of ritual behavior, which they tend to view as foreign in origin. When we have a religious group that has also a universal language, as Latin has been in the Roman Catholic Church until very recently, the combination of foreign and universal can be held without people being too greatly upset. For example, Christian behavior at Christmas and at Easter has style and depth and form.

The most perfect illustration of what Americans have done with ritual is Thanksgiving. Thanksgiving is an American religious holiday and we can certainly describe it as ritualistic. People know what they are to eat, who should come, and what time the dinner should be. Up to fifty years ago, they also went to church. It is a family festival with a definite religious element. Today, however, all normal American adults feel it their duty to disavow the "ritual" elements of the Feast. They have come to detest the traditional turkey. "We just have the turkey for the children," they say. Foreigners, on interviewing Americans about Thanksgiving, find it shocking that we Americans are alienated from our own culture and no longer believe in our institutions.

We have set up our holidays in such a way that we can repeat our rejections of it generation after generation. We have the common feeling that when Italians or Poles come over here, they bring with them their own peculiar ceremonies and ways of doing things, which we think of as ritual, while at the same time we disavow doing anything ritualistic ourselves. The Italians and the Poles find no ritual here at all, and we reinforce this view by telling them that we are not a ritualistic people.

An attitude very current in America and Great Britain equates ritual with formality. Many of us also think of ritual as something superficial, meaningless, empty, phony, lacking in depth and sincerity. Such an attitude is the exact opposite of what the term actually denotes.

A second attitude common to Americans is that we have come to think that doing anything twice has no value. I would hazard that this attitude has been influenced especially by television. The television audience expects and demands that everything be new and different. Let me cite an example.

One of the ways in which I try to give my students some sense of what it is like to work in a primitive society, some sense of wholeness, and integration, and consistency, is to have them observe the ceremonies of a religious group with which they are unfamiliar. One student, who claimed that she had never experienced anything religious, decided to tackle something extremely difficult: Roman Catholic High Mass. With notebook and sharpened senses, she was prepared to try to understand the full emotional impact of the ritual. Everything was fine, she said, until the thought struck her that "they do this *every Sunday*." An idea so shocking that she was oblivious to the remaining portion of the ceremony. Such an attitude, I submit, is widespread in America today; it is such an attitude towards the repetition of anything, ritual included, that undercuts our capacity to ritualize. As I have pointed out above, ritual depends for its efficacy on continuity. It also depends on repeating the same ritual action, because only by repetition does a certain ritual action and the realities it symbolizes become more enjoyable, and hence efficacious.

When it happens that we do develop some ritual, inevitably we soon become bored with it. A perfect example is our moon shots. Fourteen-year-old boys will say: "I used to be interested in trips to the moon when I was young, but I have heard and seen those moon shots ever since I can remember." We have definitely ritualized the whole event. The preparations are always the same, the countdown is accompanied by the same comments by the same television personalities expressing the same emotions. The splashdown is the same, the arrival on board the ship, the dinner with the President, the ticker-tape parade down Madison Avenue. Every time it happens, it matters less to us rather than more. One of the most momentous events in our period, if it happens more than once, becomes boring.

This phenomenon of boredom with anything done more than once is particularly acute among Americans, and is probably one of the reasons why we find it impossible to ritualize. One cause for this phenomenon, I submit, is that Americans are conditioned to accept and expect a high degree of irregularity in their lives. We live in so many different types of housing, and move so often, and drive so many kinds of cars, and smoke so many types of cigarettes, etc., that change, in certain areas, has become part of our lives. This is a very different type of life from that lived by people who have been reared in one house, and have died in the same bed in which they were born.

This expectation of continuous change also contributes to our inability to ritualize. Such an attitude is becoming characteristic of the whole modern world, due, I am confident, partially to our rapid rate of technological change.

This inability to enjoy repetitive events, and to develop repetitive habits, contributes to, if it is not the primary cause of, boredom. We do not know or understand very much about boredom, except that it is one of the most painful sensations a human being can experience. Intense boredom is absolutely intolerable. It is a reaction to a situation in which one has no emotional investment, in which one in no way participates. Like a movie camera or a tape recorder, the person just sits, objectively present, feeling nothing. One feels stuck in a certain place, like a formal dinner, but makes no response one way or the other. He is so bored that he does not even feel it worth while to leave. Boredom is probably one of the most serious drawbacks in our educational system, in our religious rituals, in everything that happens today.

No one was bored, I am sure, with the funeral for John F. Kennedy. This was the first thing of its kind that had ever happened, and it was extremely moving for everyone, regardless of their political views. But then Martin Luther King was assassinated, followed by Robert Kennedy. Not only were people becoming bored with televised accounts of the funerals, but they were becoming bored with assassinations. Some, in fact, telephoned the television stations and requested that the funerals be cut short and the serials restored because, they felt, "something new at least will be happening there." We become bored with even the most moving presentations of events of worldwide significance, if they carry with them any expectation of repetition.

This problem, I feel, already serious, will become increasingly more so. How can we give people rituals that will carry them through crises, rituals that will enable each individual, however deep his grief or confusion, however high his excitement, to reach out to the feelings of others who have experienced the same thing, and to his own previous experiences, and to reach out in a way that gives depth and meaning to the present?

Members of the younger generation today have, I think, sensed the lack of ritual in our lives, and have attempted to restore it. Witness the numerous protest rituals that have taken place in the past few years. Witness, in particular, this example of the incantations voiced outside the Pentagon:

Now, while an Indian triangle was repeatedly struck, and a cymbal was clanged, a mimeographed paper was passed around to the Marchers watching. It had a legend which went something like this:

October 21, 1967, Washington, D.C., U.S.A., Planet Earth

We Freemen, of all colors of the spectrum, in the name of God, Ra, Jehovah, . . . do exorcise and cast out the EVIL which has walled and captured the pentacle of power and perverted its use to the need of the total machine and its child the hydrogen bomb and has suffered the people of the planet earth, the American people and creatures of the mountains, woods, streams, and oceans grievous mental and physical torture and the constant torment of the imminent threat of utter destruction. . . .[5]

That is an attempt to make a new ritual, to take something from every ritual that they ever heard of and pile it into one utterance, attempting by simultaneity to give it a strength that has been lost with the ability that people have had before to rely on historical sequence. It is a kind of gross, really appalling simultaneity and eclecticism and it would not work but once.

The problem that confronts us is this: we should be able to make of shared events (like the funeral of Churchill, which was witnessed in some form all around the world) something that has ritual value and significance for all who participate in it. The combination, however, of never wanting to do anything twice and the self-consciousness of television leads to a somewhat cynical attitude. At present we are unable to provide for the order of ritual awareness on which the human race has depended in the past. We have an impatience with the symbols that have been used before. We sense a discontinuity of young people from their elders, since the experience

_____

5 Norman Mailer, *Armies of the Night* (New York: New American Library, 1968).

of each group has been so different. Our new form of communication has disabled us from participating in repeated events.

Although a great many people did participate in the first colored television pictures of the earth as seen from the moon, the next time they will switch channels. "We saw that before."

How are we going to build a world in which children are raised with sufficient proximity to the events relating them to their families and the ceremonies and rituals of the past, to give them a basis for continued participation of some sort, and with a cosmic awareness that can only be imparted by means of television? The only way in which I see a solution to this is for us to develop what I have described as ritual awareness, so that both types of ritual are meaningful to the young who grow up with them as well as to those of us who did not.

4

Ritual and the Definition of Space

*(or Ritual Space-making Habits among the
Western Christians, with Particular Emphasis
on Romano-American Aberrations)*

by

PATRICK J. QUINN

SINCE ANTHROPOLOGISTS AND THEOLOGIANS FIND IT HARD
to agree on a definition of the word "ritual," I must select
from the plethora of alternatives a general definition that
suits my purpose, one that borrows largely from Margaret
Mead. Ritual for me is a recognizable and repeatable
form of activity within which innovation is possible, and
which is transformed only rarely at a peak of creativity.
Architecture is, in this sense, ritual.

Patrick J. Quinn is Dean of the School of Architecture, Rensselaer
Polytechnic Institute. He has contributed articles on church architecture to *Liturgical Arts* magazine, and in 1970 he received an honor
award from the American Institute of Architects for the design of a
church at Chico, California. This paper was originally delivered to
the accompaniment of slides, which are not reproduced here.

Architecture looks more and more to the behavioral scientists for help in assessing the human milieu for which their buildings are the ritual frame. So eminent a psychologist as Robert Sommer admits, however, that he can give no advance directives to architects.[1] He can, however, do a post-factum evaluation based on observation and tell you why the building does not work. So can most people, so that does not help the space-maker too much.

E. R. Leach, the anthropologist, asserts "categorically that no interpretation of ritual sequences in man is possible unless the interpreter has a really detailed knowledge of the cultural matrix which provides the context for the rite under discussion."[2]

Perhaps, therefore, because of my lifelong intimacy with the tribe herein considered, as well as my being engaged in the art of space-making, I feel myself able to make some observations. This, then, is a loosely documented, totally unscientific series of observations on the tribe known as Western Christians, and their sometimes erratic behavior in making spaces for ritual.[3]

To begin I would like to expose my prejudices in the form of three basic assumptions. First, contrary to popular romantic myths about creativity, building becomes architecture only when it becomes ritual. Second, the link between ritual and architecture is the establishment of what the behaviorists like to call "ethnic domain," territoriality, or "sense of place." Third, the catalyst, in giving life to both ritual and architecture and thus introducing the "sense of place," is the manifold dimension of human encounter.

A brief historical perspective will clarify certain aspects for those unfamiliar with these Western Christian peo-

---

1 Robert Sommer, *Personal Space* (Englewood Cliffs, N.J.: Prentice-Hall, 1969), p. 157.

2 E. R. Leach, "Ritualization in Man in Relation to Conceptual and Social Development," *Philosophical Transactions of the Royal Society of London*, Series B, No. 772, Vol. CCLI (1966), pp. 403-408.

3 Tribe, in this context of a nongenealogical group, is hardly a scientifically appropriate term, but it serves merely as a convenient label.

ple, but this presents a paradox because the Western Christian is inclined to ritualize his historic origins without considering the vagaries of his intervening history.

I divide my historical schema into four phases of the development of the tribe's space-making endeavors: the emergent, the reflective or intellectual, the neological, and the reemergent.

The Emergent Western Christian and His Places of Ritual

I have seen no anthropological evidence that, among primitive peoples, ritual ever began full-blown — as a "given." The Western Christian, however, often seems to believe that his particular ritual was so born. There is reason to believe that he has a measure of truth in this assumption, although, as with most tribal subjects of study, he seldom questions his assumptions. Central to the act of ritual are two basic forms, currently described in tribal language as "the Word" and "the Eucharist," and these two can serve our purpose at least at the "nominal" level. Indeed, studied at this level, the ritual would appear to have been "given" in its pristine forms on the occasion that has come to be known as the "Last Supper" of the Founder, an historic feast commemorated regularly for almost two thousand years. Its setting was that of an ordinary meal, and for the first two hundred years there was little change in the spatial order it demanded. Certainly, as with any nascent ritual, the gestures and participant roles became more formalized so that the increased number in attendance could understand the symbolic language of word and gesture, yet the physical setting was never especially contrived. The great chieftain Hippolytus is credited with one of the earliest efforts to amplify the pattern established by the Founder, in an attempt to communicate the significant communal reality of it to the less enlightened. Critical to the structural order was the symbolic location of the leading participants — the presbyter or bishop and the deacons, who served as assistants, floor managers, and waiters. Frequently the presbyter, flanked by his host and assistants, sat upon a trichlinum, a three-person couch, facing the tribe across the ceremonial table. From this position he enunciated the Word and the Eucharistia, and in these positions they ate.

In its early days, the tribe was somewhat nomadic, spreading even into the territory of the rival Romans, who saw in this ritual-of-no-fixed-abode a threat to their own temple-based rite. Surprisingly, despite the threat of being captured and being forced to become the centerpieces of a sacrificial, ritual entertainment of the Roman tribe, the Western Christians found appropriate places for their ritual in the ordinary dwellings of their day. Not infrequently numbers of their warlike opponents succumbed to the mysterious power of the new rite and offered their own homes as places for its enactment. In its three hundredth year, so many new nonmembers had joined this nongenealogical tribe that it was possible openly to locate the new cult in the temples of the old. Finally, the chief Ruler of the Roman tribes declared the new mode to be henceforth the official ritual of his realm and ordered spaces designed for it everywhere. As a consequence the chieftain of the Western Christians was elevated to approximately equal status, and would later oust the Roman chief as legitimate ruler. All this through the power of ritual.

Two factors are important in this evolution. First, the Western Christians did not yet physically intimidate their rivals; they merely accepted them as members. It was probably the greatest voluntary submission of all time. The Christians did not demand the destruction of Roman Culture, and this tolerance greatly affected the changing form of the ritual and the spaces it occupied. The ceremony was expanded and lengthened by incorporating gestures of the Roman Court. As the Romans were given to pageantry, so the new ritual became extravagantly festive. Second, the Christian chieftains, or bishops, adopted many of the ceremonial accoutrements of the Roman chief, and demanded the same heroic adulation from their followers. Paul of Antioch was criticized for this, but the idea caught on, and the ritual rang with the thunderous acclaim of thousands and glowed with the lights of many torches, while the newly designed spaces were lined with great processional armies of historic tribal figures (called Saints and Martyrs) painted on the walls.

Unlike the "cha-no-yu" or tea ceremony of certain Eastern tribes, which is profound, symbolically elaborate, yet elegantly simple, the Christian supper-ceremony was no longer a simple meal with rich symbolic meaning, but a great mass celebration with all the trappings of the circus. A certain inconsistency and looseness was inevitable. In the seventh century, however, the revered chieftain Gregory successfully curbed this tendency by imposing new rules of order, which were written into the ceremonial code (later called Ordo Missae), and which included new gestures and a new hierarchical group, a team of lead-singers, called interestingly enough the "school of singers." From folk-developments in Syria Gregory borrowed a new alternating musical rhythm that seemed to work well in adding a certain order to the proceedings. The rhythm was infectious, with very repetitive beat, inducing an emotional state described in later generations as being "turned-on." It was called antiphonal singing. Such rhythmic involvement by a large crowd demanded control and even protection for the singers against the hero worship of young supporters, and so a permanent wall of marble (*cancella*) was erected around them giving a new spatial definition to the ritual order. The place of the Word, a small reading-stand (called an ambo), had to be redesigned as an elevated, walled box so that all might see and hear. Two of these were erected in each space for some now obscure reason that has contemporary students of the Primacy of the Place of the Word rather mystified. Although the rhythm and language of the singers eventually reached a level of sophistication beyond the capacities of the mass of participants, the latter at least had much open space in which to move around in time with the beat, if they so wished.

Despite such successful developments, however, the tribe was eventually forced to move its headquarters, northwards from the old Roman Center to a new home amid a hitherto alien group called the Franks, who, like the Romans, succumbed to the new, mysterious ritual power. The W.C.'s, as some called them, discovered that retention of the Roman tribal language, which of course they had adopted, was useful in accentuating that dimension of ritual later to be called "numinous." More than ever, the chant and ritual language of the singers and ceremonial leaders was incomprehensible to the populace, who became mere observers, and the space definition reflected this. The Schola Cantorum (now known as the choir of clerics) attracted many new members, who partook of its pride in achievement and built the wall higher, some say to accentuate their position, others to create a great sound amplifier. Participation in the ritual became increasingly subdivided, especially among that unique tribe of islanders, the Celtic Christians, and a tenth-century chronicler describes the effect on spatial definition, in the space built by one of the early female chieftains, Brigid. Here the participants were separated into three major rooms according to vocation, rank, and sex, yet were, according to the chronicler, fully "united in the Spirit."[4]

Vicarious participation reached an extreme when, with the efficient condensation of the ritual texts into one, individual chieftains were paid to conduct the rite alone. Apparently, according to the records, such paid, vicarious participation was effective in insuring that dead tribesmen would not lose rank in the postmortem rebirth that was attainable by all members. This private rite was apparently not highly considered by the chieftains, for they

---

[4] Cogitosus, biographer of Brigid, quoted in Ludwig Bieler, *Ireland* (London: Oxford Univ. Press, 1963), p. 28.

relegated it to small peripheral spaces called "chevets" and "side-chapels," where often ten or twenty rites took place simultanously. This mini-ritual has also been called the "service-sink liturgy," but the meaning of the term is obscure to scholars, who are still attempting to decipher its implications. The difficulty stems from the ancient word "liturgy" or *Leitourgia,* which used to mean "public work" or corporate public gesture. While this was appropriate to the major tribal gathering, its application to the solitary and silent aberrations continues to mystify our researchers. The space-makers, however, seemed to thrive on the possibility of using the chevet as a device to elaborate the geometry of the ritual place — an enrichment increasingly demanded by the chieftains.

This is curiously underlined in the recorded correspondence between the ascetic teacher Bernard and the great chieftain Suger in the twelfth century. Bernard and his followers must have had some inkling of Eastern custom, for they found that the ritual was more deeply moving in very simple spaces and with minimal furniture. Apparently, the simplicity of the space emphasized the richness of the rite. Suger, however, covered his meal table (or, altar, to use the adapted Roman term) with gold and precious stones and decorated the walls with vivid polychrome, and later his successors filled the windows with what we now call psychedelic light. Thus the space for Suger was a vibrant, glamorous ensemble, to be filled with those thousands who made special "trips" (in those days called pilgrimages) in order to participate fully.

Suger's approach is often called the "ecclesiastical" (an odd misuse of the word) and Bernard's the "monastic." (We shall see that when the W.C.'s crossed the great Western ocean they followed both approaches.) Suger may have confused the issue somewhat by his insistence that "only the best is good enough for God" (the father of the Founder), and scholars find it difficult to reconcile this view with the Founder's own statement that "in my Father's house are many mansions."

The Suger-Bernard controversy lasted many centuries, not only among the ritualists (later called "litniks") but also among the space-makers (later called "architects"), for whom it developed into the controversy of "form versus function," the aesthetics-versus-efficiency debates of interminable and boringly juvenile repetition. Suger was probably the first W.C. architect, after the employees of emperors Justinian and Constantine, to think of his spaces as an expression of faith more than a setting for ritual action. Thus he can be credited with seeing a building as "the Word made Flesh," or as Rudolf Schwarz, the great twentieth-century German space-maker, described it: "the Church Incarnate."[5]

I should point out that the latter word "Church" has also led to some confusion among chroniclers of the W.C. evolution. Interpretations range from the Founder's own notion of a "community of believers" to later designations as the "assembly of chieftains" or even the edifice designed to enclose the ritual space.

Such ambiguity is typical among tribes with writable speech, as is its consequent redundancy in communication; whereas in primitive, nonwritable speech, always coupled with gesture, there is greater clarity. This is certainly true in ritual, but it is also true when architecture is considered a three-dimensional language of space. We can see how far the development of architectural semantics among the W.C.'s has gone to have resulted in both a great ritual richness and a complexity of rules that clouded the meaning of the rite often to the extent of irrelevance.

The Reflective or Intellectual Period

In time the emerging controversies found a locus of

---

5 Rudolf Schwarz, *The Church Incarnate,* trans. by Cynthia Harris (Chicago: Regnery, 1958).

development in the establishment of what was called the University. Here ideas became the ritual food and disputation the ceremonial vehicle. Abstract technical discourse concerning the cosmos, as described in the ancient texts of the W.C.'s, vied with the measuring techniques of a new tribe called the scientists. The latter eventually waged war on the ritualist W.C.'s by using the new sophisticated weapons of observation and measurement. This little war fired up those among the W.C. architects who were already caught up in the Suger-Bernard controversy with serious consequences for the definition of ritual space. About this time we find an increasing number of new names applied to ritual edifices, such as "the House of God" with its many allegorical details; the "Mother Church" with accompanying matriarchal symbolism; "Dome of Heaven" and "Gate of Heaven"; the "Mighty Fortress" (a term reflecting defensive necessity as in the case of Albi); "Sacred Geometry" (using elaborate illustrations of mathematical proportions thought to be pleasing to the Founder's father).

Almost as a reaction to the new threat of reason, there occurred the elaboration of symbols, objects, and acts into a complexity hitherto unknown (except, perhaps, among the Far Eastern tribes of India, whom the W.C.'s had often considered misdirected in their ornate space-making and mysterious rituals). The substantive elements of the rite of bread and wine were so treated. What was once a storage box, in which leftovers were kept for absentees, became a focal symbol. This was amplified by the great mystical and scholarly breakthrough in confirming the Founder's own words as indicating his eternal presence in the midst of his followers, nay in the very elements of the ritual itself. New private rituals of devotion before the sacred box, or "tabernacle," as it was called, caused the space-makers to elaborate it in a manner that almost dwarfed the festal table itself, while the table devolved into a mere supporting shelf. This elaboration in decoration was then expanded to the entire ritual space. The cancella had to go, of course, for visual reasons, and since the Schola was really no longer needed except as a kind of added stimulus to fervor, a new group of musicians was located in a high gallery from which they poured out splendid polyphonic music. Such music through vulgarization would, as Jungmann says, produce "an enigmatic tinkling cloud hovering over the congregation and invariably condemning them to silence."[6]

The place from which the words of the Founder were repeated in ritual became caught up in the same general spirit of elaboration, and became a sculpted promontory from which it was impossible to hear the Word unless the speaker developed the familiar, sonorous, and rhythmic delivery that later became the *sine qua non* of preaching. Some new branches of the tribe, of course, mistook the message for a threatening harangue, and this element of fear was reinforced by a formidable setting.

The story of what happened spatially to the subsidiary rites of initiation and reconciliation is similar and need not be dwelt upon in any detail in this context. Suffice it to say that the increasing spatial complexity of the ritual setting coincided with a general pattern of redundancy and complexity in the system of tribal leadership, with the result that some members, wishing to recapture a pristine simplicity, dissented, revolted, and found a new tribe which for want of a better word we may call the R.C.'s or radical Christians. Their spaces reflected the austerity of their attitudes, and the symbolic complexity gave way to a more simple order.

Members of both groups eventually migrated across the Western ocean and found great difficulty in establishing ritual spaces of continuing symbolic import. In both tribes there were some, of course, who felt the need to recapture at least the image of their erstwhile edifices, which must have seemed oddly out of place to the natives of the new territory. Others developed a new kind of

---

[6] Joseph Jungmann, *The Sacrifice of the Church,* trans. by Clifford Howell (Collegeville, Minn.: Liturgical Press, 1956[?]), p. 51.

setting that served for both spiritual and nonspiritual rituals, in which the entire spectrum of tribal business was conducted. This was a true innovation and was called the New England Meeting House. Others still adapted the space-making techniques of that Urbanist tribe often called Pueblo dwellers, but they imposed the basic ritual organization of old upon those whom they persuaded to join. (What a change in tactics from the conversion methods used in Roman days!)

The constant uncertainty of direction in this new environment seems to have contributed to the development of many space-forms that were essentially hybrid, until the place of ritual could no longer be identified as W.C., R.C., or anything else.

The result of such hybridization was a certain confusion of lineage, historicity, and continuity, and anthropologists began to question whether these so-called ritual spaces were in fact so, or whether they were merely an indication of a deep tribal yearning for such historical continuity.

The Neological Era

This can be subdivided into two parallel phases: the ecclesiological-functional, and the symbolistic-mystical. In the first we find the phenomenon tribesmen have termed the Liturgical Movement, which was a real evolution. In the mid-nineteenth century, a group called the "ecclesiologists," an offshoot of the medieval University system, began to rediscover its recent history, and proceeded, without looking at its tribal roots, to reorganize its ritual and ritual spaces accordingly. The exercises in spatial geometry were complex and intriguing, and they were intended to capture some of the dynamism of medieval spaces. Unfortunately, since it was begotten of strictly academic origins, the dynamism was stillborn. It helped immensely, however, in developing a new trade in spatial antiques, which soon came into great demand. The ecclesiologists recovered from this temporary setback, and discovered that the new, emerging technology could produce at least a spatial dynamism (even if the ritual and spatial concepts did not change), and they arrived inevitably at some extremely fascinating new hybrids. A branch of this group revolted and adopted the name "Liturgical Movement" to designate its efforts at using ritual as the vehicle for a functional pastorate. Logic and efficiency combined with a sense of historic origins to give birth to several interesting approaches. The basic premise was that the space should be designed around an efficient pattern of furniture arrangement in which participant roles were clearly and simply defined, even as in Hippolytus' time. Even the concept of the house-church was reintroduced after 1700 years of abandonment, but there was a clear intent to make the idea operational in its twentieth-century setting, and in this there was a certain limited success. The assembly of tribal chieftains was skeptical and held on to the incipient medievalism of the ecclesiologists.

The symbolist-mystical phase is so called because it was generated by a combination of space-makers (who by this time were called artists) and some tribal stewards, who, while feeling the need to change, yet rejected the functionalism of the liturgical movement. They felt the growing obsolescence of liturgical symbols and sought vainly for new models. Indeed they were rewarded by the great creative space-maker, The Crow (or Le Corbusier), who created a unique and beautiful sculpture on a mountaintop at Ronchamp, France, as a locus for commemorative gatherings of the pilgrimage sort. The stewards and especially the space-makers were intrigued by his rediscovery of a truth established in the eighteenth century by the great Balthazar Neumann: "The key is light, and light illumines shapes, and shapes have an emotional power."[7] Total misunderstanding of the im-

---

[7] Le Corbusier, *The Chapel at Ronchamp* (New York: Praeger, 1957), p. 26.

port of this statement, and of the sculpture inspired by it, brought in its wake an onslaught of exercises in the manipulation of space and symbol alike. Open season was declared on structure, color, texture, etc., and this produced such attempts as a concrete reincarnation of the ancient fish symbol (ΙΧΘΥΣ) of the early days (ignorant tribesmen called it the Holy Mackerel) and the shaping of a gigantic reinforced-concrete crown to commemorate the Royal Founder. (Ritual within a crown can be limited.) Other efforts were made to answer the agonized cry of the minor tribesmen that "it should look like a church." Even the windows were infused with contrived and sentimental meaning, often of a semi-erotic nature. The great mother-symbol, the "Madonna," suffered an equally sad fate. Once standing high on a golden dome over the place of ritual, she now shared importance with a territorial symbol called the "Flag"; she was further relocated to give some dignity to ventilation systems; finally to be sold off in discount trading establishments. Last of all, in this mystifying series of aberrations, was the effort of the chieftains to place in front of the ritual spaces great structures, commonly known as "status symbols" (or campaniles, "banners," etc.) .

Confusion and controversy reigned in the tribe (which had grown to immense proportions) until a great leader emerged and, in 1963, called his subchiefs to an historic meeting in the ancient Roman center. While much tribal reorganization was proposed, the key agreement was that the minor tribesmen should be allowed greater participation in the ritual. Some interpreted this decision to mean that spaces should allow an encirclement of the ritual table, giving rise to the strange dictum "Blessed are they that run in circles, for they shall be known as wheels." Others felt that they should return to the ancient idea of ritual in a living room and the space-makers again responded, giving rise to the term "spaghetti-feed liturgy." Certain chiefs clamped down on such reform, believing that the minor tribesmen were incapable of understanding such matters. Others merely sold off their old ritual buildings and began anew. They felt that both tribal and nontribal rituals could be held in the same space, thereby insuring more efficient use. Technology overcame the difficulty of locating the sacred tabernacle by introducing the revolving bread box, which could disappear into a janitor's closet, leaving space for the nontribal symbol called the Bingo-machine. Even such ingenuity failed to satisfy the now aroused tribesmen, who felt the need for release from the bonds of ritual conformity.

The Reemergent Phase

Thus far the strange history of the ritual space-making of the Western Christians: they have currently entered the fourth phase of their evolution, the surprising phase of "reemergence." While it would be premature to analyze recent developments, we can at least make some observations on the nature and possibilities of the present turmoil.

First, people can feel alone even in a group. Second, when they attempt to cross ritual barriers, such as the Generation Gap, the results can be catastrophic. Third, on both sides of this barrier, individuals can communicate with their peers in ritual language that has unspoken and complex meaning, the origin of which is often unknown. Fourth, some members will make plaintive gestures of appeal in the face of such catastrophe. And fifth, some will be perplexed and confused by the apparent incomprehensible nature of the impasse.

*   *   *

The space-maker can come to grips with the problem of designing for such unpredictable circumstances in a number of ways. While looking deeply into the faces and minds of the young initiates who have not lived long enough to freeze their own rituals into rubrics, he can recognize that people have a strong tendency toward ritual, regardless of tribal origin. He can ignore those who point the way toward the mysterious "heavens," and attempt to understand those who search for meaning in their immediate surroundings. He can realize that a place is made sacred not by mere designation but by what takes place there, by people attempting to establish a sense of place; that people, by taking possession of a place, ritualize that place. He can realize that space becomes a "place" only through this ritual transformation. He comes to know that ritual movement transforms not only the place but also the participant; that, conversely, a place designed with human ritual in mind can evoke informal ritual encounter, indoors or out. He knows that people can be considered a random aggregate of entities that in ritual gathering becomes a dynamic, living sculpture. Finally, he knows that symbolic gesture can be magnified by a place.

Perhaps the real starting point is in the family house, for a house becomes a home only when it is "taken possession of" by the rituals of daily living. Frédéric Debuyst suggests that we look at the profound sparseness and richness in the Japanese tea-house.[8] If one begins with the concept of a ritual place, the design of a home can then evoke a response that enriches the lives of its occupants. We must be careful to understand the range and intensity of ritual involved, and consequently allow a considerable range of choice within the spatial framework. People can thus discover the place anew from time to time and make it a real home. There are the fundamental rituals of preparing a meal (why should a kitchen be just a service center?). Informal gatherings can have ritual dimensions in the living room. Even going to bed is a rite. The settings should recognize the fact. The connections between these ritual spaces can make the home one large living room if they are treated not merely as

---

8 Frédéric Debuyst, *Modern Architecture and Christian Celebration*, ed. by John G. Davies and George A. Raymond (Richmond, Va.: John Knox Press, 1968).

passages but as places of casual, transitional encounter, in which the richness of form is just as understated and just as important as elsewhere. People and light are the two chief building materials, and they are both the most neglected in contemporary design. The link between indoors and outdoors cannot be considered a guillotine, chopping off one part of life from the other, but can act as a place in itself, a doorstep, if you will, that allows for pausing, conversing, etc. The real challenge of such design problems is, as Louis Kahn would have it, to make your small spaces seem large and your large spaces small,"[9] for the evocative tension ensuing is an ingredient in richness.

Despite the nonseparation/separation of the without from the within, the privacy of the dwelling as a whole is vital. It can be aloof, yet welcoming, inviting you in, but asking you to knock first. It is a sacred place.

Perhaps it would be helpful to look further into the Eastern concept of NO TEA, which one eminent has illustrated as being akin to the "sound of one hand clapping."[10] There is profundity in both the tea ceremony and in the concept of NO TEA, which as yet eludes the Western Christian.

Yet still our ritualists and architects fiddle and faddle with obsolescent novelty in form-giving. They confuse ritual with "happening," "sensory awareness" with perception and sensitivity, and life with images. They might do well to reflect on the message of Shelley:

> . . . traveller from an antique land
> Who said "Two vast and trunkless legs of stone
> Stand in the desert. Near them on the sand,
> Half sunk, a shatter'd visage lies, whose frown
> And wrinkled lip and sneer of cold command
> Tell that its sculptor well those passions read
> Which yet survive, stamp'd on the lifeless things,
> The hand that mock'd them and the heart that fed;

---

9 Louis Kahn, Informal Seminar, Univ. of Pennsylvania, 1958.
10 Aidan Kavanagh, O.S.B. Discussion with the author.

And on the pedestal these words appear:
"My name is Ozymandias, King of Kings:
Look on my works, ye mighty, and despair!"
Nothing beside remains. Round the decay
Of that colossal wreck, boundless and bare,
The lone and level sands stretch far away.[11]

(— Perhaps to the land of NO TEA.)

[11] Percy B. Shelley, "Ozymandias of Egypt," *The Complete Poetical Works of Percy Bysshe Shelley* (New York: Houghton-Mifflin, 1901).

5

The Influence of Symbols upon Social Change: A Place on Which to Stand

by

JONATHAN Z. SMITH

THE PHILOSOPHER HAS THE POSSIBILITY OF EXCLAIMING with Archimedes: "Give me a place to stand on and I will move the world." The quest for this place finds paradigmatic expression in the almost initiatory scenario of Descartes' *dans un poêle.* There is, for such a thinker, at least the possibility of a real beginning, even of achieving *the* Beginning, a standpoint from which all things flow, a standpoint from which he has clear vision.[1] The historian or the historian of religions has no such possi-

---

1 Cf. M. Foss, *Abstraktion und Wirklichkeit* (Bern: Francke Verlag, 1959), ch. I, esp. pp. 5-7.

Jonathan Z. Smith serves as Associate Professor and Chairman of the History of Religions Field, Divinity School, University of Chicago. This paper originally appeared in *Worship,* Vol. 44 (1970), pp. 457-474.

bility. There are no places on which he might stand apart from the messiness of the given world. There is for him no real beginning, but only the plunge that he takes at some arbitrary point to avoid the unhappy alternatives of infinite regress or silence. His standpoint is not discovered; rather it is erected with no claim beyond that of sheer survival. The historian's point of view cannot sustain clear vision.

The historian's task is to complicate, not to clarify. He strives to celebrate the diversity of manners, the opacity of things, the variety of species. He is barred thereby from making a frontal assault on his topic. Like the pilgrim, the historian is obligated to approach his subject obliquely. He must circumambulate the spot several times before making even the most fleeting contact. His method, like that of Tristram Shandy, Gentleman, is that of the digression.

The historian's manner of speech is often halting and provisional. He approaches his data with that same erotic tentativeness expressed in the well-known colloquy from the "Circe" episode of Joyce's *Ulysses*:

> You may touch my . . .
> May I touch your?
> O, but lightly!
> O, so lightly![2]

And having shyly addressed and momentarily touched the object, he must let it go and return it to its place, unexhausted and intact.

The historian in his work detects clues, symptoms, exemplars. He provides us with hints that remain too fragile to bear the burden of being solutions. He is a man of insights; not, preeminently, a man of vision.

*   *   *

He was a most curious Frenchman, Seigneur de Saint-Évremond, who was born in Normandy and buried in the Poet's Corner of Westminster Abbey — a distinguished

---

[2] J. Joyce, *Ulysses* (New York: Random House, 1934), p. 561.

soldier, brigadier general in the army of Louis XIV, political critic of strong monarchy, fugitive and exile, sceptic, *philosophe,* Epicurean, friend of Hobbes and Spinoza, defender and author of English comedy, wit, and "Freethinker triumphant."[3] About 1678, writing his *Dissertation sur le mot Vaste* addressed to the Academy, he maintained:

> The *vast* and the dreadful have a great affinity to one another.... *Vasta solitudo* is not one of those solitudes which offer the sense of charming repose ... (rather) it is a wild solitude where we are afraid of being alone.... A *vast* house offers something ghastly to the sight. *Vast* apartments never tempt anyone to live in them. *Vast* gardens lack both the amenities which are the result of art and those graces which Nature bestows. *Vast* forests frighten us; the sight loses itself in looking across *vast* plains.... Savage lands that are uncultivated, landscapes ruined by the desolation of war, lands forsaken and abandoned — all partake of the quality of *vastness* which gives rise to a sense of secret horror within us.... *Vast* is almost the same thing as laid waste, spoiled, and ruined.... The most common meaning of *vastus* is too spacious, too extended, too great, immoderate.... We never say *"vast* enough" because "enough" implies something fitting and reasonable; whereas as soon as a thing is vast, there is an excess, it is too much [*de trop*].[4]

Such a sense of almost Sartrean nausea before the vast, the *de trop,* is, as R. Ternois, Saint-Évremond's most recent editor, has pointed out, in sharp contrast with definitions of *vaste* in contemporary French lexica. In diction-

---

3 See the fine, brief account of Saint-Évremond in P. Hazard, *The European Mind 1680-1715* (New York: Meridian Books, 1953; reprint), pp. 120-130. I have borrowed the phrase "Free-thinker triumphant" from p. 127.

4 *Oeuvres meslées de Mr. de Saint-Évremond* (2nd ed.; Paris: C. Barbin, 1967), pp. 90, 92, 94. See further the excellent critical edition by R. Ternois, *Saint-Évremond: Oeuvres en prose* (Paris: Didier, 1966), III, 380f., 382, 383. Compare the rendering above with the original English translation by P. Des Maizeaux, *The Works of Monsieur de St.-Évremond Made English from the French Original* (London: J. Churchill, 1714), II, 98, 100, 101.

aries such as those of P. Richelet (1680) and A. Furetière (1690), *vaste* carries the meaning of free, expansive, imaginative.[5] It is this positive sense which led de Tocqueville to use *vaste* or a synonym nine times in the first three pages of his enthusiastic physical description of America. Indeed, it has been a characteristic description of America — it peoples the pages of material collected in Henry Nash Smith's classic, *Virgin Land;* it lies behind such characteristic American expressions as Frederick Jackson Turner's well-known "frontier thesis." It is a curious, and possibly significant detail, that the three great powers in today's world are those most frequently described in traveler's reports as vast, open, almost limitless realms: America, Russia, and China.

The ambivalence here expressed in relation to the notion of vastness may be seen in analogous concepts. For example, in classical sources the nomadism (and hence the openness and vastness) of the Scyths is both idealized and abjured. On the one hand, their mobility makes them shiftless, barbaric, frightening, perpetual exiles; on the other hand, they are free, uncontaminated, wise lords of all the earth they so casually roam.[6] (A similar dichotomy may be seen in the varying assessments of the period of wilderness-wandering in the biblical texts.[7])

The difference between these two standpoints — horror in the face of the vast, and enthusiasm for expanse and

---

5 R. Ternois, *Saint-Évremond,* III, 384n. Cf. the discussion of the word *vaste* in the works of Baudelaire, in G. Bachelard, *La Poétique de l'Espace* (Paris: Presses Universitaires de France, 1957), pp. 174-181.

6 See the material collected in A. Riese, *Die Idealisierung der Naturvölker des Nordens in der griechischen und römischen Literatur* (Heidelberg: Weiss, 1875); A. O. Lovejoy-G. Boas, *Primitivism and Related Ideas in Antiquity* (Baltimore: Johns Hopkins Press, 1935), I, 315-344; G. Boas, *Essays on Primitivism and Related Ideas in the Middle Ages* (Baltimore: Johns Hopkins Press, 1948), pp. 135-137.

7 Following the magnificent traditio-historical investigations of G. W. Coats, *Rebellion in the Wilderness: The Murmuring Motif in the Wilderness Traditions of the Old Testament* (Nashville: Abingdon Press, 1968), it is no longer possible to speak of a simple dichotomy between wilderness traditions dependent upon an alleged "nomadic ideal" and negative ones.

openness — is not merely a matter of aesthetic sensibility. A total world-view is implied and involved in assuming these postures, one that has to do with a culture's or an individual's symbolization of the cosmos and their place within it. There have been many ways of naming these two basic structures of human symbolization and experience. One might speak of a centripetal and a centrifugal viewpoint. One might adopt the language of Bergson and speak of the closed/static society and the open/dynamic one. One might follow the fruitful lead of Eric Voegelin and point to the contrast between a "compact" and "differentiated" experience of the cosmos.[8]

Whatever terminology is employed, we must be careful to preserve a sufficient sense of the experiential and symbolic character of this dichotomy, and resist imposing an evolutionary scheme of development "from the closed world to the infinite universe" (to borrow the title of Alexandre Koyre's well-known history of science). We must resist as well the frequent tendency to identify the centripetal-closed with primitive or archaic society, and the centrifugal-open with the modern. Both have been and remain existential possibilities that may be appropriated whenever and wherever they correspond to one's experience. We might recall that in Greece the period of the development of the *polis,* with its characteristically bounded understanding of the world, coincided exactly with the rise of Greek colonization, with its correspondingly expansive view. Or we might point to our contemporary society with its growing reinterest in community and in rediscovery of one's roots in the earth, on the one hand, and its fascination with space exploration, on the other. Nevertheless, and bearing this caveat firmly in mind, we can point to the oscillation in human history

---

8 H. Bergson, *Les deux sources de la morale et de la religion* (Paris: Alcan, 1932; Eng. trans., New York: Holt, 1949); E. Voegelin, *Order and History*, Vol. I: *Israel and Revelation* (Baton Rouge: Louisiana State Univ. Press, 1956), p. 5: "the history of symbolization is a progression from compact to differentiated symbols."

between these viewpoints, with one and now the other giving a dominant complexion to a people or an age. The adoption of one or the other of these symbolic systems has the most profound implications for the question of social change.

*   *   *

In the Mediterranean and Near Eastern world, for some 2,000 years man's faith was predominantly informed by what Cornelius Loew (following the researches of Frankfort, Jacobsen, Voegelin, and others) has termed "a cosmological conviction," that is, "the conviction that the meaning of life is rooted in an encompassing cosmic order in which man, society, and the gods all participate." Loew goes on to specify five facets of this conviction: (1) there is a cosmic order that permeates every level of reality; (2) this cosmic order is the divine society of the gods; (3) the structure and dynamics of this society can be discerned in the movements and patterned juxtapositions of the heavenly bodies; (4) human society should be a microcosm of the divine society; (5) the chief responsibility of priests and kings is to attune human order to the divine order.[9]

This pattern of affirming and celebrating the order of the cosmos is exemplified in the typical creation myth of the Mediterranean-Near Eastern world, a creation by combat between the forces of order and chaos. Order is something won by the gods, and it is this primordial act of salvation which is renewed and reexperienced in the cult. For example, in the famous Babylonian creation myth, *Enuma elish,* Marduk the king-god and his forces are victorious over the powers of watery chaos. In victory, Marduk seals the tablets of destiny (IV.121f.), sets bounds, limits, and guards over the chaotic waters (IV.139f.), creates stations for the gods, establishes their signs in the zodiac (V.1f.) and their laws and destinies

---

[9] C. Loew, *Myth, Sacred History and Philosophy* (New York: Harcourt, Brace and World, 1967), pp. 5, 13.

(VI.78; VII.144). Man's response to these activities, slave of the gods though he may believe himself to be, is that he "rejoice in Marduk . . . [for] reliable is his word, unalterable his command; the utterance of his mouth no god whatever can change" (VII.149, 151f.).[10]

There may be periods of tension (such as the myth of the theft of the tablets of destiny by the Zu bird or the imprisonment of Marduk during the New Year festival), but the "reliable" and "unalterable" structures of destiny will ultimately win out. They will be victorious because they are real, having been established by the gods. They will be victorious because they have been annually renewed and strengthened in the great double ceremony of the fixing of the divine and human destinies that concluded the Akitu festival.

Man's responsibility becomes one of discovering, of knowing his place. The man of wisdom is the sage — the one who can discern the pattern of things and aid the king and people in fulfilling their appointed role. Man is charged with the task of harmonizing himself with the great rhythms of cosmic destiny and order. If he does rebel (as in the case of Gilgamesh, who seeks to overcome the structures of destiny and death that are the common human lot) he will learn that he "cannot rise above his human characteristics . . . and after a brief time of despair, he squares his shoulders and goes back to face reality."[11]

Indeed, it might be suggested that one of the characteristic epic figures in societies of "cosmological conviction" is what I would term the hero-that-failed. Like the Polynesian culture hero Maui, or the Greek Orpheus, the hero-that-failed was *not* successful in overcoming death or his humanity; rather, through rebellion against order

---

10 I have followed the translation of A. Heidel, *The Babylonian Genesis* (2nd ed.; Chicago: Univ. of Chicago Press, 1951).

11 T. Jacobsen, "The Epic of Gilgamesh," in J. Neusner, ed., *Report of the 1965-1966 Seminar on Religions in Antiquity* (Hanover: Dartmouth College Comparative Studies Center, 1966), p. 18. Cf. T. Jacobsen, "Mesopotamia: The Good Life," in *Before Philosophy*, ed. by H. Frankfort (Baltimore: Penguin Books, 1949), pp. 223-227.

he was initiated into, discovered and assumed his humanity. By his hard-won affirmation of both the human
and cosmic structures of destiny, he became a model for
his fellow men.[12]

This locative vision of man and the cosmos is revealed
in a variety of descriptions of the places in which men
may stand. The world is perceived as a bounded world;
focusing on the etymological roots, the world is felt to be
an *environ*ment, an *ambi*ance.[13] That which is open, that
which is boundless is seen as the chaotic, the demonic,
the threatening. The desert and the sea are the all but
interchangeable concrete symbols of the terrible, chaotic
openness. They are the enemy *par excellence*. To battle
against the power of the waters a "divine warrior" is required: Baal versus Prince Sea *(Zabul Yam)* or the seven-
headed water dragon *Lotan;* Marduk versus Apsu and
Tiamat; Yahweh against Leviathan, Rahab or the Sea
(Yam); Ninurta against Kur. Victory establishes those two
inseparable companions: divine kingship and cosmic order. Order is produced by walling, channeling, and con-
fining the waters.[14]

---

12 For the tradition concerning Maui and death, see the text con-
veniently reprinted in M. Eliade, *From Primitives to Zen* (New York:
Harper and Row, 1967), pp. 142-144.

13 W. Pax, "Sprachvergleichende Untersuchungen zur Etymologie des
Wortes 'Amphipolos,'" *Wörter und Sachen,* XVIII (1937), 1-88, esp. pp.
16-26. See further K. Michaelsen, "Ambience," *Studia Neophilologica,*
XII (1939-40), 91-119; L. Spitzer, "Milieu and Ambience," *Philosophy
and Phenomenological Research,* III (1942-43), 1-42, 169-218, reprinted
in Spitzer, *Essays in Historical Semantics* (New York: Vanni, 1948), pp.
179-316.

14 For the general pattern, the fundamental work, to which new texts
have been brought, remains H. Gunkel's classic, *Schöpfung und Chaos in
Urzeit und Endzeit* (Göttingen: Vandenhoeck und Ruprecht, 1895). See
further A. J. Wensinck, *The Ocean in the Literature of the Western
Semites* (Amsterdam: Koninklijke Akademie van Wetenschappen, 1918);
O. Eissfeldt, "Gott und das Meer in der Bibel," in *Studia Orientalia
Ioanni Pedersen* (Copenhagen: Munksgaard, 1953), pp. 76-84; O. Kaiser,
Die mythische Bedeutung des Meeres in Aegypten, Ugarit und Israel
(Berlin: Töpelmann, 1962); L. R. Fisher, "Creation at Ugarit and in
the Old Testament," *Vetus Testamentum,* XV (1965), 313-324. The im-
portant notion of the "divine warrior" is brilliantly discussed in F. M.

> The Lord [Marduk] rested, examining her dead body, . . .
> He split her open like a mussel [?] into two [parts];
> Half of her he set in place and formed the sky [therewith] as a roof.
> He fixed the crossbar [and] posted guards;
> He commanded them not to let her waters escape.[15]

> [Yahweh] shut in the sea with doors . . . put bounds upon it,
> Set up bars and doors,
> Saying, "Thus far come, but no more.
> Here your wild waves halt."[16]

Ninurta, after slaying Kur, had to set up a heap of stones over the body and form a great wall of stones in front of the land: "These stones hold back the 'mighty waters' and as a result the waters of the lower regions rise no longer to the surface of the earth. As for the waters which had already flooded the land, Ninurta gathers them and leads them into the Tigris. . . ."[17]

The same stratagem will be employed against the desert.[18] It is defeated by the erection of walls and boundaries. This is why the *Epic of Gilgamesh* begins and ends with the same sort of injunctions: praising the king's building:

> He built the wall of Uruk, the enclosure
> Of holy Eanna, the sacred storehouse.

Cross, Jr., "The Divine Warrior in Israel's Early Cult," in A. Altmann, ed., *Biblical Motifs* (Cambridge, U.S.A.: Harvard Univ. Press, 1966), pp. 1-10.

15 *Enuma elish,* IV, pp. 135-140; in A. Heidel, *The Babylonian Genesis,* p. 42.

16 Job 38:8-11, in M. Pope, *Job* (Garden City: Doubleday, 1965), p. 247.

17 S. N. Kramer, *Sumerian Mythology* (2nd ed.; New York: Harper and Row, 1961), p. 81.

18 J. Pedersen, *Israel: Its Life and Culture* (London: Oxford Univ. Press, 1926), I-II, 453-460, 467-480, 491f.; A. Haldar, *The Notion of the Desert in Sumero-Accadian and West-Semitic Religions* (Uppsala: Lundequistska, 1950); S. Talmon, "The 'Desert Motif' in the Bible and in Qumran Literature," in A. Altmann, ed., *Biblical Motifs,* pp. 31-63; J. Z. Smith, "Earth and Gods," *Journal of Religion,* XLIX (1969), 103-127.

> Behold its outer wall, whose brightness is like [that of]
>   copper!
> Yea, look upon its inner wall, which none can equal!
> Take hold of the threshold. . . .
> Climb up upon the wall of Uruk [and] walk about;
> Inspect the foundation terrace and examine the
>   brickwork,
> If its brickwork be not of burnt bricks,
> [And] if the seven [wise men] did not lay its
>   foundations! . . .
> One *shar* is city, one *shar* orchards, one *shar* prairie;
> [Then there is the] uncultivated land [?] of the temple
>   of Ishtar.
> Three *shar* and the uncultivated land [?] comprise
>   Uruk.[19]

Although this repetition may be explained as simply an example of epic "ringcomposition," I would suggest something more profound is at stake.[20] Although Gilgamesh is a hero-that-failed, although he has not been able to overcome death and bring back for his people the wondrous plant "old-man-becomes-youth-again," he can, as king, win a limited security from destruction by maintaining the walls. The walled city is a symbolic universe that serves (to borrow a term from the Vietnam war) as an "enclave," a "strategic hamlet" against the threat of the boundless, chaotic desert. The desert, which is a place of utter desolation, of cosmic and human emptiness — the place called "the howling waste of the desert" (Deut. 32:10), the "land not sown" (Jer. 2:2), the land of "no-kingdom-there" (Isa. 34:12), the place "in which there is no man" (Job 38:26) — is an active threat, constantly seeking to breach the walls.

The possession of such an "enclave" is a responsibility;

---

19 *Gilgamesh* I.9-19; XI.303-307, in A. Heidel, *The Gilgamesh Epic and Old Testament Parallels* (2nd ed.; Chicago: Univ. of Chicago Press, 1949), pp. 16f., 93.

20 See W. A. A. van Otterlo, *De ringcompositie als opbouwprincipe in de epische gedichten van Homerus* (Amsterdam: Nederlandsche Akademie van Wetenschappen, 1948).

the security won, a fragile thing. Whether the cosmography is expressed through the model of the inhabited land as a bubble of air in the midst of the dangerous cosmic waters that surround it, or as a walled mound in the midst of the raging desert, safety is not guaranteed. The walls of the "hamlet" are always vulnerable to attack, and man and the gods must ceaselessly labor to sustain, renew, and strengthen the power, to keep the walls under repair. If they fail, the vision of destruction will be fulfilled:

> I saw the earth — lo, chaos primeval!
>   The heavens — their light was gone.
> I saw the mountains — and lo, they were quaking,
>   And all the hills rocked to and fro.
> I looked — and behold, no human was there,
>   And the birds of the skies had all flown.
> I looked — and behold, the tilled land was desert,
>   Its cities all lying in ruins. . . .[21]

In such a cosmos lines must be clearly drawn. Civic officials may physically set up and maintain boundary stones with inscriptions proclaiming, "I am the border."[22] Cartographers may draw maps that show the boundaries of the world *polis,* with border peoples (Scyths, Indians, Celts, and Ethiopians) who are not like us, their strangeness expressed in either their idealization as "noble savages" or their denigration as monsters.[23] Great brazen walls (such as the one constructed by Alexander the Great to confine the peoples of Gog and Magog) may be pictured as bulwarks against chaotic forces.[24] But the con-

---

[21] Jeremiah 4:23-26, in J. Bright, *Jeremiah* (Garden City: Doubleday, 1965), pp. 30f.

[22] See the border stones described and figured in R. E. Wycherley, *The Athenian Agora,* Vol. III of *Literary and Epigraphical Testimonia* (Princeton: American School of Classical Studies at Athens, Institute for Advanced Study, 1957), p. 218.

[23] See R. Wittkower, "Marvels of the East: A Study in the History of Monsters," *Journal of the Warburg and Courtauld Institutes,* IV (1942), 159-197; R. Bernheimer, *Wild Men in the Middle Ages* (Cambridge, U.S.A.: Harvard Univ. Press, 1952).

[24] A. R. Anderson, *Alexander's Gate, Gog and Magog and the Enclosed*

cern for limits, borders, and boundaries is a far more subtle and pervasive thing than these.

One need only refer to Mary Douglas' already classic work, *Purity and Danger: An Analysis of Concepts of Pollution and Taboo,* to see a total interpretation of religious and social mores in the light of these concerns. "Holiness is exemplified by completeness. Holiness requires that individuals shall conform to the class to which they belong. And holiness requires that different classes of things shall not be confused."[25] Hence no hybridization and no "mingling of seeds," no animals are to be eaten that are on the borderline with respect to their class (i.e., the bat, which is neither animal nor bird), marital regulations of both exogamy and endogamy, the polluting capacities and magic utilization of nails, hair, excrement, mucus, etc., which come from the boundary, and hence most vulnerable parts of the human body. Or, as Claude Lévi-Strauss has noted:

> A native thinker makes the penetrating comment... "All sacred things must have their place." It could even be said that being in their place is what makes them sacred for if they were taken out of their place, even in thought, the entire order of the universe would be destroyed. Sacred objects therefore contribute to the maintenance of order in the universe by occupying the places allocated to them. Examined superficially and from the outside, the refinements of ritual can appear pointless. They are explicable by a concern for what one might call "micro-adjustment" — the concern to assign every single creature, object, or feature to a place within a class.[26]

Nations (Cambridge, U.S.A.: The Medieval Academy of America, 1932).

25 M. Douglas, *Purity and Danger* (New York: Praeger, 1966), p. 53.

26 C. Lévi-Strauss, *The Savage Mind* (Chicago: Univ. of Chicago Press, 1966), p. 10. I am appreciative of Lévi-Strauss' reversal: it is not the sacred that gives things their place, but being in their place that makes things sacred. However, his "native thinker," as quoted in A. C. Fletcher, "The Hako: A Pawnee Ceremony," *Twenty-Second Annual Report of the Bureau of American Ethnology* (Washington, D.C., 1904), Part 2, p. 34, does not imply this.

Such a locative view of the cosmos seems foreign to our tendency to idealize openness and mobility. When we confront a total system of boundaries, limits, and places such as the caste system of India, we find it difficult to conceive of it as anything but constricting and shackling. Yet *homo hierarchicus*[27] enshrines a notion of cosmic responsibility, of the unique and precious value of each individual's keeping his place. This sense of significance is often lacking among societies possessing a more egalitarian view. Indeed, it might be suggested that if lack of freedom appears to be the "sin" of a locative world view, meaninglessness is the "sin" of the open. It is the power of this vision that has made the locative understanding of the cosmos and man's role within it, along with its associated complex of symbols and social structures, one of the two basic existential options open to man.

*   *   *

As Mircea Eliade has pointed out in his important and imaginative essay, "The 'God who Binds' and the Symbolism of Knots," there is a multivalence and a depth to such symbolisms of limit-situations.[28] There is the language of the "great chain of being" into which all things are bound and in which all things, distinct as they are, share. One might talk of the affirmation of one's place, the place on which one stands, or seek to be unbound, to be liberated. Both are experiential possibilities and postures. The symbolizations and expressions flow from the situation in which a man finds himself.

In the Mediterranean world we have been describing, in the Hellenistic period, such a radical revaluation of the cosmos occurred.[29] Suffering from what might be

---

[27] I utilize the title of Louis Dumont's brilliant book on this theme, *Homo Hierarchicus* (Paris: Editions Gallimard, 1967).

[28] M. Eliade, "Le 'dieu lieur' et le symbolisme des noeuds," *Revue de l'histoire des religions*, CXXXIV (1947-48), 5-36; Eng. trans. *Images and Symbols* (New York: Sheed and Ward, 1961), pp. 92-124.

[29] Cf. H. Jonas, *The Gnostic Religion* (2nd ed.; Boston: Beacon Press,

termed "cosmic paranoia," man sees danger and threat
everywhere. Looking up at the heavens, at the stars and
the motions of the heavenly bodies, he no longer sees
the signs and guarantors of order, the guardians of a
good cosmic and human destiny, the positive limits placed
on the chaotic powers above and below and on the span
of human existence; but rather a grim system of aggres-
sors, an openly hostile army that seeks to chain him. He
finds himself in a world surrounded and hemmed in by
powers, powers one dares do no more than name in ter-
rifying titles such as the following:

> O mighty, majestic, glorious Splendors; holy and earth-
> born, mighty arch-daimons; compeers of the great god;
> denizens of Chaos, of Erebus and of the unfathomable
> Abyss; earth-dwellers, haunters of sky-depths, nook-
> infesting, murk-enwrapped; scanners of the mysteries,
> guardians of the secrets, captains of the hosts of hell;
> king of infinite space, terrestrial overlords; globe-shaking,
> firm-founding, ministering to earthquakes; terror-
> strangling, panic-striking, spindle-turning ... tempest-
> tossing Lords of Fate, dark shapes of Erebus, senders of
> Necessity; flame-fanning fire-darters, snow-compelling,
> dew-compelling, gale-raising, abyss-plumbing, calm-
> bestriding air spirits; dauntless in courage, heart crush-
> ing despots; chasm-leaping iron-nerved daimons; wild-
> raging, unenslaved; watchers of Tartarus; delusive
> Fate-phantoms; all-seeing, all-hearing, all-conquering,
> sky-wandering vagrants.[30]

In such a world-view, the structures of order are perceived to have been reversed. Rather than the positive
limits they were meant to be, they have become oppressive.
Man is no longer defined by the degree to which he

1963), esp. pp. 5-7, 241-265; J. Z. Smith, "Birth Upside Down or Right
Side Up?", *History of Religions,* IX (May 1970), 281-303.

30 "Invocation to the All-powerful Might of the Constellation of the
Great Bear," from the Great Paris Magical Papyrus (Bibl. Nat. suppl.
Gr. 574, f. 15ᵛ) in K. Preisendanz, *Papyri Graecae Magicae* (Leipzig-
Berlin: Teubner, 1928), I, 118 (lines 1345-80). I have followed, with
minor alterations, the translation by E. M. Butler, *Ritual Magic* (Cam-
bridge: Noonday Press, 1949), p. 9.

harmonizes himself and his society to the cosmic patterns of order; but rather by the degree to which he can escape the patterns. Rather than the hero-that-failed of the locative world-view, the paradigm here is the hero-that-succeeded, succeeded in escaping the tyrannical order. Every man is called upon to be such a hero. The man of wisdom is no longer the sage but the savior — he who knows the escape routes.

To escape from the despotism of this world and its rulers, exemplified in the seven planetary spheres described in brutal archaic language, becomes the goal:

> The foes, the foes — seven are they, seven are they; evil are they, evil are they; seven are they, seven are they. Seven gods, seven evil gods. . . . Seven demons of oppression. On high they bring trouble, below they bring chaos. . . . Falling in rain from the sky, issuing from the earth, they penetrate the strong timbers, the thick timbers; they pass from house to house. Doors do not stop them; locks do not stop them. They glide in at doors like serpents; they enter by the windows like the wind. Seven are they — they grind the land like grain. Knowing no mercy they rage against man. Roaring above, gibbering below, they — the seven — they are the voices which cry and pursue mankind.[31]

To ascend to another world of freedom and openness becomes the aim of Hellenistic man and the chief concern of his religion. Hellenistic man discovered himself to be an exile from his true home, a home beyond the borders. He strives to return to the world-beyond-this-world that is his true place; to the god-beyond-the-god-of-this-world who is the true god; to awaken the part of himself that is from the beyond and strip off his body that belongs to his present constricted realm.

> I no longer have trust in anything in the world
> In father and mother;

---

[31] I have adapted the rendering of R. C. Thompson, *Semitic Magic* (London: Luzac, 1908), pp. 47-50.

I have no trust in the world
In brothers or sisters;
I have no trust in the world. . . .
After my soul alone I go searching about,
Which is worth more to me than generations or worlds.
I went and found my soul. . . .
I went and found Truth where she stands,
At the outermost rim of the world.[32]

As Paul in Romans 7 was to discover about the Law of
Yahweh, that it was good *once,* but that it had been captured by the Powers and turned upside down so that "the
very commandment which promised life proved to be
death to me" (Rom. 7:10), so each locative culture was
to discover that its cherished structures of limits, the gods
that ordained and maintained these limits, and the myths
that described the creation of the world as an imposition
of limits were perverse. Each culture rebelled against its
locative traditions, developing a complex series of techniques for escaping limitation, for achieving individual
and cosmic freedom now.

*   *   *

It is tempting to continue along these lines, offering
yet further examples that might add subtlety to the extremely broad strokes with which we have painted our
portrait. We might point to the cosmogonic conflict in
Indian mythology between the Restrainers (Vritras or
Daityas) and the Non-Restrainers (Adityas) with its complex dialectic of positive and negative closure and openness. We might point to constellations of symbols that
associate spaciousness, openness, and freedom in a far
more positive way than the Hellenistic model we have
dwelt on.[33] We might point to the idealization of social

---

32 M. Lidzbarski, *Ginza: Der Schatz oder Das Grosse Buch der Mandäer*
(Göttingen: Vandenhoeck und Ruprecht, 1925), pp. 390f.; Eng. trans.
Jonas, *The Gnostic Religion,* pp. 90f.

33 For example, J. F. A. Sawyer, "Spaciousness: An Important Feature
of Language about Salvation in the Old Testament," *Annual of the
Swedish Theological Institute,* VI (1968), 20-34.

mobility so rampant in this country, which has led Samuel Eliot Morison to preface his *Oxford History of the American People* with the following quotation from Oliver Wendell Holmes: "I find the great thing in this world is not so much where we stand as in what direction we are moving." We might point to the more recent mythology of conflict between these two visions of the world: the cowboy versus the homesteader, the one with his cry of "Ride on" and "Don't fence me in," the other with his barbed wire and language of roots. [34] Or we might point to an older incarnation of the same duality: Alexander the Great and the naked sages of India.

> On the appearance of Alexander and his army these venerable men stamped [the earth] with their feet and gave no other sign of interest. Alexander asked them through interpreters what they meant by this odd behavior, and they replied: "King Alexander, every man can possess only so much of this earth's surface as this we are standing in. You are but human like the rest of us, save that you are always busy . . . travelling so many miles from your home, a nuisance to yourself and to others."[35]

But the basic dichotomy remains. The question of the character of the place on which one stands is *the* fundamental symbolic and social question. Once an individual or culture has expressed its vision of its place, a whole language of symbols and social structures will follow.

While it is beyond the scope of this paper to catalogue and explicate the variety of social forms and expressions associated with either of these basic human stances, perhaps one small but significant example will suffice. We have all learned that money is symbolic; but, symbolic of what? In an expansive, open culture money becomes an important means of expressing transcendence of place.

---

34 I owe this example to my colleague, Professor Charles H. Long of the University of Chicago.

35 Arrian, *Anabasis* VII. i.6; Eng. trans. A. de Sélincourt, *Arrian's Life of Alexander the Great* (Baltimore, 1958), pp. 225f.

Through the acquisition of money, social mobility is made possible for the individual or culture group. One may rise above his station, class, or place. Similarly, the acquisition of wealth with its attendant phenomena of conspicuous consumption and waste is, at least in part, an expression of transcendence of finitude. One is no longer bound to the limits, the necessities of life. One may waste freely.

On the other hand, in a locative culture, money, or more properly exchange, serves to establish and reinforce a sense of place. Since the work of Marcel Mauss on *The Gift,* we have been accustomed to perceive the total symbolic universe implied in the structures of reciprocity that lie behind the gift and exchange process.[36] In its Melanesian form a complex notion of not transgressing bounds is involved. To cite a recent report:

> The ideal is equivalence, neither more nor less, neither "one-up" nor "one-down".... All transgressions in Tangu may be seen as attacks on equivalence.... The accepted, public device for finding and maintaining equivalence is the *br'ngun'guni* ... and a series of feasting exchanges.... In the best of all possible worlds, since all exchanges would be equivalent and true amity reign over all, there would no longer be any need to make exchanges.[37]

Exchange, the acquisition of foodstuffs or other wealth, is ultimately a means to the keeping of one's place. By way of an aside, we may note that it is in these very same Melanesian exchange cultures that the so-called "Cargo-

---

[36] M. Mauss, "Essai sur le don: Forme et raison de l'échange dans les sociétés archaïques," *L'Année Sociologique,* n.s., I (1925), 30-186; M. Mauss, *The Gift. Form and Functions of Exchange in Archaic Societies,* trans. by I. Cunnison (Glencoe: Free Press, 1954). Cf. C. Lévi-Strauss, *Les Structures élémentaires de la parenté* (2nd ed.; Paris-The Hague: Mouton, 1967), ch. 5.

[37] K. Burridge, *Mambu* (London: Methuen, 1960), pp. 82-85. Cf. the older classic accounts of B. Malinowski, *Argonauts of the Western Pacific* (London: Routledge, 1922), chs. 3, 6; R. Firth, *Primitive Economics of the New Zealand Maori* (New York: Dutton, 1929); Firth, *Primitive Polynesian Economy* (London: Routledge, 1939).

cults" flourish. Within these highly charged, intensively studied recent examples of the phenomena of social change, great emphasis has been placed on "Cargo" as symbolic of European technology, culture, colonial power, etc. The native discovers himself to be deprived in confrontation with the white man's material wealth and seeks to obtain these goods for himself. Insufficient attention has been paid in these accounts to "Cargo" as disruptive of equivalence and place, and the requirement of some system of exchange in order to rectify this situation. Indeed, in a recent essay K. Burridge has suggested that the conflict caused by the introduction of the open-money world view into a society that has a locative-exchange view is one of the four basic scenarios leading to the widespread phenomenon of contemporary millenarianism.[38]

*   *   *

In the conclusion to his well-known study, *Social and Economic History of the Roman Empire,* Professor Rostovtzeff passed under review the variety of theories that had been suggested to account for the decline of the Roman Empire. After settling on a psychological explanation, he concluded by observing that a change in a people's outlook on the world was one of the most potent factors in social, economic, and political change, and that further exploration of change in outlook was one of the most urgent tasks in the field of ancient history.[39] Several scholars have taken up Rostovtzeff's challenge, most notably M. P. Nilsson[40] and E. R. Dodds.[41] This paper is intended as a modest continuation of these studies.

The implication of these observations would be that

---

38 K. Burridge, *New Heaven, New Earth: A Study of Millenarian Activities* (Oxford: Blackwell, 1969), pp. 143-149.

39 M. Rostovtzeff, *Social and Economic History of the Roman Empire* (Oxford: Clarendon Press, 1926), p. 486.

40 M. P. Nilsson, "The New Conception of the Universe in Late Greek Paganism," *Eranos*, XLIV (1946), 20-27.

41 Cf. E. R. Dodds' brilliant Wiles Lectures, *Pagan and Christian in an Age of Anxiety* (Cambridge, U.K., Cambridge Univ. Press, 1965).

social change is preeminently symbol or symbolic change.
At the heart of the issue of change are the symbolic-social
questions: what is the place on which I stand? what are
my horizons? what are my limits? I have suggested that
there are two basic answers to these questions, that these
two provide the description of a social or individual center of value and meaning, and that from such a center all
other symbolizations derive their meaning. Thus when
one adopts one or the other of these two basic stances,
one adopts a whole symbolic universe that is, for the individual or culture, *the* Universe. To change stance is to
totally alter one's symbols and to inhabit a different
world. And finally, I have suggested that these two stances
ought not to be looked upon as stages in social (or individual) evolution or growth, with maturity or modernity
associated with the open or limitless. Rather I have insisted that these two stances are coeval possibilities. From
this perspective, place (whether in an open or closed
structure) ought not to be viewed as a static concept. It
is through an understanding and symbolization of place
that a society or individual creates itself. Without strain-
ing the point, this active sense is crystallized in the expression "to take place" as a synonym for "to happen,"
"to occur," "to be." It is by virtue of its view of its place
that a society or an individual (that history or biography
as the description of a society or individual) takes place.
The insight of the poet Mallarmé may be extended as
the exhaustive description of history or biography: "Nothing shall have taken place but place."[42]

It is this sense of happening, of things taking place,
that allows us to conjoin the notion of symbol and social
change or history. For both of these are characteristic
human activities. Both are forms of human creativity.
Both are means by which man expresses the truth of what
it is to be human (be it a limited or infinitely open
view), establishes and discovers his existence, invents

[42] Quoted in G. Poulet, *The Interior Distance* (Baltimore: Johns
Hopkins Press, 1959), p. 281.

and participates in human culture — "the creation by man of a world of meaning in the context of which human life can be significantly lived."[43] For with Cassirer we would hold:

> We cannot define man by any inherent principle which constitutes his metaphysical essence, nor can we define him by any inborn faculty or instinct which may be ascertained by empirical observation. Man's outstanding characteristic, his distinguishing mark, is not his metaphysical or physical nature, but his work. It is this work, it is the system of human activities, which defines and determines the circle of "humanity."[44]

From this point of view — and joining with those anthropologists and sociologists who have defined man as a symbol-producing animal and society or culture as a symbol-system — we may say, by way of tautology, that social change is symbol change. Furthermore, as has already been stressed, society or culture is preeminently the construction of significance and order through symbolic activity. Social change may then be specified as the discovery or creation of new modes of significance and order.

In the preceding remarks we have deliberately introduced an ambivalence. Man, we have said, "establishes and discovers"; "invents and participates in"; "discovers or creates" the world. This reflects our conviction that one of the consistent failures in discussions of symbol and history has been to reify and value one of these terms at the expense of the other. Most usually in Western discussions it has been the symbol that has been so valued. The symbol, while possessing no ontological status of its own, has quite consistently been held to be "transparent" to the realm of being, of ultimate value. The world, and hence history as the world-process, is deficient in reality

---

43 T. F. O'Dea, *The Sociology of Religion* (Englewood Cliffs, N.J.: Prentice-Hall, 1966), p. 5. I have omitted one word from Professor O'Dea's definition of culture.

44 E. Cassirer, *An Essay on Man* (New Haven: Yale Univ. Press, 1944), p. 68.

(profane) until status is conferred on it through the symbol.[45] More recently we have seen, in historicism, this locus of values reversed.

In the works of some contemporary social scientists, much has been accomplished to overcome these unfortunate bifurcations. Thus, scholars such as Peter Berger speak of three moments in the dialectic of society: externalization, which is the "outpouring of human being into the world"; objectification, the cultural processes by which the products of human externalization attain a "reality that confronts its original producers as a facticity external to and other than themselves"; and finally, internalization, "the reappropriation by men of this same reality."[46] This fruitful development out of the tradition of Marx and Durkheim provides a "double-objectivity" for the symbolic process that grows out of the activity of the process rather than some external locus. Man creates his place in the world as he creates his world; man discovers his place as he encounters the world in which he finds himself.[47] Social change, symbolic change of the sort we have been describing, occurs when there is disjunction, when there is no longer a "fit" within all the elements of this complex process.

Each society has moments of ritualized disjunction, moments of "descent into chaos," of ritual reversal, of liminality, of collective *anomie*. But these are part of a highly structured scenario in which these moments will be overcome through the creation of a new world, the raising of an individual to a new status, or the strength-

[45] See particularly the trenchant critique of H. Penner, "Bedeutung und Probleme der religiösen Symbolik bei Tillich und Eliade," *Antaios*, IX (1967), 127-143.

[46] P. L. Berger, *The Sacred Canopy: Elements of a Sociological Theory of Religion* (Garden City, N.Y.: Doubleday, 1969; reprint), p. 4.

[47] See C. Geertz, "Ethos, World-View and the Analysis of Sacred Symbols," *Antioch Review* (Winter, 1957-58), 421-437; Geertz, "Religion as a Cultural System," in *Anthropological Approaches to the Study of Religion*, ed. by M. Banton (London: Tavistock, 1966), pp. 1-46; and especially Berger, *The Sacred Canopy*, chs. 1-2, to which I am particularly indebted.

ening of community.[48] Change — in the strongest sense of the word, a society's conversion — is required when such moments meld into history: when the world is perceived to be chaotic, reversed, liminal, filled with *anomie*. Then man finds himself in a world that he does not recognize; and perhaps even more terrible, man finds himself to have a self he does not recognize. Then he will need to create a new world, to express his sense of a new place. For man "can adapt himself somehow to anything his imagination can cope with; but he cannot deal with Chaos. . . . Therefore our most important assets are always the symbols of our general *orientation* in nature, on the earth, in society and in what we are doing: the symbols of our *Weltanschauung* and *Lebenanschauung*."[49]

---

[48] See the important work in progress of V. Turner, in particular, "Betwixt and Between: The Liminal Period in *Rites of Passage*," in Turner, *The Forest of Symbols: Aspects of Ndembu Ritual* (Ithaca, N.Y.: Cornell Univ. Press, 1967), pp. 93-111.

[49] S. Langer, *Philosophy in a New Key* (4th ed.; Cambridge, U.S.A.: Harvard Univ. Press, 1960), p. 287.

6

The Role of Ritual in Personal Development

by

AIDAN KAVANAGH

The Nature of Ritual

MY TOPIC, WHICH IS THE ROLE RITUAL PLAYS IN THE PROCESS of personal development, is obviously a difficult one for many reasons. Until recently the consensus of the Western intellectual community was fairly solid in its assumption that ritual not only had little or nothing to do with the development of the individual human person, but that it was inimical to such development — a primitive retardation to intellectual growth in a modern world, a delusion of order in a relative universe, a too simple reading of

Aidan Kavanagh, O.S.B., is Director of the Graduate Program in Liturgical Studies and Director of Graduate Studies, Department of Theology, University of Notre Dame. He is the author of *The Concept of Eucharistic Memorial in the Canon Revisions of Thomas Cranmer, Archbishop of Canterbury 1553-1556* and has contributed several articles on liturgy to *Worship* magazine.

data presented by science. Ritual was thus regarded as activity suitable for those enterprises most peripheral to *real* human existence, enterprises such as the religious, the military, and, to some extent, the political in its purely ceremonial aspects. This view of ritual's role is typical of the rationalism abroad within the intellectual establishments of the Western world; although it seems to be in its death-throes today[1] it is still with us in our assumptions and in the programs of action and research stemming from those assumptions.

The fact is that while Western man's intellectual tool box contains many devices for describing something of the gods and beasts he detects within himself, that same tool box has been found singularly wanting in devices for coping with them. Allocation of massive sums of money has not bought off man's demons; proliferating governmental agencies have not brought them to heel. This is so, according to Daniel Moynihan, because the liberal establishment has failed to state adequately the questions facing men today. These questions, he maintains, are not those of poverty, or hunger, or population control, or war and peace, or race; the questions are those of human values — of morality and ethics, of behavior, in brief, according to norms that are not within man's power alone to construct. Moynihan does not hesitate to say that the questions are radically religious in nature, and that our failure to regard them as such is nothing other than a body blow to the culture itself, a blow from which the culture may not recover.

It seems especially obvious that the political, educational, and religious structures in our culture are at present under serious pressure. The reasons for this are not of the superficial sort that more money, more bureaus, or even more laws and order will solve. In our culture, authority is well on the way to being replaced by power; that is, the persuasiveness of values clearly seen and main-

---

1 As the result of a series of assaults one would have to read, for example, the McLuhan corpus even to begin to appreciate.

tained through social patterns is giving way to coercive force, which is never persuasive but is always so much more simple to administer. Confrontations of opposing forces (no matter which side may manage to prevail) are notoriously inept at making values convincing, in producing true commonweals. Force confrontations most often inhibit such accomplishments at best; at worst, they render the common good impossible of achievement. When this happens, values, and with them cultures, perish.

To discuss the role ritual plays in the process of personal development during times such as ours may appear to be the height of irrelevance. Yet I am confident it is of the very essence of our present situation for the following reasons. First, cultures as well as the social structures and patterns of behavior that make them up do not exist of themselves, nor do they come from nowhere. Cultures are value-complexes created by real people, in real historical circumstances, for real human purposes, and they emerge through patterns of human activity that are sustained by social structures created by those same people. Second, if a culture has any root in the real order, it is to be found in the patterns of repetitive behavior by which a group of people conceives of and enacts those values which enable the group to survive its own particular context of stresses and threats that would destroy it. A group's behavior patterns, and thus its culture, are in this sense always responsive to the particular existential milieux in which the group finds itself. By this I do not mean that a group's values, in themselves, are merely relative or eclectic: I mean that the values being conceived of and enacted by the group are always contemporary and in response to the immediate stresses and threats that bear upon the group at a given time. Thus the need within the group for structures whose prime responsibility it is constantly to review and to renew the meaning of the group's values in concrete reference to the ever changing context of stress the group finds itself presently confronting. This process of reviewing and renewing values for the sake of group survival here and now is what gives the group continuity and cohesiveness in space and time, in the real order, in history. The by-product of this process is a certain group distinctiveness of life-style that sets this group off from all other groups that are engaging in the same enterprise under different circumstances and with their own distinctive results.

*   *   *

This process of review and renewal of group values is what I understand tradition to be. As such, it is not static but an ongoing and thoroughly dynamic enterprise that never stops.[2]

The agent that discharges this premier responsibility within the social group is what I understand to be the group's authority structure. I would note that this structure is multiform in direct ratio to the social complexity of the group (which has nothing to do with its being "civilized" or "primitive") , and that, as it functions on levels most closely touching the central values of the group, it progressively assumes a more "sacral" character on the one hand, and divests itself of executive jurisdiction on the other.[3]

The functions of conceiving and enacting the values of the group *ad hoc* its particular stress-context are what I understand to be cult. The conceiving aspect I take to be myth, and the enactment aspect I take to be ritual. Both myth and ritual thus appear to me as strictly cor-

2 J. R. Geiselmann, *The Meaning of Tradition,* trans. by W. J. O'Hara (New York: Herder and Herder, 1966).

3 See Ruth Benedict's account of this among the Zuni Indians, in *Patterns of Culture* (2nd ed.; Boston: Houghton-Mifflin, 1959), pp. 99-100. The same phenomenon may be detected in the American constitutional separation of the Supreme Court from the other branches of government. In this perspective, the canonical centralization of all authoritative aspects in the sacral person of the Roman Catholic Pope, who is also defined as possessing all executive power in the Church by divine right (Canons 218-219, 1431, 1518, etc.), is anthropologically extraordinary.

relative and inseparable functions: their reciprocal union is what I mean by cult. The outcome of cult, so understood, is what I understand as culture — what Margaret Mead has called ". . . the systematic body of learned behavior which is transmitted from parents to children,"[4] or what I would prefer to call the continuous and cohesive life-style by which a particular group conceives of and enacts what its values mean, thus to survive intact the stresses and threats of existence in the real order of space and time.

In brief outline, this is my position on the interlocking roles played by tradition, authority, and cult in society. Although these realities suffer currently from a bad press, no society of men can exist long without them. It may indeed be that the terms are much responsible for the negative popular reaction to the realities they stand for; for myself, I find much evidence that these central social realities are being rediscovered (howsoever painfully) in new categories by the leading edge of our society as represented in the several arts, in politics, in educational reform, and in religious sentiment welling up from below in many of our churches. Marshall McLuhan, the high priest of much of the present *avant-garde,* has noted repeatedly in his works the integratory impact of electronic media on modern living: that living "mythically" (i.e., within values rather than in a detached or "uncommitted" way in regard to those values) is rapidly becoming the life-style of youth, and constitutes the chasm separating it from older generations given more to rational discourse about reality than to enacting reality by engaging in it. Youth's alternative I regard as far and away the more human of the two and, for this reason, I am confident that it will prevail, that it has already in fact begun to do so, not only among youth but the population generally.

In support of this, and with due reserve regarding the

---

4 Benedict, *Patterns,* p. vii.

infallibility of opinion polls, Louis Harris remarked on the findings that resulted from a survey of public opinion on morality in the United States: "The results strongly suggest that the central theme of the young in protest against hypocrisy and double standards has more going for it in terms of potential public support than might have previously been imagined."[5] This shift in attitude appeared, perhaps significantly, in responses to questions that were not couched in terms of conventional moral ideology, but rather in responses to questions that posed personal situations in which respondents had to pass comparative judgment on various types of miscreants. Most notable were responses to personal moral situations in which matters of sex and property were concerned. For example, a politician who takes bribes was judged worse than an adulterer by 54 percent to 32 percent; a policeman who takes money from the prostitute was judged worse than the prostitute by 81 percent to 8 percent; a prosecutor who railroads an innocent man was judged worse than an armed robber by 78 percent to 10 percent; and a doctor who refuses a house call to someone seriously ill was judged worse than a homosexual by 71 percent to 18 percent.[6] That the matter of abortion should be solely between the prospective parents and their doctor rather than a matter of law was the judgment of 64 percent, and 60 percent of Roman Catholics thought so too.[7]

Without advocating adultery, prostitution, robbery, homosexuality, or abortion, one may detect in these responses a definite departure from conventional moral ideology learned by rote. One may also note something of an approach once again to a basic human equilibrium of moral judgment at least reminiscent of the best moral continua found in the Judaeo-Christian tradition, viz., the position of Jesus regarding the woman taken in adultery. My point, however, is that this apparent ap-

5 *Time,* June 6, 1969, p. 26.
6 *Ibid.*
7 *Ibid.,* p. 27.

proach seems to be different than it would have been a generation or two ago. The approach is, moreover, the result of a certain increased involvement in values as opposed to detached and uninvolved observation about them. Perhaps McLuhan is right in his insistence on the involvement-effect that the electronic media of instantaneous communications have had in this. He would surely be the first to admit that much more than the media is involved — and some of that "much more" is the burden of my topic.

For I must insist that tradition is the process by which values are communicated in human society; that authority is a central agent of that communication process; and that myth and ritual, the components of cult, are the enactments by which that communication of values takes place on the deepest and most critical level for the future survival of society itself. I must further insist that all of these — the process of tradition, the agency of authority, and the enactments of cult — are enterprises carried on by persons. They are not "things" that happen of themselves. Nor is the society in which these realities are found a "thing" unto itself. Every human society is a group of persons, a group of persons banded together, as Peter Berger notes, in the face of death in order to survive[8] — to have life in an abundance that constitutes the antithesis to death, both social and individual. Survival as used here is, therefore, a richly ambiguous and analogical concept that embraces everything within the ambit of human experience exclusive of chaos, death, and nonsurvival.

In this view, for man to survive and live is for him to socialize — advocates of the misanthropic fable of the noble savage to the contrary notwithstanding. For man to socialize is for him not only to engage others like himself but to involve himself with them as well. And for man to involve himself with others means that individuals must be brought to a point of development within their

---

8 See *A Rumor of Angels* (Garden City: Doubleday, 1970), pp. 1-27.

particular group through a process of psycho-social integration into the group — a point of development that makes adequate intragroup relationships not only possible but inevitable. The point of development I am talking about is, in nontechnical terms, that of true individual maturity. Such maturity is the goal of social patterns that form the individual from the cradle to adulthood through adolescence. It is this period of adolescence in which, for the most part, psycho-social integration takes place in the individual, if it takes place at all, and in taking place contributes to the individual the necessary senses of belonging, of support, and of identity without which mature individuation would be impossible of achievement.

It does indeed seem to me that the nature not only of human but of all primate maturity is social. Such maturity consists largely in the learned ability on the part of the individual to balance off the need for releasing aggression with the equally strong need for group support. Much has been written about this matter, but it seems clear that aggression is as necessary for the attainment of the individual's requisite autonomy within the group as group support is necessary for the maintenance of that same degree of individuation on the part of its members. Put more simply, an unindividuated group of human individuals is not a society, and even less is it a community: it is a mob at best or an Orwellian nightmare at worst. Totalitarianism is its political form, force its method, fear its motivation, the demagogue its prophet, and the tyrant its master.

I have said that maturity is social, and that it is acquired only throughout a long and complex process of psycho-social integration of the individual into the group. The learning process is itself thus social: it occurs on a variety of levels, many of which overlap and may be simultaneously engaged in. The learning process is as wide and continuous as is the individual's own awareness; its formal aspect (i.e., classroom learning) is only a minuscule tip of the iceberg. Yet the learning for all that is not unstructured. Taking place throughout what I have called a long and complex process of psycho-social integration, the learning follows patterns that normally correspond to stages of the individual's own psycho-physical growth from preverbal infancy at least through adolescence. These patterns are the material out of which the humanization of the individual arises. The psycho-social integratory process is the structure that gives form to the pattern-sequence: the integratory process is, moreover, the structure that enables those incommunicable subjective reactions of the maturing individual to the patterns he encounters and appropriates to become "shareable" by others of the same group — in such events as public enactment of the group's own self-awareness (i.e., in worship, political ritual, dramatic forms, judicial procedures, educational programs, etc.) .

What I mean by pattern in this context is nothing other than repetitive human activities that reduce the raw and seemingly random stuff of experience to manageable proportions on both the individual and public social levels. This reduction is not a flight from reality; even less does it have to be by definition a falsification of the real. Nor is it, I think (along with Lévi-Strauss) , an overt if initial attempt to get at the "truth" of things in a rationally discursive manner. The patterns I speak of exist in order to deal with reality, as it is encountered, by establishing not the "truth" of things but rather the coherence of human response to the real. The questions such patterns deal with are thus not those refined by the several rational disciplines: the questions are predisciplinary ones of value-relevance to the individual and of survival for him and his group. Man asks: "What must I do to live?" and then: "What must I be in order so to act?" Coherent criteria for self- and group-identification are at issue for man perennially. Answers that are found to work empirically are the compelling ones at this stage, answers that aid man to survive or, perhaps more modestly, to hold death and dissolution at least temporarily at bay. The patterns are such answers in that they (1) enable more effective communications to take place in the group, (2) reduce intragroup damage (e.g., by channeling normal release of aggression by individuals, and by containing or repressing extraordinary aggression-release that could well split the group asunder and impede its response to the stresses pressing upon it), and (3) foster the bonds that hold the group together.

The foregoing I regard as a behavioral description, if not exactly a definition, of ritual. And I regard liturgy as one sort of ritual among many.

The Role of Ritual in Personal Development

The role such patterns of repetitive ritual behavior play in the development of the human person may be seen in the dynamic process of that development itself. Such an investigation has only recently been begun by such authors as Erik Erikson, Erving Goffman,[9] and others who are bringing the disciplines of psychology and social anthropology into new syntheses centered on man as he is found to be — without the sort of *a priori* bias that so frequently in the past marred or distorted research in these disciplines. Leaving aside, for example, the absorption of clinical psychology with the pathological as the point of research departure, Erikson has recently advanced a magistral theory of the interplay between ritual and the development of the human personality. "Ritualization in man," he says, "seems to be grounded in the pre-verbal experience of infants while reaching its full elaboration in grand public ceremonies."[10] This process, which ". . . must consist of an agreed-upon interplay between two persons who repeat it at meaningful intervals

---

[9] Erving Goffman, *Interaction Ritual: Essays on Face-to-Face Behavior* (Garden City: Doubleday, 1967).

[10] Eric H. Erikson, "Ontogeny of Ritualization in Man," *Philosophical Transactions of the Royal Society of London,* Series B, No. 772, Vol. CCLI (1966), pp. 337-350.

and in recurring contexts,"[11] which is dim in contour and ambivalent in its consequences, may nonetheless aid in correlating seemingly distant phenomena such as human infancy and man's formal, social institutions (religious, judicial, dramatic, political, artistic, etc.).[12]

Beginning with infancy, Erikson contends, the first pattern (and through it simultaneously the first interpersonal involvement available to man) is the pattern-complex of mutual recognition rituals with the mother or mother surrogate. The patterns by which mother and infant initiate mutual communication are composed of recognition symbols and sense stimuli — the smile, the touch, the embrace; the effects such patterns produce in each actor, while by no means being completely the same in both mother and infant, have about the same quality. Through such patterns their individual separateness is transcended (female becomes "mother," and foetus becomes child), and yet their own individual distinctiveness is confirmed.[13] Here is afforded that wholly necessary first sensation of secure identification the infant needs in becoming not just an increasingly complex organism but a social being as well. The element most distinctive to the ritual patterns appropriate to this stage of the infant's development Erikson does not hesitate to refer to as "numinous." This I take to be the irremovable natural foundation of that sense of the sacred or the holy which overtly religious people seem to feel is their own. This ritual element, and the consequent sense it evokes in the human person already on the preverbal level, precedes formal religious training and arises out of the first involvement the infant has with another person.[14]

As the infant grows into early childhood, the ritual

---

11 *Ibid.*
12 *Ibid.*
13 *Ibid.*, p. 339.
14 The implications of this for education, and especially religious education, seem to me absolutely immense.

patterns of mutual recognition begin to modulate, especially with the onset of initial locomotive and speech abilities. These abilities necessitate further specification of recognition patterns in response to the child's need for identity here, e.g., in the living room or out of doors: is it acceptable, he says, that I am here doing this? There are, he finds, limits to his activity that he can only learn by rote — where not to be, what to say or what not to say, etc. In all this the patterns become discriminatory: the child learns to differentiate acceptable from unacceptable, i.e., the "good" from the "bad," in behavioral rather than ethical or moral terms. The limits are sanctioned from outside the child himself through positive approval or negative disapproval of the numinously endowed mother figure. Erikson terms the element distinctive of this stage of ritual specification "judicial," i.e., the child begins to judge, discriminate, differentiate vicariously through the ritual leadership of one in whom his confidence reposes and on whom his sense of secure self-identity depends. In short, here one may detect the specific source of morality at a pre-ethical stage of evolution in the emerging human person.

Ritual patterns of mutual recognition and of discrimination, then, appear both to evoke and to reinforce the "mother experience" of the child. All subsequent personality development in the child depends upon the adequacy with which this primordial experience is had. Without this first bipartite pattern-engagement, it has been found to be statistically demonstrable that the child's ability to appropriate observed acceptable behavior through play-activities,[15] and the child's ability to confront the new complexities of peer-group experience in school and in other group activities can be inhibited, if not maimed, beyond repair. Current programs of pre-school stimulative and sensitivity training, such as those

---

15 Erikson, p. 340.   Erikson notes that it is this stage in which the child begins to familiarize himself with his own particular social group in the most concrete manner.

undertaken in Head Start for children without adequate mother-experience background, are in response to this need. Without remedial stimulation such children are found to be literally unable to play, and often they engage in traumatic withdrawal antipatterns or antirituals such as crying, thumbsucking, body rocking, or even catatonia when faced with a peer-group they do not yet have sufficient security or self-assurance to face. Thus the integratory phases of their experience from play age through adolescence can be at best only partly successful: social alienation, ostracism, fear, and isolation result in the individual, and when this occurs on a large scale due to family breakdowns, a part of the social tissue goes dead. More specifically in the ritual area, the patterns of play rituals or of dramatic elaboration, together with the formal performance patterns learned during peer-group school age are missed, or engaged in partially, or are deformed; with this, Erikson observes, the ritual elements of the dramatic and the formal are reduced or disappear altogether. What has in fact taken place when this happens is that the child never adequately severs his psychic bonds with the numinously secure and autoesthetic mother-experience stage of his development, or the psychic bonds get severed in such a way that the attainment of independence from the mother security-figure results not in other figures involving the child "beyond mother security," but in little or no further involvement of the child at all. He is left merely with a most negative and traumatic sense of alienation.

Three things should, I think, be noted of the patterns Erikson describes. First, the patterns of infancy and early childhood simplify and elicit one's own sense of security and, consequently, identity. Second, the patterns of play age and school age begin to wean the child from the mother-experience of infancy and early childhood at the same time that they begin to integrate him into peer-group experience — an experience continuum in which the child's personality is no longer being confirmed in

its security, but tried, stretched, and pressured into allo-
esthetic rather than autoesthetic modes of behavior. The
transition from the mother-experience patterns to the
peer-experience patterns is crucial for maturity as I have
already described it, for in this transition the child learns,
at base, how to discharge aggression (autoesthetic) while
maintaining that group support which takes over the
mother-role in providing the child the security of self-
identification. Third, each of the stages in the evolution
of the ritual patterns requires that the pattern preceding
be recapitulated in the pattern succeeding. Thus also
the ritual elements will be found to follow in order (an
order based on normal personality development) — the
judicial on the numinous, the dramatic on the judicial,
the formal on the dramatic, etc. This sequence of ritual
patterns, and of the distinctive ritual elements to which
each gives rise, can be violated at the risk of aborting not
only the ritual sequence but also the cohesive evolution
of the individual personality to which each ritual pattern
and element corresponds. When the whole sequence
breaks down in the individual members of a group, the
group itself is already well into social dissolution.

Why is this so? Because, I think, the patterns of ritual
repetitive behavior correspond to and, therefore, may be
said to carry, the inchoate and largely incommunicable
human experience of reality — for the most part in a non-
verbal and always in a parabolic and nondiscursive manner. The whole purpose, as I see it, of assembly, of
coming together for public ritual engagements, religious
or not, is so that individuals may communicate those
experiences that are most incommunicable, publicly, in
standard symbolic patterns agreed on by the group so
that those experiences can be entered into, "put on,"
affirmed, and appropriated by the group as a whole. Such
standard symbolic patterns are richly ambiguous, but
they are also invariably and rigorously judgmental. The
point at which the group does, in fact, enter into, finally
affirm without reservation, and wholly appropriate the

incommunicable life-experiences of its members is that at which judgment falls away in the face of solid affirmation and conviction. It is at this point alone, I submit, that celebration becomes possible if we understand celebration as the single ritual enterprise that is subordinated to no further or subsequent ritual pattern. Erikson associates this ultimate ritual pattern with incipient adulthood — adolescence. Here it is, he maintains, that everything comes into focus for the first time and is able to be maintained in a stable manner in the individual: the processes of self-definition and identification, of a theoretic and ideological grasp of the formal rules of acceptable social behavior, of a solid conviction in the basic dependabilities contained in and transmitted by the behavior patterns specific to the individual and his group, and of an initially adequate ability to handle aggressive conflict and anxiety. It is usually only at this point, he notes, that social groups have appeared willing to give the social sanction of "majority" to such individuals. For what has occurred is, in ritual terms, the attainment by such individuals of the ability to be, themselves, "ritualizers" in their own right on the adult level. A dominant function of ritual in the life of an adult, Erikson thinks, is that parents are the earliest ritualizers in their children's lives; at the same time, ". . . they are participants of the instituted rituals in which the ritualizations of their own childhoods find an echo and a reaffirmation. . . ."[16] The prime contribution of adult ritual to the whole evolutionary thrust is that adult ritual "reaffirms the sanction needed by adults to be convincing ritualizers. . . ."[17] The mature needs of an adult include that need to be periodically reinforced in his or her role of ritualizer — i.e., to become a "numinous model in his children's minds" — and to act as judge and transmitter of continuity on every level to those coming into the group from infancy on.

16 *Ibid.,* p. 347.
17 *Ibid.*

In all this perhaps something of the meaning of values and their dissemination in society may be grasped. The product of this is really a most simple and knowable one, for all the apparent complexity of the processes I have only sketched. It is a human being who is limpid, kind, and filled with candor, because he has lived not just his own brief life but that enormous span of years and experience embraced by his culture: a life ". . . so old, so well-established, so integral and coherent as to give a human being the unself-consciousness, the authority, the completeness of a wild animal, a great strange creature who looks straight at you out of his eternal present."[18]

18 Ursula K. Leguin, *The Left Hand of Darkness* (New York: Ace Books, 1969), pp. 71-72.

7

Ritual as Communication

by

EDWARD FISCHER

ALL RITUAL IS COMMUNICATION. AS COMMUNICATION, RITUAL
speaks to our minds, and spirits, and intuitions by means
of words, sights, sounds, and smells. The Gothic cathedral
says one thing about God and the store-front church another. Incense and flowers speak with their fragrance.
The rose window influences the emotions in the way it
stains the light; the organ or the guitar, in the way each
fills the air with its peculiar vibrations. Any of these can
tell of grandeur or simplicity, of joy or sorrow.

Ritual was not always perceived as communication. It
was not always viewed as a living, shifting, changing form

Edward Fischer is Professor of Communication Arts at the University
of Notre Dame. He has authored two books, *The Screen Arts* and
Film as Insight. This paper, given at the conference on Roots of
Ritual, has appeared in *Worship*, Vol. 45 (1971), pp. 73-91.

of expression that varied from place to place and from time to time. Ritual was, in the past, viewed as a fixed matrix into which generations were poured.

Because of this, an unrealistic approach to ritual developed, and attempts were made to keep it alive through repetition rather than through changing, creative effort. Since ritual was, in the past, not allowed to unfold through the easy stages of evolution, it now finds itself in the throes of revolution.

To overturn traditional ritual overnight is admittedly dangerous. Too many familiar landmarks are too quickly lost from sight, which causes a loss of orientation and results in confusion. Trying to communicate with someone who lacks orientation is like trying to speak to him in a language he does not understand.

Edith Wharton once spoke of Catholic ritual as giving "a sublime frame" to the three great events of human life — birth, marriage, and death.[1] Rather than attempting to renovate the "sublime frame," ancient ritual should, perhaps, be retained, at least for the sublime occasions: weddings, funerals, baptisms, Easter, Christmas, etc. (Perhaps Mass should be offered only on such sublime occasions because any form of communication that becomes routine is apt to become perfunctory.)

Renovating ancient ritual is like renovating ancient churches: no matter how well it is done, it is always a renovation and is not truly creative. What Thomas Merton said about church architecture might well be said about church ritual:

> The perfection of twelfth-century Cistercian architecture is not to be explained by saying that the Cistercians were looking for a new technique at all. They built good churches because they were looking for God. And they were looking for God in a way that was pure and integral enough to make everything they did and everything they touched give glory to God.

---

[1] Bernard Berenson, *Sunset and Twilight* (New York: Harcourt, Brace and World, 1963), p. 533.

We cannot reproduce what they did because we approach the problem in a way that makes it impossible for us to find a solution. We ask ourselves a question that they never considered. How will we build a beautiful monastery according to the style of some past age and according to the rules of a dead tradition? Thus we make the problem not only infinitely complicated but we make it, in fact, unsolvable. Because a dead style is dead. And the reason why it is dead is that the motives and the circumstances that once gave it life have ceased to exist. They have given place to a situation that demands another style. If we were intent upon loving God rather than upon getting a Gothic church out of a small budget we would soon put up something that would give glory to God and would be very simple and would also be in the tradition of our fathers. That is why the best-looking buildings around Gethsemani are the barns. Nobody stopped to plan a Gothic barn, and so they turned out all right. If they had built the gatehouse on the same principles as the hog house it would have been beautiful. Actually it is hideous.

However, the twelfth-century Cistercians took good care to be architects. Saint Bernard sent Achard of Clairvaux out to study the village churches of Burgundy and see how they were built. And it is true that there was a clean kind of mysticism in the air of the age that made everything beautiful. One of the big problems for an architect in our time is that for a hundred and fifty years men have been building churches as if a church could not belong to our time. A church has to look as if it were left over from some other age. I think that such an assumption is based on an implicit confession of atheism — as if God did not belong to all ages and as if religion were really only a pleasant, necessary social formality, preserved from past times in order to give our society an air of respectability.[2]

Copycat architecture and copycat ritual are both uninspired and uninspiring. There is, however, one great advantage in having a ritual that is set and enduring: it

---

[2] Thomas Merton, *The Sign of Jonas* (New York: Harcourt, Brace, 1953), p. 86.

provides some insurance againt the vulgarians and the faddists. There is a difference between change and faddism: change is natural evolution, but faddism is artificial. Faddism lacks taste, judgment, and sensitivity, and seeks change for the sake of change.

If the vulgarians seize ritual, as they have seized much of life, they will, with their whims and fancies, hurry man along the path of becoming more and more a socialized insect. We already have in popularized religious thought a tendency to see theology as the handmaid of the social sciences. The social scientist-theologian has popularized a lingo that is eroding our language. It is so bad that it has become a grim joke among those who have some feeling for words. A parody on such prose appeared in a newspaper published at a Catholic women's college:

> A community, characterized by Christian love, presents a unique opportunity for growth and development. Challenging the whole person, total involvement demands a recognition of the common humanity shared by others. Initial commitment leads to in-depth dialogue, and the ensuing interpersonal relationships will lead to many a meaningful experience.
>
> The privilege of preparing one's role in society, the extension of community, demands responsibility on the part of the individual. Superficiality and mediocrity must be replaced with significant and relevant ideals.
>
> Outmoded structures must be replaced by creative attempts to reach the desired goal of total personalism. The conscience of mankind must react positively to this search for identity and encourage the process of becoming, lest man's true self be lost in meaningless tradition or existential apathy.[3]

This is only a parody, but even so it is an argument for an unchanging ritual. It is far better, I feel, to keep an outmoded ritual that has dignity and nobility than to create new forms in the spirit of that prose style.

Whether we renovate old forms of ritual or create new

---

3 *Seton Journal* (Mount St. Joseph, Ohio), October 3, 1968; Vol. 46, No. 2, p. 2.

ones, we must remember that communication is effective only if it fits its times. Communication is blurred when one attempts to use forms that are no longer fitting. To try to formulate a ritual meaningful to all people at all times in all places is a form of pride that anyone interested in communication cannot afford.

The ritual of princely pomp, which Miss Wharton referred to as a "sublime frame," lost its effectiveness in civil life; it passed with the passing of the aristocracies. Princely pomp was never as effective in the United States as it was in Europe, and yet it did speak to Americans in those years when Independence Day celebrations, the circus parades, and the secret rites of fraternal orders played an important role in American culture.

Yet even princely ritual need not be dead if the setting is right. The most impressive ritual I have known is held in Westminster Abbey. In 1973 the Abbey is still a reverential place even though a couple of million tourists pass through it each year. Religious services are held several times daily, and strict vergers make sure that all is calm during that time. As a leaflet explains, "The Abbey was built above all that God might be worshiped in the beauty of holiness and in the holiness of beauty."

I attended several services. On two Sundays I sat in the choir stalls for matins. The first line of the opening hymn was, "Lord of beauty, thine the splendour." It was so appropriate sung in a spot saturated with prayer for nine hundred years. To sit there surrounded by music and stone that declare the dignity of man, that proclaim his possibilities, is something that moves powerfully on the soul. It makes one proud to be a human being.

Yet that service, so impressive in Westminster Abbey, would be out of place transplanted to a new suburban church. It would be just as out of place as a guitar Mass in Westminster Abbey.

That ritual fit the time and the place is necessary for good communication and there may also be a moral dimension involved. Is it not a breach of personality for a man to take part in a rite for which he has no feeling? To force a man into a ritual is a form of cruelty. Physical or moral, such force treats man as less than man. If there is one thing that should be done with an open heart and embraced with both arms, it is the way in which one communicates his reverence for his God.

Required attendance at ritual presents a problem in communication. Among professional communicators, for example, a theater manager might be pleased to have a law of required attendance because that would be profitable, but the artists — the writers and performers — would feel uneasy in the presence of a captive audience, present in body but not in spirit.

We need to accept numerous ways of praising God and of being aware of his presence in the world. If we try to make one ritual for everyone from eight to eighty, learned and unlearned, civilized and semi-barbaric, we are out of touch with reality. For this crime we must always pay the price, which at times is high.

In liturgy, as in all forms of communication, there is no substitute for knowing the audience, which is as varied as the bands of coloration in a political spectrum. This varied audience is found in religion, art, education, etc. In music, for example, the preferences range from Lawrence Welk's champagne melodies to the Rolling Stones' acid rock. In poetry, from Edgar Guest to the things read in coffeehouses. In motion pictures, from Disney to underground films. Newspapers, books, and magazines also reflect this wide range of preferences.

To try to reconcile all of these groups into worshiping God in the same way is frustrating and impossible. It is easier to get a middle-of-the-road Catholic and a middle-of-the-road Jew to sit down and reason together than to reconcile either of them to the extremes of the right or left within his own religion. When free to move in a free society people tend to band together by spiritual coloration more than by religion, education, or neighborhood; but these latter do have a bearing on spiritual coloration. Birds of a feather *do* flock together.

If a priest is going to hold a Mass that might be called "Pizza and Beer/Jesus Is Here," he ought not urge everybody to come. If he intends to stand on his head at the canon just to show he is ecumenically in touch with yoga, he should be sure of his audience before he tries it. And if he is starting a litany to St. Jude the Patron of Lost Causes, he had better be sure of his audience before he makes an announcement in the bulletin, or else he might be left holding one more lost cause.

To require a person to attend a certain church because he lives at a certain address is a failure to see ritual as communication. No one buys a certain book, or reads a certain magazine, or watches a certain television program because he lives on a certain piece of property. In all forms of commercial communication men seek the things that touch them at their level of development. In religious matters a man might find his needs better filled in a church three parishes away, and yet he is expected to attend a certain church because he lives in a certain area.

The commercial communicator would feel frustrated if he were forced to make his appeal along parish lines; his aims are cultural levels. The commercial communicator knows, because dollars and cents have taught him so, that some people prefer an intellectual approach to things, others an emotional approach, and a blessed few prefer some balance.

Some of the processions in Spain, with their hooded, white-robed participants and their grotesque statues, would make American Catholics cringe. That is because the ritual reflects a cultural difference just as bullfighting and baseball reflect such differences. To expect every country to take to its heart the same ritual is as unreal as to expect every country to adopt the same national sport.

Anyone involved with ritual must face up to diverse

personalities and to diverse cultures. For example, what about the person who prefers a ritual of silence, a tradition among Quakers? And what about people who have no feeling for ritual? Processions and communal singing make them uneasy. A walk in a woods might bring them more of a religious experience, make them more aware of God's presence in the world, than a service enlivened by candles and incense. What attitude should the Church take toward these people who prefer a God-made cathedral to one made by man?

Every man needs celebration. It is usually assumed that celebration must be evident to the eye and to the ear because most people feel the need to give praise in public.

What about those who are at their best giving praise in private? Some people are able to celebrate life by moving slowly through it. If one has such inner resources, must he be made to feel guilty in the presence of those who celebrate with more outward vigor?

*   *   *

Man has a need to be creative. He needs to try to imitate God the creator. The creative side of liturgy can help people fulfill this need. What about the artist whose destiny it is to create? He may not find the need for the group creativity that is called ritual.

Artists may fall away more often because of religious rites than because of dogma. This could be true even though an artist must have an intensity of religious feeling; it is something he must have to fulfill his destiny. He may have religious feeling without much devotional feeling. Liturgy requires devotional feeling.

An artist must have such reverence for life that he cannot clutter it up with inadequacies. That is a religious attitude. Anyone whose work is of such quality that it lifts life is praising the Creator of life, even if he is unwilling to admit that such a Creator exists. If art is really communication at its best, then an artist is a man of charity, for he brings light into the world.

Celebration is an artist's destiny. It is the destiny even of those artists who do not realize that they are celebrating the Great Script that God has written. Their works reveal the many facets of man and add up to the feeling that life is Great Theatre.

When an artist lifts a man's head, by lifting his heart and spirit, he makes the theologian's way easier. When the theologian gives a man a desire to know more about God he hands the artist a ready audience. The artist and the theologian are allied even if they do not see it that way.

Through the ritual of his preference each person gives himself away, because communication is always self-revealing. For example, the less sophisticated the person in the ways of communication, the more secure he feels in repeating the same rite over and over in exactly the same way. The repetitious rite at its best lifts the heart and settles dreads; at its worst it is an aberration. The sophisticated person is interested in releasing his emotions in more subtle ways, and so he turns to the arts. Sophisticated ritual at its best is man at his best, and at its worst it is man revealing his affectations.

If ritual is communication, the development of new ritual is a task for the artist, for communication is a form of art. To develop a ritual that is genuine for a certain time and place requires all of the talents of great artists. Ritual and art are related because, whether one wants to communicate with God or with man, he works from the same basis of psychology — the self communicating with the other.

The Church has used great artists for its ritualistic settings: they built the cathedrals, they added paintings to the walls, and they composed the music, and in so doing contributed glorious chapters to the history of the Church and to the history of art. The great artists were not, however, invited to lend their talents to the heart of ritual: their talents were not tapped in the composition of the prayer texts and the accompanying ceremonial. Not only has the Church suffered the loss in this regard. Art too, says Ingmar Bergman, the Swedish film-maker, lost its creative urge when separated from worship.

Each individual creates an environment around himself. That environment is the real reflection of his inner life. We create what we are. A polluted society cannot help but create a polluted environment. Kenneth Clark, the art historian, said: "If I had to say which was telling the truth about society, a speech by a minister of housing or the actual buildings put up in his time, I should believe the buildings."

The man who leads or directs ritual must be something of an artist. He needs the ability of vibrating his feelings into others — call it charisma, call it empathy. How much of this is a gift, as the Greeks thought, and how much can be developed, no one knows. Certainly, some of the ability to communicate can be acquired. In the past it had been assumed that any ordained minister possessed by virtue of ordination alone enough charisma to make ritual come alive. Today, we are beginning to realize that every minister is not a master in the art of communication, and that, perhaps, some should lead ritual and some should not. The best conceived ritual, like the best conceived play, suffers through poor performance.

There is, however, a danger of getting "showmen" as directors of ritual. Quintilian said something worth remembering: "I hold that no one can be a true orator unless he is also a good man."[4] Goodness is, admittedly, a factor in the leader's effectiveness, but goodness alone will not bring it off. A certain degree of artistic talent is also required.

The talent for creating new ritual and directing it will not be found in abundance because artists are not found in abundance. For a practical reason, therefore, if not for a charitable one, women might well be welcomed to create and direct ritual. In all other forms of communication

---

[4] Frederick Mayer, *The Great Teachers* (New York: Citadel Press, 1967), pp. 101-102.

talented women make their contributions. Communication is an art, and art knows of no sexual monopolies.

Then there is the problem that people will use ritual as therapy. Certainly the creating of something can do good things for the psyche. Maybe this is one legitimate use for ritual; certainly it is a human use. But what about those who do not want to be a part of other people's group therapy? How many hours of their lives should they be willing to dedicate to that? It is a delicate question involving charity.

There is always the danger of liturgy for its own sake instead of for God's sake. There is a fine line between worship and idolatry. Ritual for its own sake is vanity. Ritual for the sake of the participants reflects a thoughtfulness, a concern for others, and it is charity. For the sake of God, it is love. It is easy to perform ritual for its own sake. It is more difficult to perform it for the sake of the participants. To perform it for the sake of God takes the greatness of a saint.

The Church might issue decrees on communication, but they will be just so many words on paper until more attention is paid to the technique of communication. Communication is not the same as imparting information. Dictionaries, encyclopedias, and textbooks inform, but they do not communicate. Communication is one human spirit reaching out and touching another. Communication does not consist in glittering generalities and high-flown abstractions. One who practices communication at the highest level, the artist, reaches out to touch the spirit through the hard, definite matter of the here and now. As soon as he tries to act as though he exists only from the eyebrows up he fails to communicate and merely passes on information. The same is true in matters of ritual. Techniques are just as important in ritual as they are in all other forms of communication, and they must be acquired and learned.

Seminaries are giving more attention to the arts than they did in the past. If they are serious about the arts,

however, they will accord the arts as important a status
in the curriculum as they accord philosophy and theology. An occasional "art film" followed by a discussion
can be good and valuable, but this is often a case of the
blind leading the blind. Provision of facilities in which
students can exercise their artistic talents also accomplishes
little. Many of those who take advantage of such facilities
are more energetic than discerning, and those who need
it most are not interested.

As long as the arts are considered on the same level
as sports — as recreation — they will remain fun-and-games
stuff, and not an important and serious part of education.
As long as the arts are relegated to a second-class citizen-
ship, we must continue to pay the price for such discrimination. The price is inept communication, and such
ineptness can be found in many areas of ecclesiastics,
from architecture to homily.

Some priests, weak in the skills of communicating, will
find it much easier to cling to the safe ecclesiastical terminology learned in the seminary. Such terminology, however, means little in the real world today.

Other priests, feeling that they are not communicating
with their parishioners, might attempt to "go modern."
Chances are that they will become addicted to gimmicks,
vulgarizing whatever they touch, because they have not
learned the techniques of using modern idioms. Discern-
ment needs to be developed over a long period of time.
There is no such thing as "instant taste."

Such an attempt to "go modern" (the real danger of
"Modernism") results in the degradation of words, one
of the communicator's tools. Dag Hammarskjöld wrote in
Markings:

> Respect for the word — to employ it with scrupulous
> care and an incorruptible heartfelt love of truth — is
> essential if there is to be any growth in our society and
> in the human race.
>
> To misuse the word is to show contempt for man. It
> undermines the bridges and poisons the wells. It causes

man to regress down the long path of his evolution.[5]

Thomas Merton also seemed aware of the morality of the corruption of words. It might be called the immorality of something badly done.

> Dylan Thomas's integrity as a poet makes me very ashamed of the verse I have been writing. We who say we love God: why are we not as anxious to be perfect in our art as we pretend we want to be in our service to God? If we do not try to be perfect in what we write perhaps it is because we are not writing for God after all. In any case it is depressing that those who serve God and love Him sometimes write so badly, when those who do not believe in Him take pains to write so well. I am not talking about grammar and syntax, but about having something to say and saying it in sentences that are not half dead. Saint Paul and Saint Ignatius Martyr did not bother about grammar but they certainly knew how to write.
>
> Imperfection is the penalty of rushing into print. And people who rush into print too often do so not because they really have anything to say, but because they think it is important for something by them to be in print. The fact that your subject may be very important in itself does not necessarily mean that what *you* have written about it is important. A bad book about the love of God remains a bad book, even though it is about the love of God. There are many who think that because they have written about God, they have written good books. Then men pick up these books and say: if the ones who say they believe in God cannot find anything better than this to say about it, their religion cannot be worth much.[6]

It seems to be a trait of the up-to-date swinging man, these days, to distrust professionalism. The amateur is king. In music, art, literature, drama, even in life itself, it is the amateur who is envied, especially if he has done it on his own, and has not seen it absolutely necessary to

5 Dag Hammarskjöld, *Markings*, trans. by Leif Sjoberg and W. H. Auden (New York: Knopf, 1964), p. 112.

6 Merton, *The Sign of Jonas*, p. 59.

conform in any way to the canons of the past. In our day, it seems, it is the amateur who is canonized, while the perfectionist is scorned. Inept people may be virtuous, but ineptness is not a virtue.

It is especially depressing when something is badly done in the name of God: shabby ritual, a disheveled parochial school, a sloppy church supper. All of these things communicate something to people. If only Christians could learn from the Buddhists the value of doing small things well. Anything that lifts life — even the way that tea is served — becomes ritual because it does honor to God in enhancing the world that God has made.

The Church has been blessed with individuals who have a natural gift for reaching others. By their very way of being they show a sense of anthropology. One such individual, an anonymous Franciscan, was described by Bernard Berenson in his diary. The entry is dated May 31, 1948, at a villa near Florence:

> For a week my parish church has been turned into a brilliantly lit drawing room, where the villagers were attracted to come and listen to the eloquence of a Franciscan who harangued them about their duties as Catholics, as men, as Italians. He addressed them in language of their own brew without inhibitions, and from the age of three upward they listened and had their ears filled with the rhetoric they love. Then yesterday a procession with bands, gorgeous garments, flowers, gaiety of every orderly kind to my private chapel. All in all a work of entertainment going straight to the senses and heart of the villagers (or suburbanites), that Communists and similar performers cannot rival. Think of the dreary harangue in Gorky's *Foma Gordeyev* whom his fellow picnickers, revolutionists like him, had to stop! No, anthropologically the Church has all the innings.[7]

That sermon, so effective in Italy in 1948, would not be too effective in the United States in 1969. It might be

---

[7] Berenson, *Sunset and Twilight*, p. 82.

less effective even in Italy today, because the more a culture becomes saturated with the mass media the less effective becomes the sermon as a format.

The irony is that the Catholic Church did not give a very high priority to the sermon during the years it was an effective form of communication; it was looked upon as something of a Protestant specialty, something one turned to because he had little else to recommend attending his services. Now that the sermon is declining in popularity, the Church has taken an exceptional interest in it.

The sermon and all ritual as we have known it seem near exhaustion. Maybe we should forget all the ritual we have known and develop something that we scarcely think of now as ritual. This could be a ritual that develops awareness, a ritual that seeks to organize life, more than a ritual of display.

This does not mean that ritual should be abstract or lacking in visual symbol but that the visuals should suit our times in a way the visuals of the old forms do not. The inner search for grace through definite outward signs becomes more important than ever as we become more visual-minded.

Louis Nizer, the trial lawyer, states:

> Visual evidence sticks in the mind better than oral statement. We comprehend through the eye more easily than through the ear. That is why lawyers frequently use toy models of automobiles to explain an automobile collision, or skeletons to explain injuries. Even in complicated antitrust litigations, colored charts are worth thousands of explanatory words. The old saying, seeing is believing, is true in court, although in church, the reverse is probably true. There, one must believe in order to see.[8]

In church, however, seeing can also lead to believing, because a man brings to church the same psychology he

---

[8] Louis Nizer, *The Jury Returns* (Garden City: Doubleday, 1966), p. 349.

brings to court. Some few great spirits may be able to make the great intuitive leap to God, but for most of us the ascent is a slow and painful climb, one difficult rung after another. These rungs are formed of the familiar things around us, and ritual, like poetry, should take ordinary objects and through metaphor heighten their meaning to lift them above absurdity.

Ritual can help us sense holiness, or the possibility of holiness, in the familiar. Someone said that an artist is a person who shows the importance of things. A ritual artist would also show their holiness, and he does this by lifting things above their abused state. If we see things only in their abused state we come to think of them as essentially shallow and this leads to disillusionment, even despair.

Television commercials, for example, are a familiar format of communication, much in the idiom of our time. We have seen them so often abused that we often think of them as essentially in poor taste, without concern for the spirit of man and with small possibilities of showing such concern. Yet some Franciscan Fathers in a film studio in California proved that the television commercial format can be used to promote the good life of the spirit as well as the good life of the body. They showed perception in using the television commercial format because the people they are trying to reach are accustomed to receiving their attitudes packaged in this format.

The Franciscans have made sixty-second and thirty-second tele-spots, as they call them. These are being used between television programs on three hundred stations. Here is one such visual homily that promotes right living:

Quick close-ups of two couples playing bridge. One couple leaves. All hell breaks loose when the remaining husband and wife get into an argument over what went wrong during the game. Their children awaken and listen. The sound track carries sirens, bombs, and gunfire — sounds from the dark side of the soul.

The commotion lasts sixty seconds but your meditation lasts longer. You wonder how much people degrade their

spirits with two-bit arguments. When bitterness is spewed
does it not poison the spirit, no matter what causes the
spewing? How permanently are the children scarred?
Would it be ironic for the husband and the wife to go
on a peace march? Does it make sense trying to change
the big things over which you have no control when you
do not change the little things over which you have
control? Can there be a utopian world without utopian
families, a perfect society of imperfect men? Is it possible
for nations to cease from warfare as long as individuals
continue to war among themselves?

Another visual homily that speaks of the tragedy of
conflict between husband and wife was made in California by Family Theater. This is part of a series of four-
minute films based on the Psalms. A husband and a wife
are shown packing, preparing for a divorce. The words
of Psalm 54 are heard twice, once in a man's voice and
once in a woman's:

> If some enemy had insulted me, I could bear it,
> > If my foe had risen against me, I could hide from him:
> But it was you, my fellow companion,
> > My comrade, my friend!
> How glad we once were together,
> > Walking in procession to the house of God!

Call it a visual poem, if you like, a visual meditation,
a visual homily. How long a sermon would it take to
make one feel the anguish and the tragedy of separation
the way that four-minute film can make one feel it?
What is more, it makes us realize how an ancient psalm
can fit the last half of the twentieth century once an artist
gets his hands on it.

The comic strip, another communications format developed in this century, has been misued as much as all
other formats. Then along comes a true artist, Charles M.
Schulz, and lifts the format to a level not believed possible, proving once again that the fault lies not in the
format but in the user.

Charles Schulz, a Sunday school teacher, believes that, "if you do not say something in a cartoon you might as well not draw it at all. Humor which does not say something is worthless humor."[9]

The characters in his cartoon series, *Peanuts*, say plenty. Several children and one dog reflect the insights of Kierkegaard, Barth, Tillich, Newman, Salinger, and Eliot.

Lucy is a pragmatist who might grow up to be president of a corporation; Linus is a philosopher stuck with insecurity; and Schroeder is an aesthete out of touch with his surroundings. Charlie Brown is Everyman, and Snoopy, the hound of Heaven, is capable of bringing Christian joy to all he pursues, if only they will let him.

It is unthinkable to array a crew of children against such thinkers as St. Paul, Isaiah, and Shakespeare and expect them to look good, but it works, because of the genius of Charles Schulz. The comic strip can be taken on two levels; it can be enjoyed at the surface level of kids making funny remarks, or the appreciation can be deeper when we observe children making perceptive comments on life. To have insight into the deeper level, one needs to be aware of the writing and thought ranging from Old and New Testaments to current philosophy.

It is amazing how much of a homily Schulz can crowd into a four-panel comic strip. For example, one opens with Snoopy, the hound, shivering in the snow. Charlie Brown, well bundled against the elements, says, "Snoopy looks kind of cold, doesn't he?" Linus, also well bundled, answers, "I'll say he does . . . maybe we ought to go over and comfort him." Linus says, "Be of good cheer, Snoopy," and Charlie Brown echoes, "Yes, be of good cheer," and they both walk away leaving Snoopy feeling puzzled and still shivering in the snow.

Books have been written explaining how admonitions, glittering generalities, and abstractions mean nothing to a person if you let him remain feeling as miserable as

---

9 Robert L. Short, *The Gospel According to Peanuts* (Richmond, Va.: John Knox Press, 1965), p. 11.

ever. Young people might be able to learn about such theological problems from a book; Schulz's way of putting it, however, may speak to them more directly, not because it contains more truth than the well-worn tract but because he uses an idiom of our time.

Coffeehouse theater, another modern format, also has the power to lift the mind and heart to spiritual matters. At a Catholic College a group presented a series of skits entitled, *Something for Lent*.

The program said: "*Something for Lent* tries to take a look at the small and large pain of any and every person's daily life. Using some great words of great people and some ordinary words of ordinary people we are trying to express the profound paradox of suffering most perfectly exemplified in Christ's Passion. What we want to say is that each of us is responsible for alleviating pain wherever we find it and at the same time each of us is reborn only through suffering."[10]

The students performed brief skits, each of which told of a different aspect of suffering. They used slides, film clips, tape recordings, newspaper want ads, and radio commercials. They danced, sang, and carried posters and used quotes from Pope John, Carl Sandburg, James Joyce, Dostoevski, St. Paul, Ray Bradbury, and Jacques Maritain.

The program closed with taped excerpts of a newscast of that very evening. By then members of the audience were so sensitized to suffering that they heard the newscast on a whole new level, in a way they might continue to hear newscasts from that night on. A long sermon about the need for compassion could never make an audience feel compassion the way that presentation of concrete realities did.

There is another example of how something in the idiom of our time can be used to lift the mind and the heart to God. This example translates the advice of the psalmist into a twentieth-century format. The psalmist

---

10 Program for *Something for Lent,* dramatic skits presented at Immaculate Heart College, Hollywood, California, February, 1965.

wrote: "Praise God in his sanctuary; praise him with
the sound of the trumpet; praise him with the timbrel
and dance; praise him with stringed instruments and
upon the loud cymbals and the high-sounding cymbals.
Let everything that has breath praise the Lord."

In all of these ways Duke Ellington and his orchestra
praised the Lord with a concert of sacred music in the
sanctuary of the Fifth Avenue Presbyterian Church on
Christmas night. There in front of the golden oak pews
with their burgundy seat pads, there in front of the
stained glass windows they praised the Lord in an idiom
of the twentieth century.

The whole setting spoke of tradition, conservatism, affluence. The program said, "Even a Presbyterian Church
with its starched classical image reaches far beyond its
immediate ecclesiastical connections."[11] How far was in-
dicated in the printed program's list of patrons: The Five
Spot, The Half Note, The Newport Jazz Festival, and
Father Norman O'Connor, C.S.P.

There was honest communication when Cat Anderson
praised the Lord in the one way he can praise him best
— with a trumpet that goes high . . . higher . . . highest.
John Lamb, with a bass viol, did what the psalmist said,
"Praise him with stringed instruments."

No one took the psalmist more at his word than did
the drummer. "Praise him upon the loud cymbals and
the high-sounding cymbals." Louis Bellson used six min-
utes of percussion solo to praise God for what he has
wrought. He went back to the beginning and helped push
things around, the light from the dark, the water from
the land, and he hung out a few stars while he was at it.

Duke Ellington explained: "In this program you will
hear a wide variety of statements without words, and I
think that you should know that if it is a phrase with
six tones it symbolizes the six syllables in the first four

11 Program for Christmas Concert, Fifth Avenue Presbyterian Church,
New York City, December 25, 1965.

words of the Bible, 'In the beginning God,' which is our theme, we say it many times, many ways."[12]

Ellington played a piano solo, *New World A'Coming.* He explained it as "the anticipation of a very distant place on land, at sea, or in the sky, where there will be no war, no greed, no nonbelievers, and no categorization. Where love is unconditional and no pronoun is good enough for God."[13]

Bunny Briggs tapped, *David Danced Before the Lord with All His Might.* Lena Horne sang and Brock Peters sang.

Perhaps everyone left understanding a little better three sentences printed in the program: "Sacred music in all of its forms offers a universal point of meeting. But what makes music sacred is not a rigid category nor a fixed pattern of taste. The sole criterion is whether or not the hearts of the musician and the listener are offered in response and devotion to God."[14]

Perhaps this would not have happened had not Pope John opened some windows, an event noted indirectly in the program: "With other congregations in the city the Fifth Avenue Presbyterian Church recognizes the new ecumenical spirit of understanding."[15]

Something that Duke Ellington wrote for the program brings to mind Pope John: "Communication itself is what baffles the multitude. It is both so difficult and so simple. Of all men's fears I think that men are most afraid of being what they are — in direct communion with the world at large. They fear reprisals, the most personal of which is that they won't be understood.

"How can anyone expect to be understood unless he presents his thoughts with complete honesty? This situation is unfair because it asks too much of the world. In effect we say, 'I don't dare show you what I am because

---

12 *Ibid.*
13 *Ibid.*
14 *Ibid.*
15 *Ibid.*

I don't trust you for a minute but please love me anyway, because I need you to. And, of course, if you don't
love me anyway, you're a dirty dog, just as I suspected,
so I was right in the first place.' Yet every time God's
children have thrown away fear in pursuit of honesty —
trying to communicate themselves, understood or not —
miracles have happened.''

Pope John threw away fear in pursuit of honesty and
that is how he made possible new and interesting ways of
praising the Lord. He threw open not only a window, but
many doors, to make possible a new search for communication through ritual.

Except for Ellington's concert, nothing described here
was conceived as ritual. Maybe such things can give us
hints, though, of the formats new ritual will explore
when lifted by great imaginations. The new ritual needs
to be vastly different from the old because it will be
created for a vastly different world. The uses of modern
equipment in ritual might make some people feel uncomfortable. Television, tapes, records, slides, and films
are aids that can be well used or abused. They are gifts,
like talents, and as such need to be used, or else we will
feel the frustration of being out of touch with the times.
They will be effective only if used by someone who en-
dows them with an angle of vision that is unique, alive,
and discerning.

It might be objected that the things described here
have had too much to do with entertainment to be fitting
for ritual. To be effective, however, ritual needs to have
some aspect of entertainment about it. The ritual of
pomp may have been entertaining in its time, but today
we do not find it so. All art is to some extent entertaining, something that springs from the playful side of man.

To put it the other way around, ritual should not be
dull. In a search for new ritual the problem will be to
keep alive a spirit that is open to variety. A homily that
features slides of Charles Schulz's cartoons might have
meaning to the young, but it may make older people feel

uncomfortable, just as guitars and bongo drums make them feel uncomfortable. If older people prefer the organ, the rosary, and silent meditation why not let them have those things?

The promoters of new ways usually proclaim that they are overthrowing the authoritarianism of the past. Often this avant-garde ends up becoming more authoritarian than those it rebelled against. It can happen in ritual, too.

One thing is sure, a more alive ritual will not be born without pangs and anguish. Birth, and growth, and change are what cause most of the ache of existence. As Ernst Barlach, the artist, wrote: "I once remarked to you that there is a law that no work can turn out successfully unless it goes through a series of crises that deepen and spiritualize it."[16]

Bernard Berenson foresaw the agonies of the transitional period that we are passing through when he wrote, "Ritual is what keeps societies together, and woe to the day when our traditional rituals give way to others, for that can only happen with the destruction of our societies and their being replaced by others. But in the course of time they will develop beauty, I hope."[17]

There is consolation in Barlach's observation that a severe crisis deepens and spiritualizes work. There is consolation in Berenson's hope that out of chaos some orderly beauty eventually emerges. These are worth remembering because in a transitional period, such as ours, when one moves from the known to the unknown, one needs all the consolation he can find.

It is not easy to resign ourselves to the fact that ritual is a Rorschach test. Although ritual is a blending of all

---

[16] From a letter to cousin Karl Barlach referring to the nine sculptured figures of the Frieze of the Listeners, Reemtsma Collection, Hamburg, December 12, 1935, Briefe II, 220. Quoted in *The Transformations of God, Seven Woodcuts* by Ernst Barlach, with selections from his writings in translation by Naomi Jackson Groves (Hamburg: Christians, 1962), p. 50.

[17] Berenson, *Sunset and Twilight*, p. 190.

the arts it is still something of an ink-blot test. What we like and dislike depends on what was locked into our genes to start with and everything that happened to us along the way.

This is true in all communication. What I have said in these pages gives me away. What you approve of in them and what you disapprove of also give you away. We are all biased, only in different ways.

I am made aware of how much of a Rorschach test all communication is each time I screen *The Seventh Seal* for my students. There is one part in the film that makes me think of Zen Buddhism, when probably no one else in the room is thinking of Zen Buddhism. That is because something happened to me that did not happen to anybody else in the room.

In the film a knight is returning from the Holy Land and is tired in body and soul. He dines one evening with Mary, Joseph, and their child. He says to Mary that he will always cherish the memory of that evening and will hold it gently the way he holds the bowl of milk.

At that point I think of Zen because I spent some time living in a deserted Buddhist monastery in Burma writing a history. I became interested in Zen and learned that one of its teachings is: if you want to hold something in life then hold it gently as you would hold water in the hand. Love, friendship, life itself, hold gently. If you are interested in the arts or sciences hold them gently. If you care about ritual, hold it gently like water in the hand, because if you grasp it too tightly, you will lose it.

8

Ritual and Conceptual Systems: Primitive Myth to Modern Ideology

by

DAVID B. BURRELL

Introduction: Organizing Principle

EFFORTS TO EMPLOY THE METHODS OF DIVERSE DISCIPLINES to illuminate a common human situàtion are often graced with artful constructions, yet blunted by vague and general observations. I wish to offer a very simple scheme according to which I shall organize these reflections and which I hope will lead beyond observations to understanding. The scheme states that conceptions of self differ according to differing conceptions of what-it-is-to-know or to understand. I am not speaking immediately of conceptions of myself as an individual, but rather of concep-

David B. Burrell, C.S.C., is Chairman of the Department of Theology at the University of Notre Dame. He has written two books, *The Future of Philosophical Theology* and *Speaking and Understanding in Philosophy*.

tions of myself as a man. The organizing scheme pays homage, then, to the long-acknowledged fact that understanding, intentionality, and knowledge distinguish men from everything else. But understanding is generally not easily come by, and even less frequently reflected upon. The fact that different cultures understand different things by 'understanding' turns the traditional observation into something more like a leading principle than a specific thesis.

Some feel that it is enough to remember what was said, others need to reproduce an outline, some have to sketch a diagram; still others speak of insight or being able to give an account, others worry about coherence, and some few speak of critical acumen. These attitudes are reflected in the courses students choose, the way professors teach them, the exams given and the way one prepares for them. They are also transmitted into arcane disciplines like "learning theory," and form the basis for curriculum revisions as well as account for the profits of sophisticated reactor-devices called "learning machines." The organizing principle — conceptions of self differ according to differing conceptions of understanding — is not offered as a means of discriminating among the multiple ways of understanding what it is to understand. It serves more generally to call our attention to the fact that we tend to think of ourselves in a certain way if we have been persuaded that understanding comes that same way.

Hence I will try to learn the way the learning theorists would have it that I learn. The more I try, the more their views are confirmed, and the more persuaded am I that I am the sort of thing that relates to my world in this fashion. Whatever conception one has of understanding, he cannot help remarking that the range of this capacity to survey must include understanding itself. Furthermore, the conception we have of what it is to understand will certainly affect our understanding. And since we understand both what and who we are by that same power of understanding, the conception I have of what it is to understand will feed back upon my conception of myself and influence the person I become. A relationship so mutually reinforcing as this one, and one so strategically situated as to influence action as well as reflection, serves as a paradigm example of *dialectical* (or progressively and mutually reinforcing) interaction. Hence I can say that my conception of understanding is crucial precisely because it affects me: who I am, can be, and will become.

The papers given at scholarly conferences tend to conform to a pattern. That pattern reflects a conception of what it is to understand — a conception reinforced, needless to say, by the society of scholars. This conception of understanding attends to certain types of questions, allows others to arise, and finds still others irrelevant. If the exercise aims at understanding something and refrains from marginal displays of erudition, then the types of questions invited, tolerated, or ignored present me with a conception of understanding itself. And since such a conception offers a pattern for understanding and for developing myself, the papers given at a gathering of scholars, whether they succeed or fail to establish their conclusions, always insinuate a way of looking at myself in my humanity. The same, of course, goes for a sales conference, a discussion of the role of business in urban planning, a country-store confab, or a bull session among disaffected Americans. The more expressly oriented is the gathering towards understanding, the more is my understanding of myself affected. A sales meeting or a political rally must needs manipulate forces. They do not address my self-understanding, but a discussion among intense, obviously committed friends certainly does.

The manner, then, in which we approach an issue in an effort to understand it, feeds back upon the inquirers themselves to fashion their conceptions of themselves and their style of living. It would be difficult to find a better illustration of Hegel's discovery: the inherently dialectical character of understanding. And it is this dialectical aspect which forms the organizing scheme for my investigation of ritual. By working in a manifestly dialectical fashion, I will be able to display the organizing principle of the paper as well as exorcise any shades of determinism these reflections may have raised. Whatever substance these shades have is gained by trading on a curiously abstract and thoroughly undialectical view of oneself as autonomous. Once we appreciate just how dialectical understanding is, and hence how symbiotic is man's relating to his world, we become able to understand interiority and autonomy afresh. By proceeding in a dialectical fashion to establish a more dialectical understanding of what it is to understand, I hope to elicit intimations of a fresh understanding of ourselves, and so exhibit the organizing thesis of the inquiry. Since ritual offers a pattern for understanding that initiates a dialectic of self-understanding, the paper itself attempts an illustration as well as a statement of the genius of ritual.

The final introductory point is a leading one. We have noted how patterns for understanding reinforce self-conceptions, and how these people go on to make their mark within the pattern, and so the process tends to be mutually reinforcing. Yet a reflective and critical spirit cannot be downed. The recent history of literary criticism is a useful example of a school undermined and gradually toppled by a movement, which could then not help becoming a school, only to be threatened in its turn by a rising movement. A pattern for understanding is ever vulnerable to an authenticating experience like: "But that's the way it is. I feel it, I just know it. That's all!" If this understanding involves a new pattern for understanding (which it usually does), and a new pattern entails a new conception of oneself (which it always does), then an experience that forces itself upon us in this fashion can initiate a transformation in our very style of life. Sensitivity groups are driving this point home to an American social strata that tended to conceive knowing or understanding as efficient managing, and patterned their lives accordingly.

Thesis: from Construct to the Constructor

The specific thesis that fleshes out the general scheme for the dialectic of self and understanding warns that the coordinate conceptions of self and of understanding which serve as paradigms for "modern man" or "a world come of age," or which pattern a university curriculum acceptable to professional academics, are deficient in a manner and to a degree that can only be called disillusioning. Hence, these going norms and standards for knowing and understanding can expect a furious and disheartened rejection, if they have not already received it. I shall not merely shout this charge, however, but will proceed to defend it. In the process, we shall stumble over much that is valuable to an understanding of ritual. The exploratory second phase of my thesis (which turns out to be a quite fruitful tack) suspects that understanding the manner in which the going model for self and understanding *misses* the mark will furnish us a language for speaking of ritual.

So far, this can be no more than a suspicion. The touted irrelevance of liturgy and rite to "modern man" furnishes a helpful hint. Ritual is useless and for that reason meaningless to "a world come of age." Yet no sooner has it come of age than an increasingly significant number of quite articulate and sensitive people designate themselves as "flower *children*," in quest of, among other things, cult. These cultural happenings suggest that, were we able to see our way through to a more sensitive conception of self and understanding, those ingredients missing from the going pattern would have something to do with ritual — with our performing as well as our understanding it.

Following up the hints and armed with this suspicion, I propose to show that many of the features of a more adequate model for self and for what it is to know or understand correspond with remarkable exactitude with the more salient characteristics of ritual as we have tradi-

tionally understood it or been privileged to experience it.[1]
To appreciate the dimensions of this task, imagine Socrates
being allowed to return to a latter-day Academy now
managed by Platonic sophists. He would doubtless find
it necessary to admonish them to take heed of what lies
beneath their feet as they follow their noses in peripatetic
musing. Athena had succeeded in making their form of
life possible only by propitiating the furies with a home
right there under the Acropolis. To neglect this fact
would not merely be irreverent; it would prove suicidal.
It amounts to renouncing one's origins, allowing his roots
to wither, and so, watching himself blow away.

Present Paradigms and Their Deficiencies

In order to fairly present what I have called the "going
model" for understanding oneself understanding, I shall
employ two scenarios. The first, the more mythic, identifies the model of self and understanding with Apollo and
the limiting, organizing role of reason. The counterpoint
for Apollo is Dionysus, and the rest of the story makes
daily headlines. The second way of laying out our intellectual and communal situation, a more analytic and
self-conscious approach, associates reason with the constructive role of the social sciences. A brief introduction
to Carnap's *Logical Structure of the World* provides the
setting, and a more extensive presentation of Berger and
Luckmann's *Social Construction of Reality* furnishes the
immediate context for my critical remarks. Those remarks will carry us to the threshold of ritual: the elements found to be wanting to a thoroughgoing construction of reality will provide the syntax for a language that
allows us to speak of ritual and of the self-understanding
ritual can convey.

---

[1] By a "more adequate" model, I do not mean one that leads tenden-
tiously to confirm my hypothesis, but rather one that avoids the
antinomies of the going model and incorporates entire regions of language and of experience otherwise written off as noncognitive or
obscurantist.

The Way of Protest: Apollo vs. Dionysus

In the first chapter of his key inductive work, *Symbols of Transformation,* Jung contrasts the mode of understanding forced upon him by prolonged work with mythic materials with that pronounced acceptable by the scientific community. The essay wants somewhat in epistemological sophistication, but surpasses any epistemological treatise in power and significance, because it represents one of those breakthrough moments when a pattern is brought face up to an authenticating set of experiences. In these situations, the protagonist cannot but find himself arguing against himself in spite of himself, because the prevailing pattern has preempted the domain of discussion and rational discourse. Thus, Jung insisted that he was a scientist whose findings were empirical, and he self-consciously tried to limit his assertions to generalizations from those findings. It was not simply that he desired recognition from the scientific community, which he surely did, but more radically, that no other pattern was available to him for serious investigative inquiry.

The essay itself pleads for us, nevertheless, to recognize another mode of understanding — one that Jung himself had been forced to adopt in the wake of his "scientific" investigation of mythic consciousness. The argument comes through the chapters that follow, for *Symbols of Transformation* amasses the mythic material in such a fashion as to allow the reader to feel its compelling demand for that different mode of understanding which Jung pleads for and tries to characterize. Furthermore, Jung gives witness to my general principle by refusing to treat this question as an academic one: since a pattern for understanding implicates the person in a style of life and consciousness, this new mode of understanding is not only desirable, but imperative. Predilection for the scientific pattern, to the theoretic and practical exclusion of others, has prepared us to render a highly articulate and minutely technical account of our despair. It is not merely that we need to understand something else in order to fill out the gaps in our present understanding. The situation is not that simple precisely because patterns preempt the field of consciousness; they are endemic imperialists since they vie for self-understanding as well. The result is not simply lack of foodstuffs, but an impoverished diet certified to be adequate. In the face of collective authority, it takes both insight and courage to determine that the accepted path leads to death, and an even more sustained effort to blaze another one.

For reasons quite similar to Jung's, one hesitates to set himself over against the scientific model for knowing and understanding. There is an innate pull to identify science with inquiry itself. The alternatives, which we shall examine in a moment, seem quickly to lose touch with any reasonable guidance. The way out of the box, however, is easy: all we need do is recognize that there is no single identifiable "scientific model" for knowing and understanding. We can gradually position ourselves by qualifiedly accepting or rejecting distinct models for self and understanding — each of which may appeal to the honorific "scientific." Such a procedure is certainly the more proper — if you will, the more scientific one — for philosophical reflection. Our second look at contemporary models will proceed in that fashion, but the first look summarily divides into dramatic oppositions.

Apollo represents law and order, restraint and civility. Dionysus relentlessly undermines these by calling attention to their tantalizing other side: for law and order, passion and spontaneity; for restraint and civility, vitality and reckless abandon. The passionate analysis of a Marcuse or Norman O. Brown protests the alignment of self and of understanding uniquely with Apollo.[2] The critique

2 Cf. Herbert Marcuse, *Eros and Civilization* (Boston: Beacon Press, 1955) and Norman O. Brown, *Life Against Death* (Middletown, Conn.: Wesleyan Univ. Press, 1959). For a summary of the Apollo-Dionysus drama, see Sam Keen, "Manifesto for a Dionysian Theology," *Cross Currents*, XIX (1969), 37-54.

is inevitably socio-economic, for patterns of self-understanding dialectically reinforce a culture. Hence, a reason that sees its primary task as managing and making over tends to produce a society so oriented.[3] What is unfortunate about both Marcuse and Brown is that both seem to accept the identification of reason with management, and look for something other than understanding to release us from the repressive tyranny of the dominating, manipulating reason. Enter Dionysus; yet also begin the task of showing that our fears from this new quarter are manifest prejudices of an Apollonian conception of self and of understanding. No tyranny here; it is all liberation.

The script writer is Freud, with Apollo playing *ego* and Dionysus, *id*. Freud and Freudian orthodoxy, however, have consistently failed the reflective test. The controlling conception of self is precisely that which is so aptly protested by Brown and Marcuse — the constructing, manipulating *ego* of a technological or scientific pattern of thought — insofar as this polarizes itself against the humanistic. The other elements of the Freudian self, *super-ego* and *id,* are precisely not-self. Hence the violence of the ensuing drama, as well as its futility. The Dionysus/Apollo opposition is not so much a way of understanding as one of protest. Necessary, no doubt, and most certainly inevitable. If, however, when Apollo demands law and order, Dionysus asserts passion and spontaneity, one wonders whether this opens a reliable path to justice.

It is certainly demeaning for understanding to be yoked to making over and manipulating the world, but wholeness and integrity cannot be achieved simply through release from that bondage. Being released does not amount to being free. Nothing demonstrates so clearly how little Freud had succeeded in freeing himself from the scientific or Apollonian model of reason than his structuring of the self. For those who have seen through that model, yet re-

---

[3] It is difficult to see how one differentiates actual communist societies from capitalist ones on *this* point, but that is not germane to our inquiry.

main beholden to Freud's scheme, the road to selfhood can only be defined in terms of an *ego* from which man must find release.

The opposition between Apollonian and Dionysian is especially violent because the analysis has not yet succeeded in liberating itself from an Apollonian view of understanding. Hence, conflict can only bring confrontation, whether in the theater or on the campus. The conflict is dramatic in another sense, for it also symbolizes the shift in priorities of our own self-understanding over the past half decade. When William Hamilton was casting about for images to interpret "modern secular man" to himself, he happened upon Orestes. His claim was that contemporary man, optimistic about shaping his world, could more easily identify with Orestes than with the tortured Oedipus. Orestes' guide, we remember, was Apollo.[4]

It seems a rather obvious cultural fact that an American's assessment of reason and understanding as making over and managing the world has fundamentally shifted in the past five years. Yet one wonders whether in substituting Dionysus for Apollo, we will not simply be trading idols. Certainly the scheme that finds this opposition most hospitable — Freud's *ego/id* pattern — manifests his incapacity to find a pattern suited to the therapeutic process. He remained obligated to a mechanistic paradigm. In this respect, we would have been better served by Jung's *animus/anima* mythology.[5] Whereas my sympathies lie spontaneously with Marcuse and Brown, I find their analyses deficient precisely to the extent that they remain attached to an Apollonian conception of understanding. The weakest feature of Zorba is that he remains insufficiently free; cutting the cord still leaves one oriented towards that which gave him direction. Emancipation is

---

4 W. Hamilton and T. J. J. Altizer, *Radical Theology and the Death of God* (Indianapolis, Ind.: Bobbs-Merrill, 1966), pp. 42-45.

5 As we shall see in the more sustained and analytic second approach to uncovering the deficiencies in our going model for understanding and understanding oneself.

not yet freedom. The same may be said of the recommendations of a remodeled secular theology towards celebration. They are destined to remain idle, for the Dionysiac can only escape; he is not yet free enough to celebrate.

Reality Constructed Rationally and Socially

For a closer analytic look at our situation I shall employ — both using and abusing — Peter Berger and Thomas Luckmann's *Social Construction of Reality: An Essay in the Sociology of Knowledge*.[6] My criticism of Berger and Luckmann will be an ironic testimony to their success. For no one could have so successfully anatomized a society built upon this conception of reason and understanding without utilizing a model beholden to that same outlook. The extent to which I find their model wanting in its power to illuminate myself and my understanding to myself is precisely the measure in which the same model proves effective as a way of grasping what makes our society tick. In this sense, sociology, as they so clearly and consciously expose it, becomes the science of man in his collective dimensions. And the collective of which such a man is an integral part is one that has been shaped by the managerial reason of a democratic, capitalistic society. I have chosen this work not simply because it is a well-written and sophisticated introduction to sociology, but also because I feel that the model of understanding employed here comes closer than anything else to a working image of the contemporary myth. The authors have succeeded in translating the relativizing discourse of "conceptual frameworks" from the formal logical apparatus of a Carnap to the lived social sanctions of our world. There is little question that the universities have also allowed themselves to be shaped according to the same ethos as the society they serve.

6 Peter L. Berger and Thomas Luckmann, *Social Construction of Reality* (New York: Doubleday, 1966). Perspective is also granted by Peter L. Berger, *Invitation to Sociology* (New York: Doubleday, 1963).

Hence this model not only underlies much of our characteristic understanding of ourselves, but also the reasons why we protest against that understanding. But before proceeding to this work, a short word about its roots.

The soil from which the social relativizer springs is that synthetic mixture so carefully worked up by Rudolf Carnap and his school of logical methodology. Carnap forms the bridge between the new logic and the theories and experiments of the social scientists. It was Carnap who made respectable the suspicion that human reason is first and foremost a constructing reason. In place of the classical distinction between *theoria* and *praxis,* we were given new hope of a unified science of logical construction. Methodology has always been with us, but not in the aggressive form that it could take after Carnap. He licensed it to build foundations where it had been a more modestly Socratic venture.

It may seem pretentious to credit Carnap with single-handedly providing us the model for understanding and self-apprehension. And indeed it is. His landmark monograph, *The Logical Construction of the World,* composed between 1922 and 1925, gives logical license to what was manifestly a socio-cultural movement. Indeed the warrants that Carnap himself invokes for the enterprise are not those of critical reflection so much as a prevailing mood of intellectual work.[7] This warrant itself is the

---

7 Trans. by Rolf A. George (Berkeley and Los Angeles: Univ. of California Press, 1967), pp. xvii-xviii (preface to first edition, 1928). "We feel that there is an inner kinship between the attitude on which our philosophical work is founded and the intellectual attitude which presently manifests itself in entirely different walks of life; we feel this orientation in artistic movements, especially in architecture and in movements which strive for meaningful forms of personal and collective life, of education and of external organization in general. We feel all around us the same basic orientation, the same style of thinking which realizes that the fabric of life can never quite be comprehended. It makes us pay careful attention to detail and at the same time recognizes the great lines which run through the whole. It is an orientation which acknowledges the bonds that tie men together, but at the same time strives for free development of the individual. Our work is carried by the faith that this attitude will win the future. Vienna, May 1928."

most significant fact about Carnap's view of understanding and self-apprehension, for the manner in which he seeks to construct reality is never itself justified. What one might call the reflective question is sometimes attended to, but never as a reflective question. What results rather is a certain modification of the system.[8] The precise merits of Carnap's volume lie in its logical austerity, which makes it perfectly clear that there is no room for the constructor in such a constructive enterprise of reason.[9] The system, in short, leaves no opportunity for reflection and is itself a model or a diagram of understanding in its essentials. The irony of this view of understanding comes clearer when we appreciate the intrinsic connection between a model for understanding, one's understanding of himself, and the self that he decides to become. The fact that Carnap's model rules out the self suggests that it is a paradoxical base for understanding human understanding. The model allows no purchase for the dialectic built into the very notion of understanding: that between apprehension and self-apprehension.

Let us flesh out this purely formal critique by a closer look at Berger and Luckmann's social reconstruction of reality. By exhibiting the parentage of this venture in Carnap, I can better display the deficiencies of both as models for what it is to understand or to know. The analysis of Berger and Luckmann is more concrete and hence more complex than Carnap's logical layout. The conception of reason, however, is fundamentally the same. Understanding is everywhere pragmatic, and its ordinary use can be understood only within the context of the conceptual systems or "plausibility structures" that it creates for itself. Understanding leads to a style of life, and the style of life is also maintained by that very understanding. It is these same styles of life with their correlative social institutions which, according to Berger and

8 Cf. the notion of "quasi-analysis," No. 69, pp. 110-111.

9 E.g., "... more fitting than 'I experience' would be 'experience' or 'this experience'" (No. 163, p. 261).

Luckmann, "maintain reality." Carnap had reminded us that every conception entails a conceptual system. He also gave us the rules of constructing the system which he felt to be the most perspicuous. Berger and Luckmann simply transfer this view to the social institutions we construct in response to our need for maintaining a reality within which we can function. It is the authors' *conviction* that the institutions supporting our mode of existence are themselves constructed. Their *analysis* amounts more modestly to showing how time and again our understanding functions within the parameters of embracing social institutions. They can show, of course, how the rules and patterns of institutional behavior are explicitly and appositely constructed in specific instances of societies formed to promote particular purposes. It is one of the weaknesses of their work, however, that they simply extrapolate from such clearly arbitrary societies to those which respond to needs more deeply imbedded in our aspirations as human beings.

When I say it is their conviction rather than their analysis that warrants the view that all social institutions are the products of a constructing reason, I do not so much disagree with their thesis as point out a deficiency in their analysis. Had they paid closer attention to reason in its postulated constructing role, they might have become more sensitive to different qualities of motivation, and to observe them vary from one enterprise to another. This would then allow us to graduate and type different social realities. One of the weaknesses of their model certainly is that a society of believers in Esperanto is formally the same as the society of believers in Allah or in the God-who-reveals-himself-in-Jesus.

Look more closely at the purported constructing role of reason in human institutions. The logic is avowedly dialectical: man is the creature of the society that he himself creates. The key notions are "plausibility structures" that promote "reality maintenance." Familiar sociological terms such as "socialization," "internalization," and "significant others" are of course integral to their foundational theory. Socialization results from an interaction between persons and those institutions which form the plausibility structures that help their lives take on an increasing internal consistency. One of the prime results of internalizing the policies and norms embodied in the institutions is a healthy sense of reality.

Whatever difficulties we have with the thesis will also illustrate its power. For example, the critical reason of a Socrates can only be defined as deviant on this scheme. And so he was found. Breakthroughs in understanding must amount to conversions, for the normal impulse will invariably integrate new understanding into terms already familiar to us. Anyone who has experienced within himself or in his students the kind of resistance we can muster to new overriding conceptions of understanding or of ourselves will certainly testify that something as radical as a conversion is required for learning. (I cannot help thinking of a scripture scholar who confessed to me that he—and even all of us—had much to learn from Bultmann.) Yet whence creativity? If the overriding role of understanding, the furthest reaches of which it is capable, lies in constructing plausibility structures so that day-to-day understanding can function in the only way in which it is capable—within a framework—then how is it that understanding can supply a creative impulse? If the conceptions that form the very stuff of any constructive enterprise we might undertake are themselves imbedded within a plausibility structure, how can we shape any new ones? The activity would seem to be an inexplicable or random one, for beyond the protective framework of institutional plausibility structures lies only anomie and darkness.[10]

---

10 "Society provides us with warm, reasonably comfortable caves, in which we can huddle with our fellows, beating on the drums that drown out the howling hyenas of the surrounding darkness. 'Ecstasy' is the act of stepping outside the caves, alone, to face the night" (*Invitation* . . . , p. 150).

The same criticism can be made from a more internal feature of the authors' scheme. That is the avowedly dialectical interaction between a person seeking to know and the social institutions that form the plausibility structures or perimeters of his world. On the criteria given by Berger and Luckmann, we have interaction, but hardly of a dialectical sort. That the person who constitutes is also constituted demands nothing more than the passage of time. Action, reaction, and feedback would suffice to explain socialization and internalization on their analysis. There is little or no feel for the *manner in which* the nuanced process of socialization and internalization is carried out: the role of protest, of creative dissent, of interior withholding; in short, of all the various ruses whereby men hedge their allegiance to society, and hence impede the socialization/internalization process. In fact, "internalization" seems to do nothing more than name the result of "socialization." This leaves the model no critical distance from which to appraise motives, reasons, or degrees of internalization. In fact, the entire domain of the interior or of the subjective has been evacuated in favor of what can be understood: the ideally homeostatic process of socialization.

If we trace the parentage of the authors' scheme to Carnap we shall see why this is the case. We shall also see why a genuinely dialectical relationship between person and social institution would remain inexplicable on their model. The controlling insight has man constructing his world, yet the process excludes the constructor, and hence he can find no *place* in the world that he himself has constructed. That world instead succeeds in making him over. I am not referring to the relatively innocent fact that we have long been enslaved and are on the verge of being suffocated by the machines we make, but I refer to far more insidious forms of self-destruction. We may come to learn, for example, that "the world of childhood is so constituted as to instill in the individual a nomic structure in which he may have confidence that 'everything is all right.' "[11] I have been tricked into feeling that the accident of my birth has a certain rightness or necessity about it. Imagine my disillusionment when I realize that it is "in fact a bundle of contingencies."[12] Think of the "older child [who] comes to recognize that the world represented by his parents, the same world that he had previously taken for granted as inevitable reality, is actually the world of uneducated, lower-class, rural Southerners."[13]

Were the same lad to have signed up for an American literature course as well, he might be able to challenge our authors' manner of disposing of his childhood and crudely assessing the value of his home. Poets and novelists stemming from similar soil might bring him through the fluorescent categories of a reconstructed childhood existence to a softer light where he can appreciate his own roots and discover the genuine in whatever is genuinely his own. There is a yet more basic sense of 'nomic' which undergirds specific ways of doing things: a sense that challenges any interpretation that makes of a home an accident. A framework that allows so easy recourse to what is *actually* another's world has no right to invoke dialectic. Feedback would suffice, yet feedback empties "internalization" of any distinctive meaning. Berger and Luckmann insist that "a genuine dialectic is involved because of the *realizing* potency of psychological theories. . . . Psychologies produce a reality, which in turn serves as the basis for their verification: rural Haitians *are* possessed and New York intellectuals *are* neurotic."[14] So far, perceptive. There are, however, disverifications as well, not so much of individual situations, it is true — for the schemes are omnivorous interpretants — but of the entire theory.

---

11 Berger and Luckmann, *Social Construction*, p. 136.
12 *Ibid.*, p. 135.
13 *Ibid.*, p. 141.
14 *Ibid.*, pp. 177-178.

A look at the expression "plausibility structure" can help us uncover the factors that do make for a genuinely dialectical relationship between person and society — factors that a purely external model of interaction can only obscure. The phrase "plausibility structure" packs a weighted theoretic assessment. It assumes a highly intellectual, quite detached perspective. We ask, for example, whether a witness' testimony is plausible, whether a doctor's diagnosis or a biochemist's theory is plausible. When we find a marriage implausible ("Can you imagine Susan living with Henry all her life?"), we are calling attention to notable discrepancies in status, patterns of behavior, and other factors supportive of a human relationship. Anyone can challenge us, however, by recalling the inner dynamics of their situation. Interestingly enough, we would betray gross insensitivity were we to use the term positively as a criterion *for* an enduring relationship. To speak of a community that has become as much a part of me as I have of it as a "plausibility structure" succeeds in announcing a possible perspective on our activities together, but also misses the point of most of them.

Ironically, these institutions could not function in the way in which the authors envisage them, were the participants to conceive of them as "plausibility structures." When the "supportive" role becomes deliberate, the whole thing is a charade. On the other hand, were institutions to work perfectly according to the model of Berger and Luckmann, the result would be an automaton. By evacuating the very possibility of commitment, the explanatory model that countenances "plausibility structure" as an explanatory notion *ipso facto* loses its explanatory power. Meaning, significance, vision are all integral to man and to human society. There are manifest discrepancies that would allow us to distinguish reflective (or free) from nonreflective (or automatic) "internalization." Yet a model for reason that is thoroughly pragmatic gives enough of a twist to 'meaning' and 'vision' to put those discrepancies out of focus.

Put most directly, the upshot of a "plausibility structure" analysis of man-in-society is to call our attention to one of the necessary conditions for personal growth and social consistency.[15] The thrust of my critique has been to note the antinomies or paradoxes that follow upon assuming that this model affords a complete analysis; that is, that "plausibility structures" are uniquely necessary conditions for "internalization" and hence sufficient to give body to that notion. It does not suffice once one has adopted this scheme to insist that

> ... openness to the immense richness of human life makes the leaden consequence of sociologism impossible to sustain and forces the sociologist to permit "holes" in the closed walls of his theoretical scheme, openings through which other possible horizons can be perceived.[16]

This is no longer a live option precisely because the view of understanding presupposed to a "plausibility structure" analysis is thoroughly pragmatic and brings other nonconstructed horizons into doubt. Berger and Luckmann correctly insist that the patterns that bring the suburban ad-man to face the Madison Avenue game are not essentially different from the rituals that help us to live with the death of one we love — "except that the reality confirmations have to be explicit and intensive."[17]

We have already noted the paradoxes involved for pragmatic reason in rendering "reality confirmations" explicit. It will suffice here to note how thoroughly utilitarian and bourgeois is the picture of human existence Berger and Luckmann give us. In that sense, it supplies all too accurate a picture of "modern man." But it also

---

15 Berger is not clear on the distinction between necessary and sufficient conditions. A phrase like: "the most important social condition is the availability of an effective plausibility structure" lends itself to a necessary condition, while "the religious community ... provides the indispensable plausibility structure for the new reality" sounds yet stronger (pp. 157-158).

16 Berger, *Invitation* ... , p. 168.

17 Berger and Luckmann, *Social Construction*, pp. 149, 156.

succeeds in displaying its own thesis in a fashion that
seriously threatens its theoretic status. Their view of understanding operative *reflects* the concerns of a production
society, and stands or falls with the closed ethos of that
society. In other words, the market supplies the *plausibility* for *their* analysis of man-in-society, for they have
given us an accurate if poignant portrait of man-in-the-
market.

What is missing — what the scheme cannot accommodate — is precisely what is lacking to our producing/con-
suming world: a capacity for appreciating what is, for
living where one is, for discovering and for receiving.[18]
Perhaps these cannot be social phenomena in the strict
sense of furnishing the goals for a society. To promote
them would betray them. Yet society will consume itself
without a capacity to appreciate what is. Without these
values, people become problems to be met with task
forces, and resentment fills the emptiness we feel when
appreciation and respect are absent. These values are sus-
piciously close to the "Kingdom" language Jesus used.
Yet certainly those societies which have explicitly tried to
promote the Kingdom have normally betrayed it. Perhaps
the signal merit of Berger and Luckmann's analysis has
been to show how alien is the Kingdom to human society
constructed according to the pragmatic criteria of a
thoroughgoing constructive understanding. The benefit
of the last five years of shared human experience has been

---

18 Berger himself has opened this perspective in his recent *Rumor of
Angels* (New York: Doubleday, 1969). However, his model can only
allow these rumors as static in the social system. True as that may be,
the dialectical character of his thesis is jeopardized, since the man who
listens to rumors such as these is to that extent no longer a product of
the society he has produced. Thomas Merton's observation is salutary:
"I might suggest a . . . need of modern man which is precisely liberation
from his inordinate self-consciousness, his monumental self-awareness,
his obsession with self-affirmation, so that he may enjoy the freedom
from concern that goes with being simply what he is and accepting
things as they are in order to work with them as he can." Thomas
Merton and D. T. Suzuki, *Zen and the Birds of Appetite* (New York:
New Directions, 1968), p. 31. Merton's nearly total disaffection from the
producing/consuming society confirms the direction of my critique.

to shake loose whatever putative connections there may have been between a society so constructed and a "world come of age."

An Alternative Model

In proposing an alternative model for understanding and for understanding oneself, I am clearly espousing Carnap's central contention that whatever is understood is located within a framework. Models are always operating; it is expedient to be as explicit about them as we can be. I do not pretend to a privileged intuition or to the objectivity of an all-embracing framework; I shall simply try to incorporate something of the constructor into the constructing enterprise. In Berger and Luckmann's terms, I shall offer a model that can allow for genuine dialectic, and hence explain growth and development. The secret of a progressive dialectic lies in investing one of the poles with the initiative, acknowledging that it possesses something within itself that can continue to spark the process. The results will be informed by the consequent interaction, but the initiating spark is not the result of anything else. In this manner I shall explicitly introduce the personal, interior dimension that Berger desires but cannot accommodate without necessarily denying the perspicacity of his analysis. His pattern of man-in-society must oppose the individual to that pattern if he is to become an individual.

The image I find most hospitable for man-in-society is that of a pilgrimage: individuals traveling and questing together. No one is in a position to furnish a map, yet an accumulated sense of direction is available. It remains up to us to assimilate it. Hence, this image calls for a sense and appreciation of history. It also involves meaning, significance, and vision as interpretative keys for an environment so distinctive as a pilgrimage.

What distinguishes a pilgrimage or a quest from other more modest journeys is the mythic character of the goal.

A mythic goal announces that we mean to use the image to construe human life itself. To speak of a pilgrimage or quest means to supply an horizon within which other activities can make sense. The image introduces a logical context of meaning and significance. The resulting model is quite able to handle "routine reality-maintenance" situations, like the New Haven commuter train, yet able also to discriminate what is routine from what is critical. A pilgrimage or quest model is able to accommodate both simple feedback and genuinely dialectical exchange, for it cannot itself be reduced to a constructive interaction situation. The mythic goal sees to that: whatever reinforcement there is can never be unambiguously identified. It is the mythic dimension that introduces us into the logical context of meaning, significance, and vision. Hence, the model supplies distinctive categories to interpret human society. It both allows and calls for a dialectic within man-in-society, and it will include a simple reinforcement situation as a variety of interaction — the more common, uncomplicated, and routine type.

Towards the Distinctive Dimension: Interiority

So far I have traded upon the *image* of a pilgrimage, and yet also spoken of it as a *model,* and an appropriately human one. The difficulty with such a model is that it cannot be presented independently of exhibiting it in use. That is the disadvantage of a "distinctively human model": we cannot possess it and use it as an independent tool in understanding a human reality like man-in-society. Now we can see why explanation normally entails reducing something more complex or more subtle to a simpler or more straightforward paradigm. Hence one is tempted to cling to a homeostatic linear feedback model for human social interaction in spite of the unwelcome conclusions and paradoxes that may result. For his explanatory bent is satisfied.[19] By introducing another sort of model, I am

---

19 See Berger's critique of sociologism in *Invitation . . . ,* p. 168.

suggesting that explanation does not exhaust the capacities of understanding nor is it particularly fruitful in some domains. Furthermore, it is possible to provide some illumination of a subject — illumination tantamount to a fruitful and an appropriate understanding — without pretending to furnish an explanation.[20] I shall illustrate this contention and fill out the pilgrimage model by using it to illuminate a projected use of human understanding.

As an example of an overtly constructive use of understanding, consider the shaping of a new course in humanities, the outlining of a research project in biochemistry, the planning of a youth project. Whatever I undertake in this fashion will reflect the human ideals and the goals for understanding that I have internalized. The project itself opens me to a creative interaction with others and with forces of society. That interaction, furthermore, offers occasions for me to discover something about myself: by reflecting on my involvement I am orienting myself, finding bearings for my own journey. Since the stages I have described are recurrent, the reflective moment returns to bear upon the original ideals and goals, and so modifies, and is modified by, further interaction. This process has the makings of a truly dialectical one, for the reflective phase holds promise of initiative — renewed vigor, disillusion, or conversion.

Reflective Judgment

The fact that my interaction can become an occasion for me to discover something about myself also explains

---

[20] This observation shields an involved discussion of explanation and of methodology. The context is that of Wittgenstein and the work inspired by his *Philosophical Investigations*. I can only hope here that the example and the immediate context supply sufficient direction to grasp 'illumination' as an alternative. For a useful and probably unwitting example of this distinction, compare the explanatory remarks of chapter III ("The Anthropological Condition of Religion") with the observations of chapter IV ("The Social Forms of Religion") in Thomas Luckmann, *The Invisible Religion* (New York: Macmillan, 1967). The latter chapter proceeds along the lines we have styled "illuminating" and seems more than a little at variance with the preceding one.

how I am able to judge and make assessments. It explains how I can understand the Berger-Luckmann analysis via plausibility structures, yet also understand that such a description obscures another dimension in the social situations so described. I can understand, reflectively, that some meaning-complexes can be enriching as well as supporting, and can illuminate our shared and individual situation. We *show* that they are illuminating and not simply reinforcing by the way in which we use them. The fact that we may have had a hand in shaping those same patterns for understanding is certainly relevant, but is the less interesting part of the story. Berger and Luckmann conclude their treatise, stating what they have established:

> In the dialectic between nature and the socially constructed world the human organism itself is transformed. In this same dialectic man produces reality and thereby produces himself.[21]

By incorporating a reflective moment (which includes personal stock-taking and assessment) we can enrich the dialectic beyond that of simple interaction. This more creative dialectic both licenses and forces us to speak of man as at once producing and discovering his world and himself.

Judgment and Participation

When I speak of a reflective dimension of understanding, I am normally referring to that capacity I have to catch myself in what I am doing, to move beyond what was said to assess how I said it and what I intended in saying it. It represents my limited capacity for standing, as it were, outside myself to take stock of my own position. Logically, one cannot stand outside of this reflective dimension itself and survey it. Though reflection has recursive properties, one cannot assess reflection, for it rep-

---

21 Berger and Luckmann, *Social Construction*, p. 183.

resents the last bar of judgment to which one has recourse.

This fact does not allow us to hope for a rock-bottom basis. Yet lacking a court of appeals does not render the judgments of this court any less trustworthy. What we must say instead is that if 'trust' means anything, it means learning to live a more simple and spontaneous life of reflection. This is not an over-intellectualized recommendation, for in the dramatic language of Apollo vs. Dionysus, it means allowing oneself to live more closely with one's feelings; on the critical level of treatises on the sociology of knowledge, it means moving from the temptation to describe the world as though I were standing in an independent position, to accepting the lot of conscious participant. Far from removing us from the scene, by allowing us to participate critically, reflection actually helps our participation to become more wholehearted and integral. It seems that the more natural, nonreflective move spontaneously puts distance between us and our world by permitting the illusion that we ourselves are onlookers, standing somewhere else.

How can we arrive at an understanding of where it is we stand? How can we make it available to others? Is there a method? A sensitive auditor will have felt already how difficult it will be to meet these questions. Impossible, in fact, for they are cast after the fashion of pragmatic, problem-solving reason. The initial response, therefore, must prepare us for a new mode of discourse, a new language, a different logic. There is no *method* but there are *ways;* one never "arrives" at such an understanding —namely, of where he stands— as something that he can secure or "tether down." Only when he realizes that fact dare he offer others assistance along the way.

Such remarks are designed to throw us off balance, to intimate that we who thought ourselves on the track to complete understanding and mastery are being profoundly misguided and actually carried away from vast reaches of understanding and from ourselves. We who were as-

sured we had come of age are in fact dangerously imma-
ture in our ignorance of ourselves. What remains is to
map out these reaches as best we can by sketching something of the logic of an alternative language for understanding. Only then will we be prepared to show what
might be said about ritual. Some indication that this
analysis is on the right track may be gathered from the
manner in which we have been led to that precise point
where Socrates took his stand for understanding. That
mad virtuoso of the language of faith, Søren Kierkegaard,
himself avowed that the logic for whatever could be said
about man's intercourse with God would have to be
gleaned from Socrates.

A Complementary Language of "Acceptance"

I have been arguing that Berger and Luckmann have
sold human understanding short by restricting its range
and exercise to the pragmatic role of shaping a world that
reshapes the man who has made it. My criticism questions the power and fertility of their assessment, not the
accuracy of their description. Once one adopts the language of their model, the model spells out his fate. And
since their model skillfully brings into focus that set of
priorities and values which can only be called "the contemporary myth," it is not really a matter of adopting
the language of their model. Such language comes to us
quite naturally. That is, after all, the lesson of the model
itself. It takes insight, what I have called "reflective understanding," to see through to the necessity of another
language — one that will fill out what is wanting to the
language of making, shaping, solving, and in that very
act show it to be wanting. The strategy is not one of replacement but of establishing an essential complementarity, a true dialectic. We have already seen the need for
a complementary language from the antinomies generated
by an achieving idiom — indeed from the very accuracy of
Berger and Luckmann's describing membership in the

collective. It remains to propose the complement as an alternative, and then show how it succeeds in complementing the language of achievement.

The alternative to making over a situation or doing something about it is to accept it or something within it, to give oneself over to it, to yield or surrender. Of course, this can only be described as "compromise" from the thoroughgoing pragmatic model. On the best of interpretations, it can be regarded only as a temporary accommodation or downright ethical temporizing. At this point, however, one can show the model wanting by proposing an alternative reading to "compromise." Dramatically we have Tiresias, the blind seer, who was sent to enlighten the crafty Oedipus — only to be ridiculed. His blind seeing, however, proved more accurate than the king's lightsome wit. Oedipus' strength turned out to be his fatal weakness. And so on, from tragedy to tragedy, so characteristically that Aristotle could formulate the human situation in terms of a "tragic flaw": the studious neglect of an essentially complementary element.

Jung offered the *animus/anima* pattern in an attempt to provide a logic for complementarity — where *animus* corresponds rather directly with understanding as a pragmatic venture, and *anima* insinuates a language of yielding, accepting, receiving. Analogously, freedom entails coming to terms with necessity, as (for example) we can manage to use language creatively only in the measure that we have accepted the rules, even when we choose not to abide by them. Similarly, any decision that engages my person is as much, if not more, a matter of understanding and accepting where it is that I have come as it is stepping out along a new path. What happens to me is simply not what I have achieved; it is something else. To be engaged means to be working in a fashion that respects and reflects what is happening to me. Concern is rooted in consent, as freedom, ironically enough, idles unless it is harnessed to and by necessity.

Language proposals can be argued for, but only indirectly; the available language has no choice but to pretend to completeness. Hence I have tried to show the incompleteness of an achieving idiom and propose that it needs filling out by a language of accepting. But I can only propose; the proposal has to be accepted if we are to experience a complementary language. Yet one's own experiences and values may be so circumscribed by the accepted idiom that he will find himself unable to take up another one. Since argument must be carried out in the going *lingua franca,* it soon comes up against its own limits. Nothing short of a conversion is required: an expansion of the perimeters of one's experience so that it cries for a new language to articulate it.

Coming into Possession of a New Language

It is my conviction that ritual offers a paradigmatic setting within which one can actually *use* this new and complementary language. Before showing that directly, let us recapitulate what we have so far accomplished. By calling attention to the facts of our experience as they are embodied in a language that we find ourselves compelled to use (or shown to be presupposed by a language that we ordinarily use), we have gradually come into possession of a new conception of ourselves and a new conception of what it is to know. In speaking of the "language of acceptance," I have been sketching a logic of interiority, trust, and faith. By speaking of the "language of acceptance" I have been mapping out something of the logical space within which the conceptions of trust and faith can find a place. At this level, what one might call "logical space" is nothing other than experiential space; that is, where experience itself can be appropriately thematized.

It is this language which will allow us to speak of ritual, and it is the experience of ritual that permits us actually to use this language. This is the sense in which logical space amounts to experiential space when one can actually put a language into use. To say that ritual affords us the opportunity to use a language of acceptance, trust, and faith is not to claim that ritual grounds its use in the sense of giving one warrant for using it. Rather, ritual can be said to provide the context within which it is appropriate to speak this language. The progression is from possibility to actuality: we have been able to recognize something of the contours of the language through appreciating the limitations of an achievement idiom. What adds *use* to logic is the experience of ritual — an experience that we may allow ourselves once we appreciate the logical space that it occupies.

To the Personal through the Impersonal

The way in which ritual accomplishes this will inevitably amount to an affront on the making, shaping, problem-solving *ethos*. For ritual involves a script. At the very least, there is a prearranged pattern — if only this be printed for the sake of convenience or good order. Except at the very outer limits of what might properly be called religion, there is a listening for something to be said. In the liturgical tradition of the Christian religion, one must both listen to the Word proclaimed and carry out the eucharistic liturgy according to a pattern established, at least in its essentials.

I have suggested throughout these extended reflections that "modern secular man" is hobbled by a particular conception of himself and of what it is to know, that the world is not quite yet of age, and that something else is needed to lead us to a truly personal, interior world: more specifically something that would help us expand our language to include acceptance and surrender; something that would bring us, through a variety of conceptual frameworks, to a way of understanding where it is that we stand. Ironically, that something seems to be quite impersonal: the way to a language of acceptance and surrender involves more going-along-with than it does an explicit creation (though going-along-with a sufficiently venerable and fruitful tradition inspires and is compatible with a great deal of creativity). The move to a language of acceptance and surrender involves more silence than it does expression, though this silence inspires and is compatible with the most expressive of the arts. What is precisely *not* designed to be a "peak experience" is what comes to engage more and more of us.

Perhaps a way to get at this elementary ingredient in a new conception of oneself and of what it is to know is through the juridical notion of *validity*. The logical space of "validity" is intimately related to that of "ritual." The very notion of validity represents an attempt to say what can be said about ritual, and hence, about man as a religious person — albeit in a juridical form of expression. The form of expression does not claim completeness, yet it is interesting that the only *requirement* of ritual is that it be valid. That is, if something is a ritual, then while it *should* be many things, it *must* be valid. Validity, however, is not a sufficient condition of ritual, and hence does not lead to a comprehensive understanding of it. For ritual is also something fashioned; it is a work of art as well, and this aspect is no less essential to it than its validity. Reckoning with what can be said, taught, passed on, as well as legislated, we have a sense of form — that is, formal correctness as something into which I am to fit — and a feel for continuity over time and unity over space. The last two demands might be seen as analogues for verification in an arena where truth is so elusive.

Hence, to insist that the aspect of validity is essential to ritual in the sense that it is the only thing that is strictly demanded of it — though there be many desiderata — is not to deny that ritual is a work of art and hence a human creation, but rather to insist that it must convey something impersonal. Ritual must stand over against me in some fashion, and yet at the same time, be something into which I can and must fit. I have argued that it is precisely this dual element of standing-over-against and fitting-into which is intimated by a language of acceptance, and which is conspicuously absent from an Apollonian or constructivist picture of man. Ritual both illustrates this dual element and provides the paradigmatic situations within which we can learn a complementary language of acceptance, and hence modify our conception of ourselves as well as our conception of what it is to know. To say this is to say that ritual both demands and makes respectable a language of transcendence.

Beyond the Constraints of Our Constructed World

How can *we* — the creators and the creatures of a "world come of age" — ever engage in ritual? Even to take part in it amounts not merely to a surrender but to a loss of our sophistication, of that very self-awareness which makes for our characteristic "cool." Inevitably, participation in ritual can only be a retrogression for someone who has been taught to look objectively at one thing after another, and to construct according to the model that he finds pleasing. Participation in ritual can only lead backwards to obscurantism. Here we have a contemporary variation on an older theme: Catholicism, with its archaic authority patterns and predilection for an *ancien régime,* could not help but mean a surrender of one's dearly purchased autonomy. The same must be said for *any* religious pattern.

Ironically, it is this last point which suggests how we might participate in ritual. Again the leading notion is the thin, juridical one of *validity.* What this notion reflects is a yearning for objectivity, for groundedness, for something independent of me. Neurotically, this need is expressed in a demand for certitude, and, in its extreme forms, a certitude that is assured (paradoxically) from without. In its more healthy form, I have spoken of a demand for an impersonal dimension to our lives, and we have seen that this provides a foothold for a language of transcendence. The Roman pattern has been to fill this yearning with the *dicta* of some authority, bolstered by juridical theories of succession. The difficulty with this response to a very legitimate need is that the response retains the same ambiguities as the yearning itself. It only makes them all the more obvious because now people are exercising these very ambiguities.

If we can see, however, notions like "duly constituted authority" as serving the more basic demands for unity and continuity over space and time, then we can respect it because we understand it. We understand it because we have come to appreciate what it means to be part of an ongoing tradition through participating in cultic activity. So these three — tradition, authority, and cult — are related in an ordered way, with tradition — as something in which I stand — assuming logical priority and cult the existential priority.

Even *we,* therefore, can engage in ritual worship, in the measure that we see through the pattern for human understanding that restricts it to task forces and problem solving, and allow ourselves to appreciate whence we have come, and so begin to understand where it is we stand. The actual exercise of ritual can gradually teach us how to accept our origins and begin to mine the richness therein *as our own.*

9

Liturgy and Experience

by

ROBERT N. BELLAH

IN ONE OF HIS MOST POWERFUL SONGS, BOB DYLAN ASKS:

> How does it feel, how does it feel
> To be on your own
> With no direction home?[1]

Obviously to most of us in America today it does not feel

[1] Bob Dylan, "Like a Rolling Stone," from "Highway 61 Revisited," Columbia L.P.

Robert N. Bellah serves as Ford Professor of Sociology and Comparative Studies and Chairman of the Center for Japanese and Korean Studies at the University of California at Berkeley. His published works include an essay, "The Dynamics of Worship," in *Multi-Media Worship*, ed. Myron B. Ploy, Jr.; a book, *Beyond Belief: Essays on Religion in a Post-Traditional World;* and an article, "Christianity and Symbolic Realism," in the *Journal for the Scientific Study of Religion*. This paper was originally presented at the annual convention of the Federation of Diocesan Liturgy Commissions in San Francisco, October 1971.

very good. It seems as though, almost without knowing when, we have lost the way. Thomas O'Dea has recently likened our situation to one depicted earlier by Dante, in the opening lines of the Inferno:

> In the middle of the journey of our life
> I came to my senses in a dark forest,
> for I had lost the straight path.[2]

Dante at least knew where home was, even if he felt lost. For him God and Paradise were sure. We do not even know where home is: for us there is literally no direction home. We have an immense nostalgia and longing for home, for being at home, yet our cultural reality is an acute, radical homelessness.

Most Americans have never been at home in this land. This is not only because most of us are immigrants or the descendants of immigrants who have generation after generation continued to wander over the face of this continent, but also because most of the founding fathers believed in some version of that religious tradition of which Dante was an earlier voice. For them this earth was only a temporary abode. They were to be in but not of the world. Their true home was their Father's house, and their Father was in heaven. This earth was simply the location of the long upward climb, the "Pilgrim's Progress," which was to end gloriously in heaven. Gradually, over the course of several centuries, that upward course has become truncated. The heavenly home in which it ends is a split level in suburbia supplied with all the latest electrical equipment. In this transition, hope has become gradually overpowered by fear. One cannot really be at home in a house if one feels physically and morally unsure about one's possession of it, if one needs to purchase guns to defend it. As Max Weber pointed out nearly seventy years ago, the life lived in obedience to the heavenly father when the heavenly father has dis-

---

2 Dante, *The Inferno*, Canto I, lines 1-3.

appeared is an iron cage.[3] And what we can see even more clearly than Weber is that within the iron cage there is an ever accelerating treadmill.

It is the shattering of the myth of the sky home and the deepening disillusionment with the pseudo-home called success which gradually took its place that more than anything has precipitated our present crisis. Secular values first nurtured by the myth of the sky home have wrenched themselves loose and have set our society on a course of uncontrolled acceleration. Wealth and power, when they become ends in themselves, lead inevitably to the destruction of the natural environment, other weaker societies, the less privileged within our own society, and finally and inexorably to the destruction of those most fervently and successfully dedicated to them. As this has become increasingly clear, there has occurred a massive revulsion against these dominant secular values, a convulsive reaction to the attack by those most committed to them, and so the collapse of that great consensus which has for long, though never so totally as the apologists have claimed, characterized American society.

Throughout human history, during those troubled times when the common values were collapsing, there would arise a nostalgia for a former, better time. In the late twentieth century we see that old tendency in a somewhat new form. It has been common for the nostalgia to be directed toward an earlier phase of the same society, or to a purely mythical golden age. What is new is the considerable historical and anthropological resources being utilized in the current nostalgic fantasies. What we see is nothing less than a paleolithic revival, and its hero is the one group of people who ever really felt at home in America, the American Indian.

The young Americans who have made what Thomas

---

3 Max Weber, *The Protestant Ethic and the Spirit of Capitalism*, trans. by Talcott Parsons (New York: Scribners, 1930), p. 181.

4 Thomas O'Dea, "Transformations of Thought in America," *Thought*, XLVI (1971), 339.

O'Dea calls "the great refusal,"[4] that is, the refusal to enter the iron cage, have developed a new earth mysticism.
They want to live with great simplicity and directness, as
the Indians did, in an earth home or, in Gary Snyder's
words, an *Earth House Hold.*[5] Phyllis Beauvais in her
poem "Furniture" has beautifully captured the contrast
between the old and new visions:

> there are youngsters now
> younger than I, moving as nomads
> through the makeshift camping grounds
>
> who do not hope for what was
> expected: the catalog comforts
> of minor success
>
> nor do they imagine
> changelessness, that what they encounter
> remains
>
> whose parents
> in the suburbs, in the small
> midwestern towns
>
> have set down heavy houses on the land
> and filled them
> with a weight of furnishings, and in a manner
> held them down
>
> but not their children: who dreamed of Indians
> tracking.
> and move lightly, from city
> to city
>
> exchanging
> adornments; themselves the only
> shelter they have found[6]

Unlike these young people, most of the American Indians were not nomadic. They found long ago what our
youth are still seeking. They were at home in their land,
in the cosmos, in their bodies. Among the Pueblo Indians,

---

[5] Gary Snyder, *Earth House Hold* (Philadelphia: New Directions,
1969).

[6] Phyllis Beauvais, "Furniture," *New Yorker*, Feb. 3, 1968.

the kiva, the underground ceremonial chamber built into or near every pueblo, was itself a microcosm of the universe. The kiva, according to Frank Waters, "recapitulates in structural form" the "four-world universe"[7] of Pueblo mythology:

> In the floor is a small hole, the *sipapu*, leading down into the first underworld. The floor level is the second world into which man emerged. The raised seating ledge represents the third world. And the ladder rises up to the roof opening, the fourth world to which man has climbed. . . .
>
> In the kiva, man is ever reminded that he lives in the whole of the immense and naked universe. And he is constantly made aware of the psychic, universal harmony which he must help to perpetuate by his ceremonial life.[8]

For the Navaho, who have no kivas, the hogan or ordinary dwelling has the same symbolic meaning as the Pueblo kiva. This is indeed being at home in the world.

In contrast to the traditional American heroic image of the Indian as solitary, self-reliant, and individualistic, the new image is more anthropologically informed, if still in part romantic. It is the Indian in organic harmony with himself, his communal society, and his natural environment. Not only the Indians but all the remnants of primitive and archaic culture, and their survival in the form of heresies and sects in the great civilizations, are celebrated in the new culture. Gary Snyder speaks of "a surfacing (in a specifically 'American' incarnation) of the Great Subculture which goes back as far perhaps as the late Paleolithic."[9] He sees this Great Subculture surviving in such forms as shamanism, witchcraft, Taoism, Tantrism, Sufism, and Gnosticism. Unlike the religions of the sky father, this tradition celebrates Nature as a *mother*. The sky religions emphasize the paternal, hier-

---

7 Frank Waters, *Masked Gods: Navaho and Pueblo Ceremonialism* (New York: Ballantine Books, 1970), p. 170.

8 *Ibid.*

9 Gary Snyder, *Earth House Hold.*

archical, legalistic, and ascetic, whereas the earth tradition emphasizes the maternal, communal, expressive, and joyful aspects of existence. Whereas the sky religions see fathers, teachers, rulers, and gods exercising external control through laws, manipulation, or force, the earth tradition is tuned to cosmic harmonies, vibrations, and astrological influences. Socially the Great Subculture expresses itself not through impersonal bureaucracy or the isolated nuclear family, but through collectives, communes, tribes, and large extended families. The contrast between the old American culture and the new Earth culture could hardly be more striking. Philip Slater has pointed out, however, that the two are not unrelated.[10] Each expresses what the other has repressed. Each has inner enemies on the other side; every American is, in fact, a mixture of both.

The recovery of mythical consciousness, of the archaic world view, is one of the great achievements of modern scholarship. We need not be shocked that it has at last begun to have practical consequences, that the writings of Mircea Eliade are programming the patterns of life in rural hippie communes. Civilization has indeed been based on the repression of a great deal of human experience that is now being liberated. We have much to learn from the surviving primitive and archaic cultures, and it is very late for us to become aware of it. Particularly for us in America, the existence of intact Indian cultures like the Pueblo and the Navaho is an incomparable treasure. This battered remnant of a decimated people may yet provide the saving wisdom that will make possible our renewal.

Yet the simple abandonment of civilization, science, and technology in favor of a new tribalism is not a solution. If we have seen the fatal consequences of the degeneration of sky religions, we cannot afford to overlook how constricting historically the rule of the Earth Mother

---

[10] Philip Slater, *The Pursuit of Loneliness* (Boston: Beacon Press, 1970), ch. I and particularly p. 28.

has often been, and how liberating at an earlier period was the role of the Sky Father. At its best, the earth religion has been an elaborate dance giving expression to all the forces of the universe .and to the role of each person in his society. But all too easily such patterns can harden. The divine cosmos turns out to be only a petty tribelet deifying itself and dominated by old men who oppose every innovation. Or the cosmic forces concentrate themselves in a divine king and the tribe becomes a predatory imperialist state. Our counter-culture has produced its share of despotic gurus and narrow-minded dogmas.

Under these circumstances the being-at-home so characteristic of the earth religions becomes an image not of life but of stagnation and death, and the sky father who calls one to leave home is the liberator. Moses was called to leave Egypt and lead his people to a new and more precarious home. He spent his days in wandering and died in the wilderness. Jesus too was a wanderer. "The birds of the air have their nests, and the foxes of the field their holes; but the son of man has not where to lay his head" (Matt. 8:20). Buddha declared the world to be a burning house and called on his followers to take to the road with only a begging bowl in hand. In Japan to become a monk is to *shukke,* to leave home. In all these cases there is a home, but it is a sky home, Kingdom of Heaven, Western Paradise. The tension between this earth and the sky home generates unease, and often pressure for social change, for the greater realization of values in human society. This is the significance of prophetic religion, the achievements of which we forget at our peril when we reject the modern world too radically.

It is this restless tradition of the sky religion that lies behind the great experiment which is America, and which is still not without vitality. Not all Americans outside the counter-culture are materialistic robots. Many of them still live in the tension between this world and the Kingdom of Heaven. The original intention of the founders of America was that it become a place on this earth

more like the Kingdom of Heaven. America was to be a
city set on a hill, a home for the homeless and oppressed,
a haven for the uprooted and the dispossessed. But prophetic religions have often made rather sharp distinctions between the chosen and the others. The irony is
that this great new home for the homeless was itself based
on a most massive forcible dispossession (of the Indians)
and forcible uprooting (of Negro slaves). The great experiment was tainted with sin from the beginning, and
as we know has always been far from perfect. Even now
it is far from devoid of energies for a new beginning.

*   *   *

That, then, is my initial contrast — between traditional
American Puritan Protestant culture and the contemporary counter-culture, seen as a contrast between a religion of a sky god, heavenly father, lawgiver on the one
hand and the religion of an earth mother, benevolent
and nurturant nature on the other. Catholicism, because
it has kept a wider range of religious experience alive
within its ample precincts, does not fit so neatly on the
first side of the contrast as does Protestantism. It is not
that the moralistic and prophetic side is missing in American Catholicism. The Irish heritage and the American
context have emphasized it and Catholics in America have
on more than one occasion out-puritaned the Protestants
in both the good and the bad senses of that word. And
yet, Catholicism has never been and can never be exclu-
sively moralistic and prophetic. It also embraces in its
own way much of the range of experience I have attributed to the counter-culture. If the cult of Mary does
not worship her as God it at least mediates divinity
through a feminine image, the image of the mother of
God, and so retains a dimension of religious experience
that Protestantism has ruthlessly repressed. Indeed, much
of traditional Catholic piety is redolent of earth religion.
The cult of the saints tends to localize and concretize
religious experience, and the emphasis on sacrament tends

to give material form to spiritual vision. Yet, due to the special historical vicissitudes of the Catholic Church in America — its largely urban setting, the continual movement of the faithful — there is little connection, outside, perhaps, some of the older Spanish-speaking enclaves in the Southwest, between religious life and the American land. American Catholicism is not of the American earth the way Italian, French, or Spanish Catholicism are of the Italian, French, or Spanish earth.

But there is more to be said. Catholicism does not see God only as paternal and morally demanding or as maternal and loving. Catholicism has also seen God, and here too, much more than Protestantism, as reason and truth. Again, perhaps in part because of the difficulty in transporting to America certain other dimensions of Catholic experience, American Catholicism was for a long time intoxicated with philosophical theology, scholasticism, and Thomism. At its lower levels this Catholic intellectualism or rationalism maintained a clarity and control that avoided the excesses of Protestant revivalism with its peculiar mixture of moralism and emotion. At its highest level it transmitted an intellectual vision of God that is surely one of the great authentic moments of religious experience. The American poet Wallace Stevens has magnificently expressed that experience, even though he deliberately uses the past tense:

> There was a heaven once,
> ...   It was
> The Spirit's episcopate, hallowed and high,
> To which the spirit ascended, to increase
> Itself, beyond the utmost increase come
> From youngest day or oldest night and far
> Beyond thought's regulation. There each man,
> Through long cloud-cloister-porches, walked alone,
> Noble within perfecting solitude,
> Like a solitude of the sun, in which the mind
> Acquired transparence and beheld itself
> And beheld the source from which transparence came;

And there he heard the voices that were once
The confusion of men's voices, intricate
Made extricate by meanings, meanings made
Into a music never touched to sound.
There, too, he saw, since he must see, the domes
Of azure round an upper dome, brightest
Because it rose above them all, stippled
By waverings of stars, the joy of day
And its immaculate fire, the middle dome,
The temple of the altar where each man
Beheld the truth and knew it to be true.[11]

Such moments were always rare in America and have become rarer. Catholic rationalism like Protestant biblicism has tended to become mechanical and rigid. For many, in Stevens' image, the black smokestacks of reality have jutted up and torn through the clouds of that particular heaven. The intellectual formulas are like gutted empty houses, offering no protection against the cold wind of contemporary reality, not because they are untrue, but because contemporary Americans cannot discern their meaning.

*   *   *

At the moment, American society seems to be coming apart at the seams, and neither the earth home nor the sky home (of either moral reward or intellectual vision) are very comfortable places in which to dwell. In the midst of the collapse of our common beliefs and our division into ever hardening and more polarized groups, more and more of our people are encountering, as other peoples have before us, what Michael Novak has recently called "the experience of nothingness."[12] In this experience we find that the bottom has dropped out, that in the depth of the earth home and the sky home there is no

---

[11] Wallace Stevens, *Opus Posthumous* (New York: Knopf, 1957), pp. 53-54.
[12] Michael Novak, *The Experience of Nothingness* (New York: Harper and Row, 1970).

home at all, that at the root of every belief there is an absolute doubt, and at the core of every self and every culture there is absolute nothingness. Such a radical and shattering experience is not, however, ultimately an experience of despair. The powerful element of death in it is overcome by the possibility of rebirth. The experience of nothingness exposes man, in some deep and not wholly conscious way, as the creator of his own myths: not only a frightening but also an immensely liberating experience.

The experience of nothingness is of course not new in human history. It is one of the great archetypal religious experiences like the encounter with the earth mother or the sky father. It was perhaps first experienced by a Paleolithic shaman. In any case, it is reported, especially by mystics, in all the great traditions. Novak himself points to Saint John of the Cross and his image of the dark night and the happy night. There is no religion that has meditated more deeply on nothingness and emptiness than has Buddhism, and no culture more influenced by such meditation than the Japanese. When the experience of nothingness first burst upon modern Europe in the nineteenth century it was frightening and shattering, as the word nihilism implies, because there were few resources in the available tradition to help deal with it. Perhaps now in the twentieth century, when the experience becomes ever more commonplace, we can draw on the Japanese tradition to help us cope with it.

The Japanese, especially after the devastating experiences that they underwent in their early middle ages, developed what might be called an art of insecurity. They glorified the fleeting and the transient — the cherry blossoms that quickly fall, the dew that rapidly evaporates — as the truest expressions of the nature of reality. In the culture that Zen Buddhism had much to do with shaping, it was precisely in poverty and loneliness that one might most readily know one's Buddha nature. Among other

things the Japanese developed in the haiku a poetic art
of the utmost brevity devoted precisely to revealing the
ultimate emptiness in the minutiae of everyday life. Just
to give one example appropriate to our theme:

Furusato mo   ima wa karine   wataridori

My old home
Now but a night's lodging;
Birds of passage.

The Japanese, it seems, have gone far to make the no-
home comfortable, or to create a no-home home. This too
is dangerous, for if the experience of nothingness becomes too comfortable it can become constricting and
lose its potential for creativity. Still for us the Japanese
experience is very instructive. In particular we might
explore the suggestion of Kitarō Nishida, Japan's greatest
modern philosopher, who combined the vocabulary of
Zen Buddhism and Western philosophy, that nothingness, *mu,* or absolute nothingness, *zettai-teki mu,* might
be thought of as a place, a topos, or in Japanese, *basho.*
In such a place "the individual lives through dying," that
is, he affirms himself through negating himself.[13]

Of course we have numerous American cultural expressions of the experience of nothingness. In an earlier
generation there was Thomas Wolfe's "You Can't Go
Home Again."[14] One of Bob Dylan's most moving songs,
"Desolation Row,"[15] is an almost pure expression of the
experience of nothingness, and a line from the same song
that I quoted earlier is a beautiful example of the simul-
taneous emptiness and fullness of that experience: "When
you ain't got nothin' you got nothin' to lose,"[16] which in

---

13 Kitarō Nishida, *Fundamental Problems of Philosophy,* trans. by
David A. Dilworth (Tokyo: Sophia University, 1970), p. 9. The original
was written in 1933.

14 Thomas Wolfe, *You Can't Go Home Again* (New York: Harper and
Brothers, 1940).

15 Bob Dylan, "Desolation Row," also on "Highway 61 Revisited."

16 See footnote 1.

turn suggests Shakespeare's line: "And nothing brings me all things."[17]

A number of recent commentators on the American cultural scene have described it as bifurcated, as a culture and a counter-culture, an old culture and a new culture, a house divided, half slave, half free. My distinction between those seeking a sky home and those seeking an earth home is roughly parallel to that of these other commentators. I have also tried to delineate another archetypal religious mode, the experience of nothingness or no-home, which is increasingly affecting Americans on both sides of the cultural divide. But I do not see the third mode as a category on the same level as the other two producing a triple rather than a double division of our national culture. Rather, following Paul Tillich, I would see the experience of nothingness as the dimension of depth in both the others.[18] As such it does not offer simply another degree of fracture, but the possibility, however remote, of reconciliation and rebirth. The experience of nothingness does not involve rejection of the other experiences. Once one has felt the ultimate emptiness of the sky home and the earth home one can still dwell in those houses and with much less danger of stagnation, constriction, arrogance, and pride. Indeed, the experience of the place of absolute nothingness, because it is continuously self-negating, makes it possible to live in many houses, in many mansions. It also makes possible the recovery of twofold vision, the apprehension of old myth in new ways, and the creation of new myth. It may help provide a key to the genuine pluralism which we have sought in America but which so far has always eluded us.

The starting point for a genuine pluralism has to be the realization that the American tradition, the Western tradition, or even the biblical tradition provides insuf-

---

17 William Shakespeare, *Timon of Athens*, Act V, Scene I.
18 Paul Tillich, *Theology of Culture* (New York: Oxford Univ. Press, 1959), ch. I.

ficient resources to meet the desperate problems that beset us. Rich as those traditions are and much as we still need to study them, if we cling obstinately to them alone we will be guilty of a narrow and probably ultimately self-destructive parochialism. We must be able to embrace the experience of the rootedness of the American Indians, the uprootedness of the Blacks, the emptiness of the Asians, not out of some charitable benevolence but because our own traditions are simply not enough. Cultural defensiveness will be fatal. If we are to survive on this earth, we must embrace the entire human tradition, make all of it, potentially at least, available to our imagination.

Because of the absolutism that is so much a part of Western philosophical and religious thought, what I have just said may conjure up some notion of what is usually called syncretism: some fluid pudding in which all of the world's religions and cultures will lose their integrity in the general swill. But it is precisely the experience of nothingness that can allow us to expand our cultural horizons indefinitely without losing the integrity of the several visions. Let me turn to the words of Herbert Fingarette to help explain how this can be. He says:

> It is the special fate of modern man that he has a "choice" of spiritual visions. The paradox is that although each requires complete commitment for complete viability, we can today generate a context in which we see that no one of them is the sole vision. Thus we must learn to be naive but undogmatic. That is, we must take the vision as it comes and trust ourselves to it, naively, as reality. Yet we must retain an openness to experience such that the dark shadows deep within one vision are the mute stubborn messengers waiting to lead us to a new light and a new vision.[19]

Those dark shadows within every vision are precisely the emptiness and the nothingness of which I have spoken. They deprive every vision of its absoluteness, though not

<hr>

[19] Herbert Fingarette, *The Self in Transformation* (New York: Harper and Row, 1963), p. 236.

of its integrity. Fingarette uses our central motif, home and being-at-home, to shed light on this aspect of the problem as well:

> We must not ignore the fact that in the last analysis, commitment to a specific orientation outweighs catholicity of imagery. One may be a sensitive and seasoned traveler, at ease in many places, but one must have a home. Still, we can be intimate with those we visit, and while we may be only travelers and guests in some domains, there are our hosts who are truly at home. Home is always home for someone; but there is no Absolute Home in general.[20]

There is no Absolute Home. Once again we see that in the depths of every home is its own provisionality, its own emptiness, its own no-home.

*   *   *

Our condition, then, is homelessness, or to vary the metaphor, landlessness. "But," as Melville said, "as in landlessness alone rests highest truth, shoreless, indefinite as God — so better is it to perish in that howling infinite, than be ingloriously dashed upon the lee, even if that were safety!"[21] Landlessness is a condition of being "at sea," and that indeed is where we are, and in a rising storm. But it is a condition that, though it contains despair, invites celebration, as in Hart Crane's prayer in direct response to Melville:

> Bind us in time, O Seasons clear, and awe.
> O minstrel galleons of Carib fire,
> Bequeath us to no earthly shore until
> Is answered in the vortex of our grave
> The seal's wide spindrift gaze toward paradise.[22]

If we would be true to our present condition, then, to

---

20 *Ibid.*, p. 237.
21 Herman Melville, *Moby Dick*, ch. 23.
22 Hart Crane, "Voyages, II," *The Complete Poems and Selected Letters and Prose* (New York: Liveright, 1966), p. 36.

the dark and shoreless depths that we are in, the place
to start — for most of us the only place we can start — is
mutely, with gesture, motion, and dance, with liturgy and
sacrament. In our moral confusion and our intellectual
doubt perhaps the ordering of gesture — of the most ele-
mental gestures, kneeling, eating, drinking, touching — is
all that we are capable of. There is a natural movement
from liturgy, which is communion, to brotherhood, to
caring and curing, to social concern, though for most of
us social ideology has sagged and collapsed as utterly as
theology. Being men, we must speak, and speech is first
of all praise — praise for all that is given, and praise for
all that we see through what is given. And then, tentatively, speech about brothers, speech about community.
Intellectual speech about ultimate things comes last — is
now in abeyance and must wait until we have a fuller
and less fragmentary imaginative vision.

And if our need now is gesture and sacrament and the
community of shared gesture and sacrament because
those are the only things that seem to translate reality in
an otherwise rimless sea, then the Catholic tradition
among us in America has a peculiarly important role to
play.

Guard the real presence! Do not let the Eucharist sink
into memory and commemoration as the Protestants have
done. I do not mean guard theories about the real presence, transubstantiation or whatever, for the real presence
is not a theory — it is an experienced, present spiritual
reality. That is its power for us. Of course, regardless of
theory, it may be, and I am sure in some places even in
the Catholic Church is, transmitted as a memory of
something that used to be real, that was experienced once
by someone else. Emerson condemned the Protestantism
of his day when he said in his famous Harvard Divinity
School address, "Miracles, prophecy, poetry, the ideal
life, the holy life, exist in ancient history merely, they are
not in the belief, not in the aspiration of society."[23] The

---

23 Ralph W. Emerson, "An Address delivered before the Senior Class

present reality of spiritual experience, first of all in the sacraments, is something that Catholics have to transmit to Protestants and to all men. As the Catholic Church moves toward larger freedom, becomes in many ways more Protestant, I hope it will not allow the immediacy of spiritual life, of sacramental life, to fade, as Protestants have.

I am suggesting that the immediacy of the sacramental life needs to be, not entirely or forever, but tentatively and for a time, cast adrift from theology. The interplay between reason and experience is part of any healthy religion. But for too long the disembodied intellect, Protestant literalism or Catholic rationalism, has tyrannized over experience. Theology is a servant of a totally embodied religious experience and religious vision; it is not its master. The great symbols of the Eucharist cannot be finally captured in any theology. Their inexhaustible depth of meaning can be explained in different and even contradictory ways by a variety of theologies without their own inward vitality being affected.

At the moment we need not so much an overall abstract explanation as to hear what the symbols — the bread and the wine, the fraction and the communion, the stone and the water — are saying. We need to let them speak and we need to listen. In our technological age we have been too concerned with the technique of liturgy, with its manipulation, rather than with listening and contemplation.

The Eucharist can, if we let it, speak to our condition, as the Quakers used to say, with peculiar appropriateness, for it makes no assertion except out of negation and it sees no wholeness except out of annihilation. It is the supreme ritual expression of brokenness and death, of homelessness and landlessness. It consecrates all the good things of the earth and it promises renewal and rebirth

in Divinity College, Cambridge, Sunday evening, July 15, 1838," *The Prose Works of Ralph Waldo Emerson* (Boston: Fields, Osgood, 1870), I, 69.

not only for the individual but for society and the cosmos. And yet it makes us restless on this earth: it makes us see the conditional, and provisional, and broken quality of all things human. If it is working as we hope it is working, it makes us feel a oneness with the brokenness of our brothers — Christians in whatever sense — or not Christian at all. The glimpse we have of a regenerated mankind, one body, the branches of one vine, gives us courage to undertake the healing action that the one whose life and death and resurrection we reenact began. I say glimpse, though there are moments, after receiving the sacrament, when we experience Crane's "wide spindrift gaze toward paradise." Or if I may express my meaning with another passage from Hart Crane that combines magnificence of language with the tentativeness that is so characteristic of our present hour:

> Then in the circuit calm of one vast coil,
> Its lashings charmed and malice reconciled,
> Frosted eyes there were that lifted altars;
> And silent answers crept across the stars.[24]

---

[24] Hart Crane, "At Melville's Tomb," *The Complete Poems*, p. 34.

Bibliography

Ambrose, J. A. "Ritualization in the Human Infant-Mother Bond." *Philosophical Transactions of the Royal Society of London*, Series B, No. 772, Vol. CCLI (1966), pp. 359-362.

Anderson, A. R. *Alexander's Gate, Gog and Magog and the Inclosed Nations*. Cambridge: The Medieval Academy of America, 1932.

Ardrey, Robert. *African Genesis*. New York: Dell Publishing Company, 1961.

———. *The Territorial Imperative*. New York: Dell Publishing Company, 1966.

Bachelard, G. *La Poétique de l'Espace*. Paris: Presses Universitaires de France, 1957.

Barlach, Ernst. *The Transformations of God. Seven Woodcuts*. Trans. by Naomi Jackson Graves. Hamburg: Christians, 1962.

Bateson, Gregory, et al. "Toward a Theory of Schizophrenia." *Behavioral Science*, I (1956), 251-264.

Bateson, Mary Catherine. *Our Own Metaphor*. New York: Alfred A. Knopf, 1972.

Beauvais, Phyllis. "Furniture." *New Yorker*, Feb. 3, 1968.

Beidelman, Thomas O. "Swazi Royal Ritual." *Africa*, XXXII (1966), 373-405.

———. "Some Nuer Notions of Nakedness, Nudity and Sexuality." *Africa*, XXXVIII (1968), 113-132.

Benedict, Ruth. *Patterns of Culture*. Boston: Houghton-Mifflin and Company, 1934.

Berenson, Bernard. *Sunset and Twilight*. New York: Harcourt, Brace and World, 1963.

Berger, Peter. *The Noise of Solemn Assemblies*. New York: Doubleday and Company, 1961.

———. *The Precarious Vision*. New York: Doubleday and Company, 1961.

———. *Invitation to Sociology*. New York: Doubleday and Company, 1963.

————. *The Human Shape of Work*. New York: Macmillan, 1964.

————. *The Sacred Canopy*. New York: Doubleday and Company, 1967.

————. *Marxism and Sociology*. New York: Appleton-Century-Crofts, 1969.

————. *A Rumor of Angels*. New York: Doubleday and Company, 1969.

————, and Luckmann, Thomas. *The Social Construction of Reality*. New York: Doubleday and Company, 1966.

————, and Neuhaus, R. J. *Movement and Revolution*. New York: Doubleday and Company, 1970.

Bergson, Henri. *Les Deux Sources de la Morale et de la Religion*. Paris: Alcan, 1932.

Bernstein, B.; Elvin, H. L.; and Peters, R. S. "Ritual in Education." *Philosophical Transactions of the Royal Society of London*, Series B, No. 772, Vol. CCLI (1966), pp. 429-436.

Bieler, Ludwig. *Ireland, Harbinger of the Middle Ages*. London-New York: Oxford University Press, 1963.

Blackham, H. J. "Ideological Aspects: A Revaluation of Ritual." *Philosophical Transactions of the Royal Society of London*, Series B, No. 772, Vol. CCLI (1966), pp. 443-446.

Boas, George. *Essays on Primitivism and Related Ideas in the Middle Ages*. Baltimore: Johns Hopkins Press, 1948.

Bohannan, Paul. "Extra-Processual Events in Tiv Political Institutions." *American Anthropologist*, LX (1958), 1-12.

Bouyer, Louis. *Rite and Man*. Trans. by M. J. Costelloe. Notre Dame: University of Notre Dame Press, 1963.

Bowra, Maurice. "Dance, Drama and the Spoken Word." *Philosophical Transactions of the Royal Society of London*, Series B, No. 772, Vol. CCLI (1966), pp. 387-392.

Braestrup, F. "Social and Communal Display." *Philosophical Transactions of the Royal Society of London*, Series B, No. 772, Vol. CCLI (1966), pp. 375-386.

Brearley, Molly. "Play in Childhood." *Philosophical Transactions of the Royal Society of London*, Series B, No. 772, Vol. CCLI (1966), pp. 321-326.

Brown, Norman O. *Life Against Death*. Middletown, Conn.: Wesleyan University Press, 1959.

Burridge, Kenelm. *Mambu*. London: Methuen, 1960.

————. *New Heaven, New Earth: A Study of Millenarian Activities*. Oxford: Basil Blackwell, 1969.

Butler, E. M. *Ritual Magic*. New York: Noonday Press, 1949.

Calder, P. R. "Ritualization in International Relations." *Philosophical Transactions of the Royal Society of London*, Series B, No. 772, Vol. CCLI (1966), pp. 451-456.

Carnap, Rudolf. *Logical Structure of the World*. Trans. by Rolf A. George. Berkeley: University of California Press, 1967.

Carstairs, G. M. "Ritualization of Roles in Sickness and Healing." *Philo-

sophical Transactions of the Royal Society of London, Series B, No. 772, Vol. CCLI (1966), pp. 305-310.

Cassirer, E. *An Essay on Man.* New Haven: Yale University Press, 1944.

Chesterton, Gilbert Keith. *Orthodoxy.* London: John Lane, 1908.

Coats, G. W. *Rebellion in the Wilderness: The Murmuring Motif in the Wilderness Traditions of the Old Testament.* Nashville: Abingdon Press, 1968.

Crane, Hart. "Voyages, II." *The Complete Poems and Selected Letters and Prose.* New York: Liveright Publishing Corporation, 1966.

Cross, F. M., Jr. "The Divine Warrior in Israel's Early Cult." *Biblical Motifs.* Ed. by A. Altmann. Cambridge: Harvard University Press, 1966.

Cullen, J. M. "Reduction of Ambiguity through Ritualization." *Philosophical Transactions of the Royal Society of London,* Series B, No. 772, Vol. CCLi (1966), pp. 363-374.

Des Maizeaux, P., trans. *The Works of Monsieur de Saint-Évremond Made English from the French Original.* London, 1714.

Douglas, Mary. *Purity and Danger.* New York: Praeger, 1966.

———. *Natural Symbols: Explorations in Cosmology.* New York: Pantheon, 1970.

Duggan, Sister Eileen May. *New Zealand Poems.* New York: Macmillan, 1940.

Dumont, Louis. *Homo Hierarchicus: An Essay on the Caste System.* Chicago: University of Chicago Press, 1970.

Dunne, John. *The City of the Gods.* New York: Macmillan, 1965.

Durkheim, Emile. *The Elementary Forms of the Religious Life.* Trans. by J. W. Swain. New York: Free Press, 1965 (1915).

———, and Mauss, Marcel. *Primitive Classification.* Trans. by R. Needham. Chicago: University of Chicago Press, 1963 (1903).

Eissfeldt, Otto. "Gott und das Meer in der Bibel." *Studia Orientalia Ioanni Pedersen.* Copenhagen: Munksgaard, 1953.

Eliade, Mircea. *Birth and Rebirth: The Religious Meanings of Initiation in Human Culture.* Trans. by W. R. Trask. New York: Harper and Row, 1958.

———. *Yoga: Immortality or Freedom.* Trans. by W. R. Trask. New York: Pantheon, 1958.

———. *Cosmos and History: The Myth of the Eternal Return.* Trans. by W. R. Trask. New York: Harper and Row, 1959.

———. *Myths, Dreams and Mysteries.* Trans. by Philip Mairet. London: Harvill Press, 1960.

———. *Images and Symbols.* Trans. by Philip Mairet. New York: Sheed and Ward, 1961.

———. *The Sacred and the Profane.* Trans. by W. R. Trask. New York: Harper and Row, 1961.

————. *The Forge and the Crucible.* Trans. by S. Corrin. New York: Harper and Row, 1962.

————. *Myth and Reality.* Trans. by W. R. Trask. New York: Harper and Row, 1963.

————. *Patterns in Comparative Religion.* Trans. by Rosemary Sheed. Cleveland: World Publishing Company, 1963.

————. *Shamanism: Archaic Techniques of Ecstasy.* Trans. by W. R. Trask. New York: Pantheon, 1964.

————. *Mephistopheles and the Androgyne.* Trans. by J. M. Cohen. New York: Sheed and Ward, 1965.

————. *Rites and Symbols of Initiation.* Translated by W. R. Trask. New York: Harper and Row, 1965.

————. *Cultural Fantasies and History of Religions.* Middletown, Conn.: Center for Advanced Studies, Wesleyan University, 1967.

————. *From Primitives to Zen. A Thematic Sourcebook of the History of Religions.* New York: Harper and Row, 1967.

————. *The Quest: History and Meaning in Religion.* Chicago: University of Chicago Press, 1969.

————. *Two Tales of the Occult.* Trans. by W. A. Coates. New York: Herder and Herder, 1970.

————, and Kitagawa, Joseph, eds. *The History of Religions: Essays in Methodology.* Chicago: University of Chicago Press, 1959.

Emerson, Ralph W. "An Address delivered before the Senior Class in Divinity College, Cambridge, Sunday evening, July 15, 1838." *The Prose Works of Ralph Waldo Emerson.* Vol. I. Boston: Fields, Osgood and Company, 1870.

Erikson, Eric H. "Ontogeny of Ritualization in Man." *Philosophical Transactions of the Royal Society of London,* Series B, No. 772, Vol. CCLI (1966), pp. 337-350.

————. "A Discussion on Ritualization of Behavior in Animals and Man." "Concluding Remarks." *Philosophical Transactions of the Royal Society of London,* Series B, No. 772, Vol. CCLI (1966), pp. 523-526.

Evans-Pritchard, E. E. *Witchcraft, Oracles and Magic Among the Azande.* Oxford: Clarendon Press, 1937.

————. "The Nuer Concept of Spirit in Its Relation to the Social Order." *American Anthropologist,* LV (1953), 201-214.

————. "A Problem of Nuer Religious Thought." *Sociologus,* IV (1954), 23-41.

————. *Nuer Religion.* Oxford: Clarendon Press, 1956.

————. *Theories of Primitive Religion.* Oxford: Clarendon Press, 1965.

————, and Fortes, Myer. *African Political Systems.* Oxford: H. Milford, 1940.

Fingarette, Herbert. *The Self in Transformation.* New York: Harper and Row, 1963.

Firth, R. *Primitive Economics of the New Zealand Maori.* New York: E. P. Dutton, 1929.

————. *Primitive Polynesian Economy.* London: G. Routledge, 1939.

Fisher, Loren R. "Creation at Ugarit and in the Old Testament." *Vetus Testamentum,* XV (1965), 313-324.

Fletcher, A. C. "The Hako: A Pawnee Ceremony." *Twenty-Second Annual Report of the Bureau of American Ethnology.* Washington, D.C.

Fontenrose, Joseph E. *The Ritual Theory of Myth.* Berkeley: University of California Press, 1966.

Fortes, Myer. "Religious Premises and. Logical Technique in Divinatory Ritual." *Philosophical Transactions of the Royal Society of London,* Series B, No. 772, Vol. CCLI (1966), pp. 409-422.

Foss, Martin. *Abstraktion und Wirklichkeit.* Bern, 1959.

Geertz, Clifford. "Ethos, World-View and the Analysis of Sacred Symbols." *Antioch Review,* XVII (1957-58), 421-437.

————. "Religion as a Cultural System." *Anthropological Approaches to the Study of Religion.* Ed. by M. Banton. London: Tavistock, 1966.

Geiselmann, Joseph R. *The Meaning of Tradition.* Trans. by W. J. O'Hara. New York: Herder and Herder, 1966.

Gennep, Arnold van. *The Rites of Passage.* Trans. by M. B. Vizedom and G. L. Caffee. Chicago: University of Chicago Press, 1960 (1909).

Gluckman, Max. "Les Rites de Passage." *Essays on the Ritual of Social Relations.* Ed. by Max Gluckman and C. D. Forde. Manchester: Manchester University Press, 1962, pp. 1-52.

Goffman, Erving. *The Presentation of Self in Everyday Life.* New York: Doubleday and Company, 1959.

————. *Asylums: Essays on the Social Situation of Mental Patients and Other Inmates.* New York: Doubleday and Company, 1961.

————. *Behavior in Public Places: Notes on the Social Organization of Gatherings.* New York: Macmillan, 1963.

————. *Stigma: Notes on the Management of Spoiled Identity.* Englewood Cliffs: Prentice-Hall, 1963.

————. *Interaction Ritual: Essays on Face-to-Face Behavior.* New York: Doubleday and Company, 1967.

————. *Strategic Interaction.* Philadelphia: University of Pennsylvania Press, 1969.

Gombrich, W. H. "Ritualized Gesture and Expression in Art." *Philosophical Transactions of the Royal Society of London,* Series B, No. 772, Vol. CCLI (1966), pp. 393-402.

Gunkel, H. *Schöpfung und Chaos in Urzeit und Endzeit.* Göttingen, 1895.

Haldar, A. *The Notion of the Desert in Sumero-Accadian and West Semitic Religions.* Uppsala: A. B. Lundequistska Bokhandeln, 1950.

Hamilton, William, and Altizer, T. J. J. *Radical Theology and the Death of God.* Indianapolis: Bobbs-Merrill, 1966.

Hammarskjöld, Dag. *Markings.* Trans. by Leif Sjoberg and W. H. Auden. New York: Alfred A. Knopf, 1964.

Hazard, P. *The European Mind* (1680-1715). Trans. by J. L. May. London: Hollis and Carter, 1953.

Heidel, A. *The Gilgamesh Epic and Old Testament Parallels.* 2nd ed. Chicago: University of Chicago Press, 1949.

———. *The Babylonian Genesis.* 2nd ed. Chicago: University of Chicago Press, 1951.

Horton, Robin. "Ritual Man in Africa." *Africa,* XXXIV (1964), 85-104.

Huxley, Julian. "A Discussion on Ritualization of Behavior in Animals and Man." "Introduction." *Philosophical Transactions of the Royal Society of London,* Series B, No. 772, Vol. CCLI (1966), pp. 249-273.

Jacobsen, T. "Mesopotamia: The Good Life." *Before Philosophy.* Ed. by Henri Frankfort. Baltimore: Penguin Books, 1949.

———. "The Epic of Gilgamesh." *Report of the 1965-1966 Seminar on Religions in Antiquity.* Ed. by J. Neusner. Hanover: Dartmouth College Comparative Studies Center, 1966.

Jonas, H. *The Gnostic Religion.* 3rd ed. Boston: Beacon Press, 1963.

Joyce, James. *Ulysses.* New York: Random House, 1934.

Jung, Carl G. *Psychological Types.* Trans. by H. G. Baynes. New York: Harcourt, Brace and Company, 1926.

Jungmann, Joseph. *The Sacrifice of the Church.* Trans. by Clifford Howell. Collegeville, Minn.: Liturgical Press, 1956.

Kaiser, O. *Die mythische Bedeutung des Meeres in Aegypten, Ugarit und Israel.* 2nd ed. Berlin: Töpelmann, 1962.

Keen, Sam. "Manifesto for a Dionysian Theology." *Cross Currents,* XIX (1969), 37-54.

Kramer, Samuel N. *Sumerian Mythology.* 2nd ed. New York: Harper and Row, 1961.

Laing, R. D. "Ritualization and Abnormal Behavior." *Philosophical Transactions of the Royal Society of London,* Series B, No. 772, Vol. CCLI (1966), pp. 331-336.

Langer, Susanne K. *Philosophy in a New Key.* 4th ed. Cambridge: Harvard University Press, 1960.

Leach, Edmund. "The Epistemological Background to Malinowski's Empiricism." *Man and Culture.* Ed. by R. W. Firth. London: Routledge and Kegan Paul, 1957, pp. 119-137.

———. "Golden Bough or Gilded Twig?", *Daedalus,* XC (1961), 371-381.

———. *Pul Eliya: A Study of Land Tenure and Kinship.* Cambridge: Cambridge University Press, 1961.

——. "Frazer and Malinowski: On the Founding Fathers." *Encounter,* XXV (1965), 24-36.

——. *Political Systems of Highland Burma: A Study of Kachin Social Structure.* Boston: Beacon Press, 1965 (1954).

——. "Ritualization in Man in Relation to Conceptual and Social Development." *Philosophical Transactions of the Royal Society of London,* Series B, No. 772; Vol. CCLI (1966), pp. 403-408.

——. "Ritual." *International Encyclopedia of the Social Sciences.* Ed. by D. Sills. New York: Macmillan, 1968, pp. 520-526.

Le Corbusier (Charles Edouard Jeanneret-Gris). *The Chapel at Ronchamp.* New York: Praeger, 1957.

Leguin, Ursula K. *The Left Hand of Darkness.* New York: Ace Books, 1969.

Lévi-Strauss, Claude. "Do Dual Oranizations Exist?", *Structural Anthropology.* Trans. by C. Jacobsen and B. G. Schoepf. New York: Basic Books, 1963 (1956).

——. *Totemism.* Trans. by R. Needham. Boston: Beacon Press, 1963.

——. *Structural Anthropology.* Trans. by C. Jacobsen and B. G. Schoepf. New York: Basic Books, 1963 (1956).

——. *Tristes Tropiques.* Trans. by J. Russell. New York: Atheneum, 1964.

——. *Du Miel Aux Cendres.* Paris: Plon, 1966.

——. *The Savage Mind.* Trans. by G. Weidenfeld and Nicholson, Ltd. Chicago: University of Chicago Press, 1968.

——. *L'Origine des Manières de Table.* Paris: Plon, 1968.

——. *The Elementary Structures of Kinship.* Trans. by J. H. Bell, J. R. von Sturmer, and R. Needham. Boston: Beacon Press, 1969.

——. *The Raw and the Cooked.* Trans. by John and Doreen Weightman. New York: Harper and Row, 1969.

Lidzbarski, M. Ginza: *Der Schatz oder Das Grosse Buch der Mandäer.* Göttingen: Vandenhoeck und Ruprecht, 1925.

Lorenz, Konrad Z. "Evolution of Ritualization in the Biological and Cultural Spheres." *Philosophical Transactions of the Royal Society of London,* Series B, No. 772, Vol. CCLI (1966), pp. 273-285.

Lovejoy, A. O., and Boas, G. *Primitivism and Related Ideas in Antiquity.* Baltimore: Johns Hopkins Press, 1935.

Luckmann, Thomas. *The Invisible Religion.* New York: Macmillan, 1967.

Malinowski, Bronislaw. *Argonauts of the Western Pacific.* London: G. Routledge and Sons, 1922.

Marcuse, Herbert. *Eros and Civilization.* Boston: Beacon Press, 1955.

Mauss, M. "Essai sur le Don: Forme et Raison de l'Echange dans les Sociétés Archaïques." *L'Année Sociologique,* I (1925), 30-186.

——. *The Gift, Form and Functions of Exchange in Archaic Societies.* Trans. by I. Cunnison. Glencoe: Free Press, 1954.

Mead, Margaret. *Growing Up in New Guinea: A Comparative Study of Primitive Education.* New York: Blue Ribbon Books, 1930.

———. *Coming of Age in Samoa.* New York: Morrow and Company, 1932 (1928).

———. *From the South Seas: Studies of Adolescence and Sex in Primitive Societies.* New York: Morrow and Company, 1939.

———. *And Keep Your Powder Dry.* New York: Morrow and Company, 1942.

———. *Male and Female: A Study of the Sexes in a Changing World.* New York: Morrow and Company, 1949.

———. *The School in American Culture.* Cambridge: Harvard University Press, 1951.

———. *Soviet Attitudes Toward Authority: An Inter-Disciplinary Approach to Problems of Soviet Character.* New York: McGraw-Hill Book Company, 1951.

———. *Childhood in Contemporary Cultures.* Chicago: University of Chicago Press, 1955.

———. *New Lives for Old: Cultural Transformation.* New York: Morrow and Company, 1956.

———. *An Anthropologist at Work: The Writings of Ruth Benedict.* Boston: Houghton-Mifflin, 1959.

———. *The Golden Age of American Anthropology.* New York: G. Braziller, 1960.

———, ed. *Cooperation and Competition among Primitive Peoples.* Boston: Beacon Press, 1961.

———. *Anthropology, A Human Science.* Princeton: Van Nostrand, 1964.

———. *Continuity in Cultural Evolution.* New Haven: Yale University Press, 1964.

———. *The Changing Culture of an Indian Tribe.* New York: Capricorn Books, 1966.

———. *Culture and Commitment: A Study of the Generation Gap.* Garden City: Natural History Press, 1970.

———, and Bateson, G. *Balinese Character.* New York: Academy of Sciences, 1942.

———, and Metraux, Rhoda. *The Study of Culture at a Distance.* Chicago: University of Chicago Press, 1953.

———, and ———. *Themes in French Culture.* Stanford: Stanford University Press, 1954.

———, and Calas, Nicolas, eds. *Primitive Heritage: An Anthropological Anthology.* New York: Random House, 1953.

———, and Heyman, Ken. *Family.* New York: Macmillan, 1965.

Melville, Herman. *Moby Dick.*

Merton, Thomas. *The Sign of Jonas.* New York: Harcourt, Brace and Company, 1953.

——, and Suzuki, D. T. *Zen and the Birds of Appetite*. New York: New Directions, 1968.

Michaelsen, K. "Ambience." *Studia Neophilologica*, XII (1939-40), 91-119.

Middleton, John and Winter, E. .H., eds. *Witchcraft and Sorcery in East Africa*. New York: Praeger, 1963.

Morris, Desmond. "The Rigidification of Behavior." *Philosophical Transactions of the Royal Society of London*, Series B, No. 772, Vol. CCLI (1966), pp. 327-330.

Needham, Rodney. "Blood, Thunder and the Mockery of Animals." *Sociologus*, XIV (1964), 136-149.

Nishida, Kitarō. *Fundamental Problems of Philosophy*. Trans. by David A. Dilworth. Tokoyo: Sophia University, 1970 (1933).

Nizer, Louis. *The Jury Returns*. Garden City: Doubleday and Company, 1966.

Novak, Michael. *The Experience of Nothingness*. New York: Harper and Row, 1970.

O'Dea, Thomas F. *The Sociology of Religion*. Englewood Cliffs: Prentice-Hall, 1966.

——. "Transformations of Thought in America." *Thought*, XLVI (1971), 339.

Orwell, George. *Keep the Aspidistra Flying*. London: Secker and Warburg, 1954.

——. *Nineteen Eighty-Four*. New York: Harcourt, Brace and Company, 1949.

Otterlo, A. R. van. *De Ringcompositie als opbouwprincipe in de Epische Gedichten van Homerus*. Amsterdam, 1948.

Paterson, T. T. "Emotive Rituals in Industrial Organisms." *Philosophical Transactions of the Royal Society of London*, Series B, No. 772, Vol. CCLI (1966), pp. 437-442.

Pax, W. "Sprachvergleichende Untersuchüngen zur Etymologie des Wortes 'Amphipolos.'" *Wörter und Sachen*, XVIII (1937), 1-88.

Pedersen, Johannes. *Israel: Its Life and Culture*. London-Copenhagen, 1926.

Penner, H. "Bedeutung und Probleme der religiösen Symbolik bei Tillich und Eliade." *Antaios*, IX (1967), 127-143.

Pieper, Joseph. *In Tune with the World: A Theory of Festivity*. Trans. by Richard and Clara Winston. New York: Harcourt, Brace and World, 1965.

——. *Leisure, The Basis of Culture*. Trans. by A. Dru. New York: New American Library, 1963.

Pope, M. *Job*. Garden City: Doubleday, 1965.

Poulet, G. *The Interior Distance*. Trans. by E. Coleman. Baltimore: Johns Hopkins Press, 1959.

Preisendanz, K. *Papyri Graecae Magicae. Die griechischen Zauberpapyri.* Leipzig-Berlin: G. Teubner, 1928.

Radcliffe-Brown, A. R. *The Andaman Islanders.* Glencoe: Free Press, 1964 (1922).

Rahner, Hugo. *Greek Myths and Christian Mysteries.* Trans. by Brian Battershaw. New York: Harper and Row, 1963.

———. *Man at Play.* Trans. by Brian Battershaw and Edward Quinn. London: Burns and Oates, 1965.

Riese, A. *Die Idealisierung der Naturvölker des Nordens in der griechischen und römischen Literatur.* Heidelberg: G. Weiss, 1875.

Robertson-Smith, W. *The Religion of the Semites.* London: A. and C. Black, 1894.

Rostovtzeff, M. *Social and Economic History of the Roman Empire.* Oxford: Clarendon Press, 1926.

Sawyer, F. J. A. "Spaciousness: An Important Feature of Language about Salvation in the Old Testament." *Annual of the Swedish Theological Institute,* VI (1968), 20-34.

Schwarz, R. *The Church Incarnate.* Trans. by Cynthia Harris. Chicago: Henry Regnery, 1958.

Shelley, Percy Bysshe. "Ozymandias." *The Complete Poetical Works of Percy Bysshe Shelley.* Ed. by George Edward Woodberry. New York: Houghton-Mifflin, 1901.

Shils, E. "Ritual and Crisis." *Philosophical Transactions of the Royal Society of London,* Series B, No. 772, Vol. CCLI (1966), pp. 447-450.

Slater, Philip. *The Pursuit of Loneliness.* Boston: Beacon Press, 1970.

Smith, Jonathan Z. "Birth Upside Down or Right Side Up?" *History of Religions,* IX (1970), 281-303.

———. "Earth and God." *Journal of Religion,* XLIX (1969), 103-127.

Snyder, Gary. *Earth House Hold.* Philadelphia: New Directions, 1969.

Sommer, Robert. *Personal Space: The Behavioral Basis of Design.* Englewood Cliffs: Prentice-Hall, 1969.

Spitzer, Leo. "Milieu and Ambience: An Essay in Historical Semantics." *Philosophy and Phenomenological Research,* III (1942-43), 1-42, 169-218.

Steiner, Franz. *Taboo.* New York: Philosophical Library, 1956.

Stevens, Wallace. *Opus Posthumous.* New York: Alfred A. Knopf, 1957.

Swartz, M., Turner, V., and Tuden, A., eds. *Political Anthropology.* Chicago: Aldine Publishing Company, 1966.

Talmon, S. "The 'Desert Motif' in the Bible and in Qumran Literature." *Biblical Motifs.* Ed. by A. Altmann. Cambridge: Harvard University Press, 1963, pp. 31-63.

Ternois, Rene, ed. *Saint-Évremond: Oeuvres en prose.* Vol. III. Paris: M. Didier, 1966.

Thompson, R. Campbell. *Semitic Magic: Its Origins and Development*. London: Luzac, 1908.

Thorpe, W. H. "Ritualization in Ontogeny. I. Animal Play." *Philosophical Transactions of the Royal Society of London,* Series B, No. 772, Vol. CCLI (1966), pp. 311-320.

Tillich, Paul. *Theology of Culture.* New York: Oxford, 1959.

Turner, Victor. *Schism and Continuity in an African Society.* Manchester: Manchester University Press, 1957.

————. *Chihamba: The White Spirit: A Ritual Drama of the Ndembu. Number 33 of the Rhodes-Livingston Institute Papers.* Manchester: Manchester University Press, 1962.

————. "A Discussion on Ritualization of Behavior in Animals and Man." "Anthropological Epilogue." *Philosophical Transactions of the Royal Society of London,* Series B, No. 772, Vol. CCLI (1966), pp. 521-522.

————. "Color Classification in Ndembu Religion." *Anthropological Approaches to the Study of Religion.* Ed. by M. Banton. No. 3 of ASA Monographs. New York: Praeger, 1966.

————. *The Forest of Symbols: Aspects of Ndembu Ritual.* Ithaca: Cornell University Press, 1967.

————. *The Dreams of Affliction. A Study of Religious Processes among the Ndembu of Zambia.* Oxford: Clarendon Press, 1968.

Voegelin, E. *Order and History.* Vol. I: *Israel and Revelation.* Baton Rouge: Louisiana State University Press, 1956.

Waters, Frank. *Masked Gods: Navaho and Pueblo Ceremonialism.* New York: Ballantine Books, 1970.

Weber, Max. *The Protestant Ethic and the Spirit of Capitalism.* Trans. by Talcott Parsons. New York: Scribners, 1930.

Wells, Herbert George. *Tono-Bungay.* Boston: Houghton-Mifflin, 1966.

Wensinck, A. J. *The Ocean in the Literature of the Western Semites.* Amsterdam, 1918.

Winter, Gibson. *The New Creation as Metropolis.* New York: Macmillan, 1963.

Wittkower, R. "Marvels of the East: A Study in the History of Monsters." *Journal of the Warburg and Courtauld Institutes,* V (1942), 159-197.

Wolfe, Thomas. *You Can't Go Home Again.* New York: Harper and Brothers, 1940.

Wood, Barry. *The Magnificent Frolic.* Philadelphia: Westminster, 1970.

Wycherley, Richard Ernest. *The Athenian Agora.* Vol. III: *Literary and Epigraphical Testimonia.* Princeton: American School of Classical Studies at Athens, Institute for Advanced Study, 1957.

Index